TOTAL QUALITY PROJECT MANAGEMENT FOR THE DESIGN FIRM

TOTAL QUALITY PROJECT MANAGEMENT FOR THE DESIGN FIRM

How to Improve Quality, Increase Sales, and Reduce Costs

FRANK A. STASIOWSKI, A.I.A.
DAVID BURSTEIN, P.E.

JOHN WILEY & SONS, INC.
New York / Chichester / Brisbane / Toronto / Singapore

Library of Congress Cataloging in Publication Data:

Stasiowski, Frank, 1948–

    Total quality project management for the design firm : how to
improve quality, increase sales, and reduce costs / Frank A.
Stasiowksi, David Berstein.

      p. cm.

    Includes index.

    ISBN 0-471-30787-4 (alk. paper)

    1. Architectural firms—United States—Management. 2. Engineering
firms—United States—Management. 3. Small business—United
States—Cash position. I. Burstein, David, 1947– . II. Title.

NA1996.S755   1994

720'.68'5—dc20   93-19850

PREFACE

Much has been written about quality assurance and quality control techniques for design and construction projects. These techniques have been developed over many years—and they work. Design firms that apply them properly produce high quality designs that can be built without the need for excessive field changes.

The problem with these traditional techniques is their *cost.* According to a study conducted by the corporate engineering department of Owens-Corning Fiberglass Corporation, approximately 20% of design budgets are expended for reviews and corrections conducted after the design documents have been completed. Adding the costs of interim reviews and corrections, an average design project can easily require 30 to 50% of its budget to locate and correct errors!

Attempts to impose ever more stringent quality control methods to reduce design errors have resulted in a spiral of ever-increasing design costs. As clients become increasingly resistant to higher costs and increasingly demanding of higher quality, design firms are caught in a squeeze that forces them to sacrifice either quality or design cost or both. These sacrifices result in lost profits, lost clients, or both.

Fortunately, there is an escape from this dilemma. The same quality improvement methods that have been used so successfully in manufacturing can be adapted to design projects. In fact, they can also be adapted to solve sales, administration, budget control, and other problems that often plague design firms. This book describes how. It is written by design professionals who have had direct experience with Total Quality Project Management in design firms. The concepts presented are not theoretical. They have all been tried—and they work!

FRANK A. STASIOWSKI
July 1993   DAVID BURSTEIN

v

ACKNOWLEDGMENTS

The authors would like to personally acknowledge the efforts of every individual who helped develop this book, but this list would be too long to be practical. Particular thanks go to the officers and employees of the Ralph M. Parsons Company and Engineering-Science, Inc., whose pioneering efforts in Total Quality Project Management have provided much of the material presented in this book. Among these are Colin Knight, Quality Improvement Administrator for The Ralph M. Parsons Company; Nick Preseran, Manager of Technical Direction for Engineering-Science, Inc.; and Rose Deslaurier, Quality Improvement Administrator for the Engineering-Science, Inc. Atlanta office. The authors also thank Julia Willard for her valuable reviews and incisive comments.

CONTENTS

INTRODUCTION

It is in vogue to criticize the poor quality of American goods and services. Consider the fact that IBM, known for its high quality standards, spent $2.4 billion in warranty costs in 1989*. Unfortunately, the record of engineering, architectural, and other technical service firms is no better, often worse. Do any of these quality problems sound familiar?

Case History #1. A civil engineering firm was hired by a municipality to design 20,000 feet of new sewer lines and inspect their construction. Poor compaction of backfill by the contractor resulted in collapse of the paving in many sections of the new sewer system. The municipality sued the contractor for poor construction and sued the engineering firm for poor inspection.

Case History #2. A representative of an engineering firm visited a textile plant and promised to send the client a report on the findings. The report was sent late and the client refused to pay for the costs of the visit. The engineering firm suffered an $8,200 loss in uncollectible costs plus loss of reputation with a long-term client.

Case History #3. An architectural firm contracted with a client for a small project that was scheduled to last three and a half months. Midway through, the project was delayed by the client. By the time it was restarted, the design firm's personnel had been diverted to other jobs and had lost interest in this project. Agreed-upon completion dates came and went without any information to the client from the design firm's project manager. Result: although the client was satisfied with the technical qual-

*Source: "Pursing Zero Defects Under the Six Sigma Banner," *New York Times,* January 13, 1991.

1

ity of the work, the design firm's numerous delays precluded the firm from working there on any future jobs.

Case History #4. A surveyor was retained by a large engineering firm to perform a topographic site survey and to locate existing underground utilities. During a routine site visit by the engineering firm, some apparent discrepancies were noted between the elevations shown on the surveyor's drawings and the actual elevations in the field. More detailed spot-checks by the engineering firm revealed several significant discrepancies. The engineering firm refused to pay the surveyor's $14,000 invoice, hired another surveyor to redo the work, and will never again use the first surveyor's services.

Case History #5. As part of the design of a chemical plant expansion, an engineering firm asked a vessel manufacturer for its recommendation on the best protective coating. The sales representative provided the recommendation, which was then included in the design without being reviewed by the coating manufacturer or the engineering firm's in-house corrosion expert. Shortly after start-up, the coating failed, requiring the tank to be shut down for several months and relined with a more suitable material. The client spent $45,000 to reline the tank and $125,000 in extra operating costs to compensate for this unit being out of service. The engineering firm agreed to bear $38,000 worth of engineering costs; its reputation with the client also suffered greatly.

Case History #6. An architectural firm had a contract to design a small building. The soils report called for removal and recompaction of the top few feet of soil prior to construction of the building foundation. The project's lead structural engineer assumed that this requirement was being handled in the earthwork specs (written by the civil engineer). The civil engineer assumed it has been taken care of by the structural engineer. The problem was not discovered until the construction contractor noticed major cracks appearing in the floor slab. The owner had to issue a major change order and sued the architectural firm for negligence.

Case History #7. A systems engineering firm was contracted to install a computerized maintenance system for a chemical plant. The due date came and went with no product delivered and no contact by the engineering firm's project manager. The client eventually called the firm's project manager, who apologized and gave him a second due date. When this date also passed without product being delivered or the project manager contacting the client, the client called a principal of the firm and expressed his dissatisfaction. The product was finally delivered on the third due date. The firm's poor performance on this "front end" project killed its chances of securing the lucrative follow-on activities.

Case History #8. A hydrogeologic firm was required to do packer testing of a well. The firm's project manager requested that a pump be sent to the site. The pump worked properly when installed, but failed after six hours. A second pump was requested and was sent via Federal Express the next day. Because of an incorrect address label, Federal Express sent it to the wrong city, delaying its arrival by another day. When it was finally installed, it also failed after about six hours. The field crew finished by hand bailing the well. The result was over $8,000 in uncollectible costs due to driller downtime.

Are these foul-ups unavoidable? Must firms spend more and more money attempting to fix these kinds of problems? Does the answer lie in more sophisticated and costly quality assurance and quality control programs? Are clients willing to pay the added costs required for such programs? *NO!* Quality problems in design firms can (and must) be prevented while *at the same time* reducing costs! How? By a concept called Total Quality Project Management (TQPM).

This book does not focus on quality as defined by the U.S. legal system (although legal issues are addressed). It does not dwell on elaborate procedures for checking drawings (although such procedures are discussed). It does not focus on shop drawing review or construction inspection techniques (although some information on these subjects is provided). It does not concentrate on handling quality assurance paperwork (although some suggested documentation methods are presented).

This book presents an entirely new way of looking at quality in engineering, architectural, and other technical service firms. The word "quality" doesn't just mean how easily a design can be built, how functional the resulting facility will be, or how attractive it will look. The discussion of quality also includes such issues as how close the project came to its original schedule and budget, how happy the client is, and how satisfied the firm's employees are. In short, it includes every aspect of how a technical service firm conducts its business.

Total Quality Project Management is not new. The concept of controlling quality by using measurement techniques, conforming to requirements, and targeting zero defects was developed in the United States during World War II. After the war, General Douglas MacArthur sent Dr. W. Edward Deming to Japan to help that defeated and largely destroyed nation rebuild its economy. Deming's approach was simple: you look for waste, measure its cost, determine what caused it, and get everyone involved to fix it so that it doesn't happen again. Japan's industry leaders listened to Deming and heeded his advice; the rest is history.

By the early 1980s, it had become apparent to U.S. industrial leaders that the Japanese were beating them at their own game — producing high quality products at reasonable prices. They therefore consulted with Deming as well as other quality experts such as Dr. J. M. Juran and Philip Crosby. They even read quality manuals prepared by Japanese experts such as Masaaki Imai and Masao Nemoto. The result has been a dramatic improvement in the quality of American manufactured goods, faster cycle times in getting new products to market, and reduction of costs resulting from waste and rework. The impact on the competitiveness of the U.S. economy has been dramatic, as evidenced by the following*:

1. Productivity in U.S. manufacturing has increased at an average rate of 3.1% per year since 1983, faster than either Japan or Germany.
2. U.S. exports have grown by 9.5% per year since 1985.
3. By the end of 1990, the U.S. had regained its position as the world's largest exporting nation.
4. The U.S. overall trade deficit, which had deteriorated to $146 billion by 1987, has decreased to $7 billion by the end of 1991.
5. Importation of foreign capital has been reduced from a peak of $150 billion in 1987 to virtually zero in 1991.

To date, professional service firms have generally remained on the sidelines, seeing no reason to change the business

*Source: "The World's Most Competitive Economy," *Forbes*, March 30, 1992.

practices that have proven successful for them over the years. But history has shown that those who fail to adapt to changes in the marketplace eventually will fall by the wayside. And those changes *are* taking place. Consider the following trends in the markets served by architects, engineers, geologists, and other technical professionals:

1. Clients are insisting on a higher standard of perfection than ever before.
2. They are more eager to sue if they don't get it.
3. At the same time, they are insisting on lower costs and shorter schedules.
4. Foreign firms are entering the market, particularly from Europe and Japan, increasing competitive pressures.
5. Capital requirements for CAD and other major investments require design firms to become more profitable in spite of these obstacles.
6. There are not enough qualified technical professionals available to meet the needs of growing firms.
7. Fewer design professionals are serving in formal apprentice programs; instead, design firms (and their clients) are demanding full performance from day one.
8. Employees are becoming less willing to dedicate their lives to their companies and are demanding more from their employers.

Do you see any of these trends in your organization? Do you believe that traditional approaches will deal with them adequately? Are you willing to bet your company's and your personal future that they will? If not, read on. Find out how the same quality improvement approaches used so successfully by Japanese and American manufacturers can be adapted to the kinds of problems you routinely encounter.

1

A COMMITMENT TO TQPM IS A MARKETING ISSUE

At the heart of all litigation, is the absence of quality.

The idea that each individual in a firm should continually improve his or her work is neither novel nor easy. Yet in today's marketplace, excellent quality design and construction are no longer selling points, but are expected and even demanded by the client. A program devoted to continual upgrading and preening of a company's resources will be the key to business longevity in the 1990s.

Touting your assets by proclaiming "We provide quality work" is no longer the way to go. In fact, such an approach will only place your firm among the ranks of thousands of other firms out there who, believe that "good work" is their greatest asset. It's no great step in the direction of improving design or your image in the marketplace to say you are improving your quality. And that's not what Total Quality Project Management is all about. TQPM is about taking your clients to greater heights through a planned program of continual improvement of your firm's work processes and project management techniques. Taking the client to greater heights means that you are providing greater service, faster production, better ideas, more cost-effective ways in which to produce the work. This translates into client benefits such as saving the client money, accelerating schedules, and reducing problems during construction and startup.

THE ORIGINS OF TQM

You may recall that the source of Total Quality Management was the industrial engineering expert Dr. W. Edward Deming, who helped post-war Japan rebuild its industrial base after World War II. By the late 1980s it had become evident to U.S. manufacturing firms who had ignored TQM, that the system was working for the Japanese and that they'd better get in on it too. Corporate executives with manufacturing firms began to adopt Total Quality Management concepts and apply them to their organizations. Since that time, production in American manufacturing firms has greatly increased (and statistics on this are cited later in this text). The design professions have, however, not as yet succumbed to TQM, mainly because until now, they were not pushed to do so. Now the time has come.

Today, many governmental and industrial clients are demanding that design firms have Total Quality Management practices in place in order to bid projects. But merely having a TQM is not "enough" design; professionals find themselves with no choice but to incorporate TQM into the way they do their projects. This book explains how to use Total Quality Management techniques in your firm to deliver high quality projects to your clients: hence the term Total Quality Project Management.

If you do not adopt a policy of leadership in innovation and customer service delivery, at this point, you'll be left behind by those firms scrambling to sell the best service at the lowest possible price—touting Total Quality Project Management all the way.

HOW DO YOU "THINK" TQPM?

If you are like most design professionals, your first thought in setting up a Total Quality Project Management program is marketing and, beyond marketing, client satisfaction. Marketing in and of itself is a necessary, but increasingly outdated, concept. Because "marketing" implies internal processes and actions, "client-focused service" is a better way to consider the process. Total Quality Project Management is an integral part of the client-focused service element of your firm. And, naturally, as with traditional "marketing," the better job you do at providing, aiming, shooting for, and targeting "client service," the more money you make, the more work you have, and so on.

There are basically going to be three different types of design firms in the 1990s, with regards to client focus:

1. Internally Focused

These companies focus on their own products/services and believe that internally focused quality is the only way to get the "best" clients. These firms will not prosper, because quality alone, without faster and better service, eats up profits and is not enough of a selling point to attract demanding, high-grade clientele.

2. Service Focused

These firms do exactly what their clients ask for . . . construct buildings, provide exacting designs . . . and nothing more. These firms will struggle for profitability in the 1990s, because they are not adding their own value to the project.

3. Externally Focused, Value-Added

The third class of firms will truly succeed. These companies take clients to heights that the client never expected. They have working Total Quality Project Management processes to continually evaluate and revamp their services. They will position themselves as being providers not only of top quality design, but of excellent service (quickness of delivery, saving the client money, and so on). These firms use "expeditionary" marketing tactics to distinguish themselves from their competitors.

Figure 1.1 Internally vs. externally focused firms.

Total Quality Project Management is an outgrowth of that process. It is a new way of servicing the client that is more client-focused, that will bring the client to greater heights than he or she ever expected. Gary Hamel, Associate Professor of the London Business School, and C. K. Prahalad, Professor of Corporate Strategy at the University of Michigan, have expounded an idea they term "expeditionary marketing." They feel that in order to market service businesses in the 1990s, you have to expand your "corporate imagination" and embark on an "expedition" to excel beyond your peers. In design, the boat on which to ride for the expedition is Total Quality Project Management.

This book shows you how to better your project management processes, so that you may improve client service. This is an external, not an internal focus (see Figure 1.1). By improving upon the services you provide to the client, you will improve your "marketing" effort. After all, your job as the design professional is to truly inspire the client to reach for greater heights than they could have imagined, to look beyond their own horizon.

UNCOVERING THE CLIENT'S HIDDEN AGENDA

The Mayor of Denver, Colorado, recently spoke at a meeting of the American Society of Consulting Engineers in Denver. He made the point of meeting a client's needs—the hidden agenda—very clear. He spoke of the new Denver airport. There were many levels of satisfaction going on during the project. In addition to the issues of quality, budget, and schedule, he had his own concerns with getting the project finished on time, since he was up for reelection the year it was to be completed. He was extremely disturbed by the thought of having to go back to the city's building committee with any news of delaying the project. As Mayor of the city, he wanted to make this the gem of his administration. The true job of the architects and engineerings on the project, then, was to realize this end goal: to create a fabulous "gem" of an airport, on time, before election season. That was the true need of the mayor in question, and since the mayor was in charge of hiring future design professionals, his opinion of the airport mattered most.

HOW DO YOU DETERMINE THE CLIENT'S HIDDEN AGENDA?

By listening! Read up on listening techniques. There isn't enough space in this text to explain the entire concept of listening to your client's expectations, but suffice it to say that if you don't truly know how to listen, you will never get to the crux of the client's issue. If you don't get to the heart of the client's needs and wants, you won't get hired again, your firm will not be talked about by your client, and it will not be recommended to others!

Let's not be bound by what we traditionally believe is the way that design practices must be run. The client should feel as if he or she is the only client the firm is dealing with. Instead of telling the client how great you are, show him that you feel he or she is. This attitude speaks for itself!

HERE'S AN EXAMPLE

Engineering-Science, of which one of the authors is Vice President, assigns a senior staff member as "client sponsor" for every significant client. The client sponsor is required to keep in touch with the client periodically to assume satisfaction and to obtain a written evaluation at the end of every project. You can only imagine what their track record is with clients, which is largely responsible for the growth and financial success of the firm.

THE CLIENT NOTEBOOK

Here's a simple way to start off every project right, in an organized fashion that will allow you freedom from worry and the opportunity to manage beyond the paperwork. It's simple—just keep a three-ring binder for each and every project you manage.

Every project should have a three-ring binder notebook with seven tabs in it, for the following sections:

Tab #1: Client Expectations. This is a written list of the client's expectations, signed off—reviewed and agreed to by the client. It is very seldom that clients ever agree to this, only because they are never asked. "I will receive an award for the design of this building; we will get our picture in five newspapers, and so on." Make them concentrate, get them to let down their guard and tell you what they *really* expect. Only then will you be prepared to deliver.

Tab# 2: Schedule. Place a schedule in this section, in whatever format necessary. This may be only a simple end date, or it could be an elaborate CPM schedule. Either way, commit to a schedule and stick with it!

Tab #3: Budget. Break this section into three parts—up front planning, project management, and post-project management. Job costs seldom stop when the job stops. Whenever a new report comes out on the budget, place it here.

Tab #4: Contract. Describe the technical part of the project, or scope of services. Notice that you are four tabs in before you talk about contract. The first three tabs are the important issues to settle, before settling on a contract type.

Tab #5 Team. Put in a complete list of people working on the project. Include all staf members that will be working on the project, any consultants, contract workers, and so on. For each individual, include his or her name, address, telephone number, home telephone, home fax, car phone, and any other number the person may have, organized in a chart format so that anyone who picks up that binder can tell at a glance just exactly what is going on in the project. The goal is to be able to reach everyone at any time of the day. Disasters inevitably happen at 8 o'clock on Saturday morning when no one is accessible, or at 9 o'clock at night. For this reason, you must have access to all of their numbers, in order to reach them any time.

Tab #6: Change Orders. This section should describe exactly how you will handle design and/or construction changes throughout the project. The client should review and sign off on this section.

Tab #7: Communications Procedures. This final section should talk about how and when you will communicate with the client. Be sure to specify precisely the purpose and frequency of telephone calls and meetings, your mail system, invoice system, accounts receivables, billings, and any other communications procedure. For example, establish a time each week to call the client to discuss any issues—in this way, the client will not be calling you every day to check up on your progress. Be sure to get the client to review and sign off on this section.

This seven-tab three-ring binder system provides a quick review in a glance of project progress, and anyone from either team can pick up the binder at any point and understand project progress immediately. All schedule reports should be placed in the schedule section in chronological order, all budget reports in the budgeting section, and so on.

CLIENT SATISFACTION IS NOT ENOUGH

Don't fall into the trap of thinking that client satisfaction is synonymous with repeat business. In a recent survey*, between 65 and 85% of customers who defected said that they were satisfied or very satisfied with their former suppliers. In the auto industry, satisfaction scores average 85 to 95%, while repurchase rates average only to 70%*. Design firm clients act the same way. To retain clients over the long term, you must do more than satisfy them; you must continually provide them with something they can't get from your competitors.

MARKETING IS SUCCESS AT TOTAL QUALITY PROJECT MANAGEMENT

Successful marketing in the 1990s has little to do with fancy brochures, slick graphics, or any of the normal, traditional "marketing techniques." Instead, it is *expeditionary marketing* ... taking clients to heights they never before imagined ... giving clients more than they expected, and certainly more than they asked for ... and through the most efficient and effective project management systems, focus on quality of delivery, showing them that you are intense and active and focused on their project, and their project alone.

*Reichheld, Frederick, F. "Loyalty Based Management," *Harvard Business Review*, March–April 1993.

2 THE DESIGN FIRM AS FISHING VILLAGE

Many design firm managers view Total Quality Project Management (TQPM) as a way to avoid lawsuits, motivate employees to work harder, or improve the firm's reputation. These are all *by-products* of the quality process but they are not its *goals*. To explain how quality can fundamentally affect the way a design firm does business, this chapter presents a parable in which the *fishing village* is a design firm, its *fishermen* are the firm's marketers, and the *fish* are the projects required to keep the firm's employees (*the villagers*) well fed.

THE FISHING VILLAGE

Once upon a time, there was a fishing village whose existence depended upon the ability of its fishermen to catch enough fish to feed the villagers. Being good managers, the village's leaders knew how many pounds of fish were required each day to: (1) feed the villagers, and (2) allow the village to grow and prosper. The fishing boats sought locations where the fish were large, so that fewer fish were required to produce each day's quota. Also, large fish could be easily gutted, filleted, and refrigerated to provide increased storage life. Small fish were less desirable, since they had to be eaten immediately.

This system worked reasonably well as long as there was an ample supply of fish to keep the villagers well fed. However, there were occasional periods during which it became very difficult to catch enough fish. Some shortages resulted from normal cyclical fluctuations in the supply of fish. Other shortages were man-made, the result of too many fishermen from too many villages overfishing the same waters. During these periods of poor fishing, the village had to: (1) devote virtually all its resources to fishing activities, and (2) lower its standards for the size and quality of fish pursued by the fishermen. Sometimes, despite these increased fishing activities, there were still not enough fish caught to feed the entire village. When this occurred, some of the villagers moved to other villages that had a more ample food supply; others were unwilling or unable to move to other villages and, tragically, starved to death.

After several boom-and-bust cycles, the village leaders met one day to develop a way of smoothing out these cycles. They decided to freeze a portion of each day's catch, so that food reserves would be available during hard times. This plan improved the situation somewhat, but had drawbacks. There was a limit on the amount of each catch that could be frozen, a limited time that the fish could be frozen, and a limited storage capacity for the frozen fish. These limitations meant that freezing the fish could not prevent food shortages during extended periods of poor fishing. There was another problem with freezing the fish—the fish did not respond well to being frozen and, as a result, did not taste as good after they were defrosted and cooked.

DIVERSIFICATION OF FISHING ACTIVITIES

It soon became apparent that freezing a portion of each day's catch would not eliminate the cycle of feast and famine that had always plagued the village. In response, one of the village leaders recommended that the village diversify its fishing activities by sending fishing boats into multiple fishing areas instead of merely working the same waters over and over. Because none of the fishing boat captains were familiar with waters other than those traditionally used by the village, no one knew which waters held the best fishing prospects. A task force was assigned to visit the University and research which waters were likely to contain the most fish. The task force returned with a recommended plan for some of the fishing boats to try their luck in several nearby lakes and coastal areas.

When they got to these new locations, the fishermen found that there were indeed plenty of fish. However, these waters were already being fished by fishermen from other villages who were much more knowledgeable of the waters and the habits of the fish that lived in these waters. Despite much hard work by the fishermen and dedication of substantial resources by the village, most of the fishermen returned with meager catches containing few large fish. Furthermore, the diversification efforts diverted resources away from the village's traditional fishing waters, thus reducing the total size of the catch. Eventually, these diversification efforts succeeded in developing a few new fishing areas. But this effort had become extremely costly and often did more harm than good to the village's goal of stabilizing the food supply.

HIRING FISHING CAPTAINS FROM OTHER VILLAGES

During a meeting of the village council, one of the councilmen observed that the diversification effort was a sound strategy but was not succeeding because the village's fishermen did not adequately understand foreign waters and the habits of the fish that inhabited them. A suggestion was made to hire some of the fishing boat captains from other villages who were successful in waters that were believed to be good prospects for diversification. One of the councilmen was assigned to visit other villages in order to recruit some fishing boat captains.

After several months of recruiting, it became apparent that the best captains were held in high esteem and treated very well by their local villages. It was virtually impossible to convince these individuals to exchange the prestige they had developed over many years for an uncertain future in a new village. As a result, the village's recruiter had to settle for hiring a few captains who were, for one reason or another, dissatisfied with the way they were treated in their own village.

The new captains were brought to the village and introduced to the villagers with great fanfare. They would go to waters they knew well, diversify the village's fishing areas, and lead the village into the promised land of stable food supplies!

After a few months, the initial euphoria had worn off and reality began to sink in. These new captains were totally unfamiliar with the kinds of ships and fishing gear owned by the village. They were also unfamiliar with their newly assigned crews, many of whom resented being put under the command of foreign captains. Despite a few widely scattered successes, the hoped-for benefits never materialized.

To make matters worse, new problems arose that the village leaders had never anticipated. The foreign captains had customs that were quite different from the village natives and never quite fit into the village's culture. Also, several of the most capable *native* captains began grumbling about the fact that the immigrant captains received better pay and benefits in spite of the fact that they caught fewer fish. The morale of the entire village began to suffer.

MERGERS AND ACQUISITIONS

By this time, it had become apparent to the village leaders that hiring captains from other villages was no panacea. They convened another meeting of the village council to seek new solutions to the village's age-old problem of a fluctuating food supply. After considerable discussion, a plan emerged. The mayor would meet with the leaders of nearby villages to discuss possible annexation or mergers. This approach would provide the village with *all* the resources of some neighboring villages including their best captains, ships, fishing gear, and crews. Negotiations were eventually concluded with several neighboring villages and announcements were sent to all their villagers proclaiming a new era of inter-village cooperation and an end to the long-term problem of unstable food supplies.

Almost immediately upon signing the annexation and merger agreements, problems began to surface. Because they had different customs and languages, the people in the various villages did not mix well with those from other villages in the newly formed confederation. There was growing concern about loss of identity and favoritism toward certain villages. This mutual distrust made it difficult to resolve problems such as which ships should be sent to which waters. (None of the villages wanted to give up any of their traditional fishing areas in spite of the fact that it would be more efficient to limit the number of ships fishing in these waters.)

Eventually, many of the villagers became disenchanted and moved away to join friends and relatives in other villages. Other unhappy villagers left to form new villages that could be independent from the confederation. These departing villagers continued to fish in their traditional fishing areas, putting a further strain on the limited food supply. In time, the confederation fell apart, each village going its own way.

By this time, the villagers were up in arms. Their leaders had tried all manner of means to improve the stability of the food supply—without success. Periods of famine continued and a variety of new social problems had been created.

THE RISE OF THE Q PARTY

Among the disenchanted villagers were a few young radicals. They called themselves the "Q Party" and met secretly to work out a revolutionary approach that would fundamentally change the way the village was run. The result was a plan that the radicals called the "Q Program." The radicals met with the village leaders to propose their new strategy: *Stop* freezing a portion of each day's catch; instead, fence off a portion of the harbor, place these fish in the fenced-in area, feed and care for the fish so they would grow and eventually increase the size of the food supply. The *Q Program* was met with ridicule by most of the village leaders. The mayor laughed at the young radicals and responded, "Feed the fish? The fish are supposed to feed us! How can we increase our food supply by taking food away from our hungry villagers and giving it to a bunch of fish? That is the most outrageous idea I've ever heard! I suggest you go back to the fishing boats and spend your time catching fish. That is how we can increase our food supply."

Despite the strong negative response from the village's leaders, the young radicals still believed in their idea. They met secretly to plot the overthrow of the village leadership. The radicals were greatly assisted by a few young village councilmen who secretly supported the radical plan but were afraid to speak out during council meetings for fear of being censured. Support of the *Q Party* gradually grew among the villagers, who were becoming convinced that their current leaders were incapable of providing long-term stability for the village's food supply. A recall petition was circulated and enough signatures were obtained to call a special election for the mayor and council positions. The *Q Party* candidates campaigned on a platform of radical reform. The existing leaders responded by attacking the radicals' ideas and lack of experience in running the village. Despite a well-funded, vigorous campaign, the "old guard" had lost the confidence of most of the villagers and was unceremoniously voted out of office. They were replaced by the young radicals in the Q Party.

Upon taking office, the new leadership immediately began to implement their proposed new *Q Program*. They fenced off an area of the harbor and started stocking this area with a portion of each day's catch. They sold the freezers (which were no longer being used) in exchange for fish food. They diverted some of the villagers from their traditional fishing duties and sent them to the University to learn how to feed and care for fish.

PROBLEMS IN INITIATING THE Q PROGRAM

The village experienced considerable hardship immediately following the adoption of the *Q Program*. Fewer fish were being caught because many of the village's fishermen were no longer catching fish—instead, they were now learning how to feed and care for the captive fish. Because the freezers had to be sold, frozen fish were no longer available to level the daily fluctuations in the volume of fish that were caught. A portion of each day's catch was being diverted to the fenced-in area, further reducing the food supply. But it was still too early to supplement the food supply by harvesting any of the captive fish. During this period, the previous village leaders tried to rally the villagers in an effort to return to power and restore the old ways. But the radical new leaders successfully convinced the villagers to be patient and give the new *Q Program* time to work.

Finally, the day came for the first harvest of captive fish. Though only a few pounds of fish were harvested, it provided a glimmer of hope for the future. But it would still be many months before the volume of captive fish being harvested would equal that lost due to reduced fishing under the new program.

THE Q PROGRAM BEGINS TO WORK

Once the *Q Program* began to achieve steady-state operation, the village leaders began to learn how to make the system work even better. They came to realize that, no matter how carefully they built the fence in the harbor, the fish could always escape if they really wanted to; the "captive" fish were not really captive. This realization led to greater emphasis on the care and feeding of these fish so that they would have *no desire* to leave the fenced-in area. The fish and the villagers evolved a symbiotic relationship: the fish received food, protection against predators and other fishermen, and assurance of a long life; the villagers received a reliable food supply. Eventually, the villagers stopped building fences since most of the fish were quite content to remain in the fish farm, even though they could escape if they wished.

The village leaders also discovered that the ultimate size of the harvested fish had little to do with how big they were when caught at sea. The *species* of fish was much more important in determining their ultimate size at harvest time. For example, a one-pound grouper would eventually grow much larger than a two-pound snapper.

This discovery led to a fundamental change in the village's fishing strategy. Instead of seeking the largest fish, regardless of species, the fishing captains now sought those species that would grow to the largest ultimate size. The initial size of each fish became irrelevant. Because all the other villages were still pursuing the large fish, competition for small fish was minimal. Therefore, relatively few fishermen could catch a very large number of small fish. As long as these fish were of a desirable species, they could be grown to a very large size prior to harvesting. The village gradually reduced the percentage of its resources devoted to fishing and increased the resources devoted to raising fish in the constantly expanding fish farms.

By this time, it began to appear that the dream of a steady food supply for the village was actually achievable! This could be done by establishing a steady-state condition in which the number of small fish caught by the fishermen would equal the number of much larger fish that were harvested from the fish farms. A constant supply of fish would always be available to feed the villagers. Because it was relatively easy to catch the requisite number of small fish, the village leaders believed that the food supply could be assured even during periods of poor fishing.

UNEXPECTED BENEFITS OF THE Q PROGRAM

One day while harvesting fish, one of the villagers observed that the total number of fish in one of the fish farm areas appeared to be increasing. This observation was brought to the attention of the village leaders. They first checked the calculations used to establish the desired steady-state fish population and concluded that no errors had been made. Reports from several other fish farms also indicated a growing population of fish.

A team of divers was dispatched to determine how the fish population was increasing in spite of the fact that the number of fish harvested equalled the number of fish caught. After a week of observation, the divers issued their report to an astonished village council: the additional fish were coming from two different sources. Some were the spawned offspring of fish in the fish farms; others were being attracted from the ocean by the high level of care provided in the village's fish farms. (Because the fish farms were no longer fenced, fish could enter these areas at will.) These findings were very significant; the village's expenditures on fishing activities could now be further reduced without adversely affecting the long-term food supply The village leaders decided to further reduce the size of the fishing fleet, devoting it entirely to catching breeding stocks of the highest quality, tastiest fish.

SOCIETAL IMPACT OF THE Q PROGRAM

As time went on, profound changes began to take place in the village. In the past, the village had devoted most of its resources to catching fish, gutting them, and storing them. These activities now consumed only minor expenditures of money and man-hours. They were replaced by increasing expenditures on development of better ways to raise fish and on education and training of the villagers, most of whom were now involved with some phase of fish farming.

As fish farming became more sophisticated, it also required more specialization of labor. Specialists were being developed in fish nutrition, environmental controls, veterinary medicine, genetics, and other technical fields. This specialization soon reached a point where no single person understood or could manage all the steps in the fish farming process. The old command-and-control management structure that had worked well in simpler times was no longer viable. A new management structure was emerging based on the interdependence of each worker with many other workers. Orders issued from the village leaders now required buy-in from the villagers. Areas of needed improvement were now being identified not by the village leaders, but by the village themselves. Many problems were becoming too complex to be solved by the village leaders alone; they often required a task force approach involving several villagers who had an in-depth understanding of these problems and their potential solutions.

THE FINAL RESULTS

The village continued to grow and prosper, providing a high standard of living for all its residents. Increased leisure time became available to enjoy music, sports, art, travel, and other forms of recreation. And the villagers lived happily ever after.

Meanwhile, at villages that maintained the old fishing tradition, an unstable food supply continued to plague the lives of the villagers. They continued to suffer all the problems associated with traditional fishing villages. As far as leisure time was concerned, there was none. Most of the villagers had only two choices as to how they would spend their lives— either fish or cut bait.

EPILOGUE

Although the *Q Program* succeeded in eliminating the problems that had historically plagued the village, as time passed, new problems emerged. The large number of happy, healthy fish in the harbor attracted the attention of the village's traditional competitors, fishermen from other villages. An even bigger problem was an entirely new set of competitors— sharks that had previously stayed clear of the harbor were now making periodic raids. Also, some of the new fish that were coming into the harbor brought with them diseases for which the previous inhabitants had no resistance.

These and other new problems led to increased level of understanding among the village's leaders. The *Q Program*, as effective as it was, could not remain static. It had to be continuously reinvented to meet the new challenges of each passing day. Only by such a continuous improvement process could the village be assured of long term prosperity.

3

CHANGING THE WAY WE THINK ABOUT QUALITY

This chapter describes how Total Quality Project Management (TQPM) differs from traditional ways of thinking about quality in design firms and other technical service firms. We compare traditional "defensive" methods of quality assurance and quality control—which are intended to protect the firm against lawsuits—with some innovative "offensive" ways that seek to make the firm more client-oriented, more employee-oriented, most cost-competitive, and more profitable. The philosophies of some of the noted "quality gurus" are summarized and related to the kinds of issues that are typical of design firms and other technical service firms.

WHAT IS QUALITY?

The word "quality" can have a number of different meanings. It can be defined from an aesthetic, legal, or functional point of view. The ramifications of each meaning on a typical design firm are described below.

The Aesthetic Definition of Quality

Some design professionals believe that quality is measured by the aesthetic properties of the facilities they design. This traditional definition of quality is based on such issues as:

- How well a building blends into its surroundings.
- A building's psychological impacts on its inhabitants.
- The ability of a landscaping design to match the theme of adjacent structures.

- The use of bold new design concepts that capture peoples' imaginations.

Because these aesthetic definitions of quality are largely subjective, major disagreements arise as to whether "quality" has been achieved. Consider the Eiffel Tower in Paris. Shortly after it was built, there was strong sentiment by many Parisian architects to have it demolished because it was so ugly! One hundred years later, there is still widespread disagreement as to the aesthetic quality of this famous structure.

Since objective definitions of aesthetic quality do not exist, design professionals generally take it upon themselves to define the aesthetic quality of their designs. If the client doesn't happen to agree, then the client is merely demonstrating his or her lack of taste. Such clients are tolerated only because their money is needed to enable the design professional to create an artistic achievement that will be admired for generations to come.

Frank Lloyd Wright exemplified the arrogance often associated with the aesthetic definition of quality when he once wrote to a client*:

It appears that an attitude has developed on your part—"what does the architect know about what I want—I am going to live in this house—not he." Now I have heard that provincialism from women but never before from a man. And it isn't too late yet for you to get an architect that does know what you want.

I don't know what kind of architect you are familiar with but it apparently isn't the kind I think I am. You seem not to know how to treat a decent one. I have put so much more into this house than you or any other client has a right to expect that if I haven't your confidence—to hell with the whole thing.

Frank Lloyd Wright was able to get away with that attitude. Can your firm?

The Legal Definition of Quality

The law defines design quality in terms of professional liability, a legal concept that requires all professionals (doctors, dentists, lawyers, etc.) to know their trade and practice it responsibly. Every architect, engineer, geologist, surveyor, biologist, chemist, landscape architect and interior designer who

*Source: *Fallingwater: A Frank Lloyd Wright Country Home*, Edgar J. Kaufmann, Jr., ed. Abbeville Press, New York, 1986. Copyright Cross River Press.

markets his or her expertise to clients is subject to professional liability laws.

WHAT IS PROFESSIONAL LIABILITY?

Many technical professionals and clients have serious misunderstandings about professional liability. They believe that the costs of *any* mistake made by their consultants should be paid by the consultants. Contrary to this often-held belief, the law does *not* require technical professionals to do perfect work, nor does it require them to pay for all the mistakes they make. The law *does* require a technical professional to be competent; that is, to provide services that conform to the standards of his or her respective profession. In other words, to do as good a job as most of his or her competitors.

NEGLIGENCE

"Negligence" is the failure to mcct the standards customarily provided by a professional experienced in his or her field. There is a legal distinction between a mistake (which anyone can make) and negligence (which competent professionals should not make). The law does not require perfection, only competence. For example, on a multi-million dollar project, it is not reasonable to expect the design to contain *no* interferences and *no* inconsistencies. However, a competent professional *is* expected to take precautions to minimize such mistakes. Furthermore, their magnitude should not be excessive.

ERRORS AND OMISSIONS

The term "errors and omissions" is often used to describe professional liability. This term actually combines two different legal concepts. An "error" is a mistake that will require rework to correct. For example, if an engineer specifies a 20-horsepower pump, but calls for a Size 1 motor starter (which will only handle up to 10 horsepower), the starter will have to be removed and replaced in order for the pump to operate. An omission is a mistake in which something is left out. For example, if the mechanical engineer who specified the pump forgot to tell the electrical engineer about the need for a motor, the motor control center will be installed without a starter for that pump. The construction contractor will therefore require a change order to purchase and install the missing starter.

DAMAGES

"Damages" are the costs incurred by the owner that result from a mistake made by a professional service firm. In the case of the 20-horsepower pump with the improperly sized motor starter, the damages would be:

- The cost of removing the Size 1 starter.
- The additional cost of the Size 2 starter.
- Any shipping and restocking charges that might apply.
- The cost of installing the Size 2 starter.

In the example of the motor starter that was *omitted* from the design, there are theoretically no damages. This is because the cost of the starter would have been included in the contractor's original price (and therefore paid by the owner) had the starter not been omitted from the design. We use the word "theoretically" because the owner may pay a premium to have the starter installed as a change order, compared to having it included in the original price. Determining whether such a penalty exists is difficult. Determining its magnitude is even more difficult. There are no commonly accepted procedures for handling this issue, so it is generally dealt with on a case-by-case basis.

WARRANTEES AND GUARANTEES

A design firm may provide a warranty or guarantee that its work will conform to a *higher* standard of quality than the law normally requires. For example, if an architectural firm guarantees that a building can be constructed for no more than $10 million, it has made a legal commitment even though the law would not normally hold architects accountable for construction costs. If the building ends up costing $11 million, the owner is entitled to recover any resulting damages from the architect.

CONSEQUENTIAL DAMAGES

The examples presented so far have been "direct damages," that is, they have resulted directly from mistakes made by the engineer or architect. Let's say that the omission of the motor starter was responsible for a two-week delay in the start-up of a new manufacturing facility and that this delay resulted in a loss of $100,000 in orders for the owner's product. This $100,000 is known as a "consequential damage," a consequence of the omission made by the design firm.

LIMITATION OF LIABILITY

Design firms generally charge fees that represent a small fraction of the total capital cost of a project. These fees are an even smaller percentage of the total life cycle cost, usually less than 1%. However, as shown in the previous example, the damages resulting from an error or omission can be many times the design firm's fees. The concept of "limitation of liability" is intended to place the design firm's risk in line with its compensation. For example, an owner may agree to limit the liability of a design firm to the amount of its profit, the amount of its total fees, or the amount of its insurance coverage.

INDEMNIFICATION

"Indemnification" (also referred to as "hold harmless" clause) means that one party is relieving the other of its normal liability. For example, if an owner has an urgent need to complete a project in an extremely short time, the engineer may set out a plan that shortcuts his or her normal design review procedures in order to meet this tight schedule. The owner, realizing that this is the only way to get the job done on time, might be willing to indemnify the engineer for any damages resulting from design errors or omissions.

Indemnification can also be used to favor the owner. For example, a chemical company may have created a hazardous waste problem and hired an engineering firm to provide all services required to clean it up to the satisfaction of the environmental regulatory authorities. The chemical company may also ask the engineering firm for indemnification from third party liability. In this case, the engineering firm would be responsible for any and all claims or lawsuits brought by third parties as a result of the cleanup effort. The engineering firm is therefore providing more than professional services—it is also providing an insurance policy to the chemical company.

THE SMOKING GUN

Perhaps the most overlooked source of legal liability is the firm's own quality control procedures! If the firm has published manuals, memos, or other documents that dictate what quality control measures are required, the law expects that such procedures will be followed. For example, many design firms have documents that *require* that all designs be reviewed prior to being issued for bidding. If, for any reason, a project manager fails to conform to this requirement and quality problems are later found in the design documents, the fact that he or she did not conform to the company's own quality control requirements is *prima facie* evidence of negligence.

A better approach is to divide these procedures into two categories; essential and desirable. Essential procedures must include, as an integral part of the procedure, a method of monitoring compliance. For desirable procedures, the firm can publish "guidance documents" to assist the project managers and technical staff. These guidelines should permit managers to deviate somewhat from the firm's standards without automatically incurring liability.

This problem is a bit more complex when viewed for a specific project. A project manager cannot publish "guidance documents" for project reviews. Each project *must* have a detailed quality control plan, it must be distributed to the appropriate members of the project team, and it must be executed.

The Functional Definition of Quality

"Quality" can be defined by how closely the project conforms to its requirements. By this functional definition, a high quality design can be described by such terms as:

- Easily understood drawings.
- Few conflicts in drawings and specifications.
- Economical to construct.
- Easy to operate.
- Easy to maintain.
- Energy efficient.

Describing a high quality study is a bit more nebulous. Commonly used terms include:

- Well written.
- Thoroughly researched.
- Correct grammar.
- Proper use of charts and graphs.
- Accurate.
- Objective.

CAN QUALITY BE MEASURED?

Aesthetic quality is difficult, if not impossible, to measure quantitatively. Attempts to do so have resulted in numerous design awards, each of which is based on predefined criteria for quality. Unfortunately, many awards are made for political considerations as well as aesthetic quality. Other award-winning projects are highly controversial and lack a true consensus regarding their aesthetic quality.

Legal quality can be measured by such criteria as the number of lawsuits filed, amounts paid for professional liability claims, and insurance company risk categories. However, such measurements are often based on factors other than design quality (such as litigiousness of clients and political circumstances).

Functional quality is also difficult to measure, but tools do exist to make such measurement possible. As an example, let's take the traditional attribute of "easy to operate" to describe a well-designed facility. Instead of requiring that the facility be "easy to operate," let's define the desired operational staff as "a total of four people, including an experienced superintendent." If the facility can indeed be operated successfully by this staff, the requirement has been met. If it turns out that an additional person is needed to maintain sophisticated equipment and instrumentation, then the requirement has not been met. Many other examples of measurement techniques are described later in this book.

WHO MEASURES QUALITY?

Ultimately, our clients measure the quality of our projects by how well they conform to the clients' requirements. It is the job of the design firm to identify all these requirements and document them in terms that can be readily measured.

However, there are others who also pass judgment on the quality of our projects. Designs and reports must often be approved by zoning commissions, planning boards, building departments, architectural review committees, environmental protection agencies, and other third parties. The client's objectives cannot be met if these agencies don't approve the project.

Others who also pass judgment on the quality of our projects include equipment vendors, construction contractors, and building maintenance personnel. If they are not pleased with the quality of our designs, their displeasure will probably be conveyed to the client.

For future reference, it is useful to define a term that encompasses all the people who must use the products of our work. Let's call them "customers." Let's further expand this term to include anyone who uses the products produced by the work of someone else. Thus, a geologist would be the "customer" of a word processor who types a handwritten draft of a report. This "customer" may measure quality by the number of typographical errors in the completed report.

There is yet another group of people who are involved in measuring quality. They are the people who provide the input needed for someone else to do his or her job. Let's call them "suppliers." For example, the geologist in the previous example relies on a laboratory to provide the proper data required for the geologist's report. If any of this data is incomplete or incorrect, the result will be a poor quality report and an unhappy client.

In measuring quality, the needs of *every* customer and supplier must be considered. Unhappiness on the part of any customer or supplier will ultimately manifest itself in reduced quality in the eyes of the client.

WHY TRADITIONAL APPROACHES ARE BREAKING DOWN

Design firms have traditionally used quality control (QC) reviews, which are designed to catch errors. More recently, technical service firms have also employed quality assurance (QA) to look at a broader range of project quality issues. These have included quality assurance (QA) audits to verify that the QC reviews are being conducted properly. However, these QA and QC techniques add cost and time to every project. The more thoroughly they are applied, the more they cost.

Perhaps the most extreme example of applying traditional QC and QA has been the nuclear power plant industry. During the 1950s, it became apparent that the design and construction of nuclear power plants had to conform to extremely high quality standards. In response to this requirement, the firms performing these projects (along with various regulatory agencies) developed a highly detailed system of quality control and quality assurance. The results have been multi-billlon dollar cost overruns and years of delay in virtually every major nuclear power plant project. In spite of these exhaustive QA and QC efforts, many facilities are still plagued with serious quality problems.

These same problems are evident on smaller projects. They result from Pareto's Law of Diminishing Returns, which states that every increment of additional quality costs more (in time and money) than the previous increment. After a while, the cost to achieve small improvements in quality becomes excessive.

WHAT CAN WE LEARN FROM THE "QUALITY GURUS"?

To break away from the problems described above we, as technical professionals, must change the way we think about quality. Instead of trying to improve the quality of our projects, we must improve the *process* we use to perform our projects.

Since manufacturers in Japan and the U.S. have been working on solving quality problems for many years, maybe we can learn something from them. A good place to begin is with the teachings of the three most famous "quality gurus," Dr. W. Edward Deming, Philip B. Crosby, and Dr. J. M. Juran. Figure 3.1 describes Deming's "14 Points," Crosby's "Quality Improvement Process," and Juran's "Journey from Symptom to Cause." A good comparison of these three philosophies was made by Ted A. Lowe and Joseph M. Mazzeo, two senior quality managers at General Motors*, and is summarized below.

*Lowe, Ted A. and Mazzeo, Joseph M., "Crosby*Deming*Juran: Three Preachers, One Religion," *Quality*, Hitchcock Publications, September 1986.

Dr. W. Edwards Deming's 14 Points

1. Create constancy of purpose for improvement of product and service.
2. Adopt the new philosophy of refusing to allow defects.
3. Cease dependence on mass inspection and rely only on statistical control.
4. Require suppliers to provide statistical evidence of quality.
5. Constantly and forever improve production and service.
6. Train all employees.
7. Give all employees the proper tools to do the job right.
8. Encourage communication and productivity.
9. Encourage different departments to work together on problem solving.
10. Eliminate posters and slogans that do not teach specific improvement methods.
11. Use statistical methods to continuously improve quality and productivity.
12. Eliminate all barriers to pride in workmanship.
13. Provide ongoing retraining to keep apace with changing products, methods, etc.
14. Clearly define top management's permanent commitment to quality.

Dr. Deming's 14 points are contained in his book, *Quality, Productivity, and Competitive Position.*

J.M. Juran's "Journey from Symptom to Cause"

Quality Improvement in Action

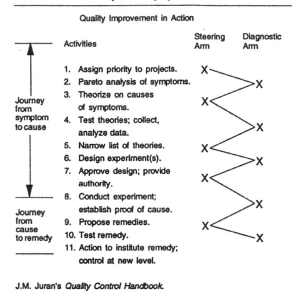

| Activities | Steering Arm | Diagnostic Arm |

Journey from symptom to cause

1. Assign priority to projects.
2. Pareto analysis of symptoms.
3. Theorize on causes of symptoms.
4. Test theories; collect, analyze data.
5. Narrow list of theories.
6. Design experiment(s).
7. Approve design; provide authority.
8. Conduct experiment; establish proof of cause.

Journey from cause to remedy

9. Propose remedies.
10. Test remedy.
11. Action to institute remedy; control at new level.

J.M. Juran's *Quality Control Handbook.*

Philip B. Crosby's Quality Improvement Process

1. Management commitment.
2. Quality improvement team.
3. Quality measurement.
4. Cost of quality evaluation.
5. Awareness.
6. Corrective action.
7. Zero defects day.
8. Quality education.
9. Zero defects planning.
10. Goal setting.
11. Error cause removal.
12. Recognition.
13. Quality councils.
14. Do it all over again.

Philip Crosby's Absolutes of Quality Management

Definition of quality:
    Conformance to requirements.

System:
    Prevention.

Performance standard:
    Zero Defects.

Measurement:
    Cost of quality.

Phillip B. Crosby's books, including *Quality is Free* and *Quality Without Tears.*

Figure 3.1   Work breakdown structure for an environmental study.

Definition of Quality

To Crosby, quality is conformance to requirements. Juran defines quality as fitness for use. Deming describes quality as a predictable degree of uniformity and dependability, at low cost, and suited to the market. Juran's definition relates to Crosby's in stating that a company's quality mission is fitness for use, whereas the quality mission of departments or individuals is conformance to requirements.

Management Commitment

Each expert begins his road map by emphasizing management commitment. All 14 of Deming's points are obligations of management commitment.

Similarly, Juran urges all management levels to provide hands-on leadership in quality management by taking on their own quality projects. Upper management must ask itself, "Since we are asking everyone else to make a new commitment to quality, what are we going to announce as *our* part of the commitment?" Juran's breakthrough sequence starts with a breakthrough attitude. He uses cost of quality as a tool for providing the need to secure top management commitment.

Crosby's 14-step process is geared toward bringing about this breakthrough in attitude. His process also starts with management commitment. Crosby says management must understand that quality is a definable, measurable, and manageable function requiring constant attention. Furthermore, management must communicate its understanding and commitment. His four "absolutes" provide the new philosophy to which Deming alludes in his second point. Although all three of the quality experts agree that quality improvement must start with management commitment, Crosby provides the most well-defined road map for attaining a new management quality commitment and culture.

Strategy

A signpost in the journey of quality improvement is structure and strategy. For example, Deming's 14th point is to create a structure in top management that will push every day on the other 13 points. Juran specifically recommends that a council be formed to guide the quality improvement process. He states that problems can be thought of as projects and that all improvements can be made project-by-project.

The third step in Juran's breakthrough sequence is to prepare for a managerial breakthrough in knowledge by creating problem-solving steering arms and diagnostic arms. This step provides the problem-solving machinery required to achieve improvement. The steering arm guides the overall problem-solving effort by establishing the direction, priorities, and resources. The diagnostic arm is a work group that has the investigative skills and mobility to track a problem to its root cause. Juran divides the problem-solving effort into two journeys: a journey from symptom to cause and a journey from cause to remedy. He says the hardest journey is from symptom to cause, because it is unclear where the responsibility lies.

Crosby's 14-step process provides an explicit, structured approach to launching the improvement process and changing the culture. It does the same for building a quality improvement attitude throughout the organization. A quality improvement team is formed in step 2 to run the improvement process.

Training

As the journey to world-class quality continues, Juran, Deming, and Crosby all emphasize education and training, but with different focuses. Juran covers quality management practices and problem-solving techniques. He provides a systems approach to QC and improvements for all parts of the organization. Deming's focus is on statistical techniques. Crosby's training is targeted toward developing a new quality culture and implementing the quality improvement process.

Quality Measurement

Crosby, Juran, and Deming all recognize the importance of measurement to track progress and assure that the plan stays on course. Although they all promote direct measures of quality performance, such as assembly line defects or billing errors, Deming places more emphasis on statistical analysis than do his counterparts. He uses statistics to understand whether the process is stable, capable, and on target.

The three experts provide different directions with regard to the cost of quality, Crosby and Juran both view the cost of

quality as the main quality measurement tool and use it to select quality improvement projects. Deming opposes the use
of cost of quality as a measurement tool. He believes that the
largest factor—the cost of customer dissatisfaction—is almost impossible to identify, and therefore is left out of the
cost of quality analysis.

The need for a cost-of-quality measurement system is in
proportion to the extent that top management requires cost-
justification for quality improvement projects. Direct measures, cost of quality, and statistical measures are all required,
but will receive different emphasis in different parts of the organization.

Eliminate Problem Sources

One of the most important milestones on the journey to improvement is removing sources of problems. Juran and Deming both maintain that 85% of the problems are management
controllable and not worker controllable. Deming uses statistical techniques to separate common versus special causes.
Workers use control charts to identify and remove special
causes of variation. The up and down movements of the
points should be disregarded by the production worker as
long as they remain in control. It is management's job to correct the causes of variation and improve the operation's process capability. Juran also urges management to address both
chronic and sporadic problems.

Juran also provides instruction for reducing operator errors. He divides these errors into three types: inadvertent,
technique, and willful. He explains why each type happens,
develops the cause for it, and suggests remedies. Juran provides the how-tos in helping operators achieve Corsby's performance standards of zero defects (ZD).

Step 11 of Crosby's process focuses on removing the
causes of error. That step, plus his emphasis on conformance
to requirements, help address the category of problems that
Juran calls the "trivial many."

All three experts believe that management's job is to improve the system with the help of the workers. When Juran
and Deming state that 85% of the problems are management
controllable, they are not implying that only management can
solve these system problems. Rather, management must give
the workers the tools to address the system problems as well
as the local problems.

Instilling Ongoing Improvement

Deming, Juran, and Crosby all preach the need for instilling a culture of continual improvement. Juran urges mangement to create an annual quality improvement program with goals and to see that specific projects are chosen each year with clear responsibility for action. His approach fits in best with management by objectives. He advises that quality objectives must be set according to the marketplace and not be limited by factors outside the firm's immediate control, or by what it thinks can be realistically achieved with current resources.

Deming also emphasizes the need for ongoing improvement. His fifth point is to constantly and forever improve production and service. This concept is illustrated by the Deming circle, which serves as a model for a quality improvement cycle: planning and designing a product, making and selling it, checking customer satisfaction, and acting to further improve customer satisfaction.

In instilling the culture of continued improvement, Crosby, Juran, and Deming do not view improvement strictly in terms of final products. Rather, they focus on internal customer/supplier relationships. Every company has individual products and customers. How do customers perceive the quality of individual products? And what are their requirements? Most people within a company also have internal suppliers who provide them with products and services that they use to complete their tasks. What are individuals' requirements for their suppliers? How do individuals provide feedback to their suppliers on the quality of the work they provide?

Key Points of Each Approach

Although the routes of Deming, Juran, and Crosby cover the same ground, each consultant's road map is unique. Reviewing each expert's major points can help mesh their approaches.

In a broad sense, Deming removes major roadblocks to quality improvement through his 14 obligations of management and by requiring management's commitment. And it was Deming and his 14 points that started the renaissance in quality attitude. His 14 points also promote a participative management style. According to Deming, it is management's duty to give employees meaningful work that gives them a sense of pride and self-esteem. Stressing the use of statistical techniques to control processes and to reduce variations, Deming has provided the statistical tools—the mile markers for the journey.

Juran's quality improvement methodology stresses a project-by-project implementation, and the "breakthrough sequence." He warns against taking shortcuts from symptom to solution without finding and removing the cause. Juran also provides several problem-solving tools in addition to statistical process control. With his "fitness for use" definition of quality, Juran is strongly oriented to meeting customers' expectations.

The main strength of Crosby's program is the attention it gives to transforming quality culture. Crosby involves everyone in the organization in his process by stressing individual conformance to requirements. These 14 steps, a "how-to" for management, provide an easy-to-understand, structured approach to launching the quality improvement process and starting the journey to world-class quality.

Because of this focus on first changing the management culture, Crosby's approach is clearly a top-down process. Besides defining the new management culture with his four absolutes, Crosby gives management a very explicit plan for managing the transition. In contrast, Deming's emphasis on statistical tools tends to make his approach a bottom-up process. Juran's focus on managing improvement and the project-by-project orientation makes his concept most useful to middle managers and quality managers.

Tailor-Making an Improvement Process

The methods from each expert are necessary, but not sufficient in themselves, for reaching the world-class quality destination. Crosby, Deming, and Juran are interdependent. Their concepts can be combined.

In establishing a quality improvement process, a company should fit Crosby, Deming, and Juran into its process, rather than try to fit its process into one of their programs. Tailor a quality strategy based on all three ideologies, and avoid the conflict involved with trying to chose the proper "champion."

Any organization would benefit by using the concepts of all three experts to provide a complete strategy for quality improvement. However, all of their major concepts must be clearly understood and related to each other to assure an integrated approach to quality improvement. Companies must be cautious to not implement a Juran, Deming, or Crosby "process" as if following an easy cookbook approach. Rather, each firm's quality improvement process must be consistent with its own culture and values.

This tailor-made approach will not be as easy as simply adapting a program from an expert or another company. But a greater level of acceptance and commitment will be achieved with an internally developed approach rather than through a "packaged" program. Companies can learn from the quality professionals' experiences and can follow their directives, but there are no shortcuts. Only by creating its own route will a company have the greatest chance of achieving world-class quality products and services.

An example of this tailor-made approach is the Westinghouse Corporation, a recent winner of the covered Malcolm Baldrige Award for quality. Westinghouse has combined all these concepts into what they call the "triangle of quality" (see Figure 3.2). Another example is PPG Industries, which has developed ten strategic elements as the guiding principles of its quality process (see Figure 3.3). This process has succeeded in rescuing PPG's Chemical Division from near oblivion and turning it into one of the most profitable units of the company.

ARE THESE PHILOSOPHIES APPLICABLE TO DESIGN FIRMS?

At this point, it is necessary to point out two short-comings of all three systems. First, these systems were developed for the manufacturing industry, which makes standardized products. Design and other technical service firms produce few, if any, standardized products. The kinds of tools developed by Deming, Crosby, and Juran do not work as easily when they seek to measure nonconformances in reports, designs, manuals, and other customized products from technical service firms. The remainder of this book describes how measurement can successfully be used to improve the quality of studies, designs, construction services, administration, and client relations.

The second difference is the higher education level and smaller size of most architectural, engineering, and other technical service firms when compared to a typical manufac-

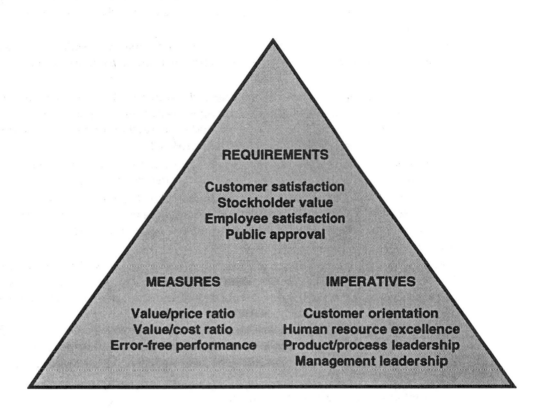

Figure 3.2 The Westinghouse Triangle of Quality.

1. *Leadership Commitment.* Create policies and basic principles for quality improvement throughout PPG; show support by individual example and by maintaining ongoing attention to quality.

2. *Organizational Implementation.* Through Quality Leadership Teams (QLTs), guide and coordinate quality efforts at different levels; communicate goals, efforts, and results. Quality Advisory Councils, whose members represent either a single organizational unit or a larger set of functions, advise QLTs about significant quality-related issues and exchange Quality Process information. Quality Councils also monitor progress throughout PPG and share their findings to promote synergy.

3. *Education.* Provide conceptual foundation and practical training in all aspects of the Quality Process, from basic instruction to more specialized training.

4. *Quality Environment.* Promote heightened awareness by everyone of our quality improvements and our new challenges; contribute to a positive environment for quality through flexibility, trust, and constructive problem resolution, encouraging commitment to quality standards by all.

5. *Measurement.* Assess the state of all work processes to identify and communicate priorities, establish improvement goals, and determine progress.

6. *Cost of Quality.* Define, quantify, and communicate the costs to ensure conformance to requirements and prevent nonconformance and to correct/eliminate nonconformances. Incorporate these concepts into PPG's strategic management process.

7. *Quality Action.* Foster individual initiative to set goals, as well as to identify and take preventive and corrective action; establish and support team-based corrective action at all levels, both within work units and across organizational lines.

8. *Customer/Supplier Processes.* For internal as well as external customers and suppliers, conduct detailed requirements anslyses, and planning and communication efforts to ensure mutual agreement and satisfaction on an ongoing basis.

9. *Recognition.* Provide formal and informal ways to recognize quality improvement efforts as well as accomplishments.

10. *Renewal.* Continuously evaluate progress, encourage new initiatives, and broadly communicate our commitment to the evolving Quality Process and its perpetual importance to PPG's success in the world marketplace.

Figure 3.3 Strategic elements of the PPG quality process.

turing company. The highly structured procedures required by Deming, Crosby, and Juran tend to be a bit stifling and bureaucratic when applied to most technical service firms. Such rigid procedures may not be necessary to obtain the kind of top-to-bottom motivation that is needed to realize dramatic improvement in quality in most design firms. Looking at the

1. Quality is defined as "conformance to requirements"—*all* requirements, including budget and schedule.

2. Requirements must be *mutually* agreed upon with the client and among the entire project team.

3. Requirements must be defined *quantitatively* so that nonconformances can be measured and made visible to everyone involved.

4. The traditional concept of the "project team" must be expanded to include all "suppliers" (people who provide input) and "customers" (people who use the products of our work).

5. Solving quality problems requires the efforts of a *broad cross section* of this extended project team.

6. There must be a *firmwide* system to seek out nonconformances that recur from project to project.

7. Nonconformances should be expected, but not tolerated. In striving for "zero defects," everyone must *continually* reduce the number of nonconformances.

8. Nonconformances that affect client satisfaction are the most serious; they should receive the highest priority.

9. Prevention is cheaper than damage control; the *earlier* you catch a problem, the *less costly* it is to fix.

10. There must be a *firmwide* commitment to quality from the CEO all the way down to the most junior clerical assistant.

11. Everyone in the firm must be trained so that they *understand* the new ways of looking at quality.

12. Individuals and groups who achieve the goals of quality improvement must be appropriately *recognized and rewarded.*

13. Total Quality Project Management (TQPM) cannot be viewed as another program in addition to the firm's "normal" business; it must become *the way the firm does its business.*

Figure 3.4 Burstein and Stasiowski's rules of quality.

"typical" design firm, we have developed a list of basic principles (see Figure 3.4).

LET'S DEFINE SOME TERMS

Over the years, a standard vocabulary has developed to describe the principles of Total Quality Project Management (also known as the Quality Improvement Process). It is important to understand these terms so that meaningful discussions can be held among those who are applying the principles. The items that are used frequently in this book are defined below. A more complete glossary of terms is presented in Appendix A.

Audit. A type of review used to ensure that the required work processes and procedures are being followed and that the work produced is conforming to the requirements.

Brainstorming. A method of generating ideas within a group about problems, their causes, and their solutions; members take turns speaking, record suggestions without immediate comment, and defer discussion or evaluation until everyone has finished contributing.

Conformance. A condition in which a product, service, or work process meets the requirements of the customer.

Corrective Action. Specific actions taken to eliminate the root cause(s) of a nonconformance so the problem is eliminated. The corrective action should be followed up at a later date to verify that it was effective.

Customer. Anyone who receives or uses the output of a process. There are both internal and external customers.

Diagnostic Arm. A group of employees who are assigned by management to solve a specific quality problem.

Measurement Chart. A graphic presentation of facts that highlights raw data, trends, or unusual activities or that presents information on status. It is used to monitor a process or focus attention on a nonconformance so that appropriate actions can be taken.

Nonconformance. Work that does not meet the previously agreed-to requirements of a customer.

Pareto Principle. The "80/20" rule; 80% of the results (problems *or* successes) come from 20% of the causes.

Price of Conformance (POC). What it costs to "get things done right the first time," to ensure that work processes conform to requirements.

Price of Nonconformance (PONC). What it costs to do things wrong; the cost of wasted time, effort, and money plus the cost resulting from dissatisfied customers.

Quality. Conforming to defined and agreed-to requirements; fit for the intended use; predictable in uniformity and dependability; work that will not have to be redone.

Quality Assurance (QA). Actions necessary to provide adequate confidence that a system and its components will perform satisfactorily in service.

Quality Control (QC). Checking a product to determine if it conforms to requirements.

Quality Improvement Process (QIP). The series of actions that aids each employee in producing higher quality work.

Quick Fix. Taking immediate, short-term steps to keep a job or process running while the root cause of the problem is analyzed and eliminated.

Requirement. Expectations for a product, service, or work process, which should be mutually agreed upon by suppliers and customers.

Root Cause. The primary source(s) from which a nonconformance originates.

Run Chart. A measurement chart used to record the data gathered (usually on the vertical axis) over a period of time (on the horizontal axis).

Steering Arm. The role of senior management in guiding the solution of specific quality problems.

Supplier. Anyone who provides the input to a process. Suppliers can be external or internal to an organization.

Total Quality Management. The integration of effective methods for Quality Control, Quality Assurance, and Quality Improvement.

Zero Defects. The intent to meet requirements the first time, every time.

IS THE QUALITY IMPROVEMENT PROCESS SUICIDAL?

There are those who argue that the Quality Improvement Process is a path toward professional liability disaster because it focuses so heavily on documenting instances where the firm did *not* conform to requirements. Indeed, in the hands of an aggressive attorney representing a litigious client, a design firm's carefully maintained records of nonconformances can serve as evidence of the firm's negligence.

In reacting to this legitimate concern, it is necessary to remember that the existence of errors and omissions does not in itself demonstrate negligence. The test is whether the quality of the work conforms to the standards of the profession—a profession in which errors and omissions are a fact of life.

If the design professional and the client can agree on the project's objectives in *quantitative* terms *before* the work is begun, misunderstandings that lead to law suits will often be avoided. Properly applying the principles of Total Quality Management will not totally eliminate errors or omissions, but it will result in projects that meet the client's objectives. Successful projects yield happy clients and happy clients don't sue!

Even if a professional liability claim is made by a client, Total Quality Project Management can aid in the design firm's defense in two ways:

1. The statistical data compiled regarding nonconformances can be used to demonstrate that the firm makes *fewer* errors than the norm in the industry.
2. The fact that a firm is implementing a well-recognized quality management process is strong evidence of a responsible, professional attitude.

In the final analysis, each firm's principals must decide what course they will chart for the future. Will their firm become more and more defensive, afraid to take risks for fear of legal repercussions? Or, will it strike out boldly, with an objective of becoming the best it can possibly be?

SUMMARY

This chapter concludes the discussion of basic principles and concepts of TQPM. The remainder of this book describes how these techniques developed for use in manufacturing can be adapted to improve the quality of work performed by design and other technical service firms. But implementation of these techniques goes far beyond the objectives of reducing design errors. It is the door to a new way of doing business, one that will result in more satisfied clients, more motivated employees, and higher profits.

4 IMPROVING THE QUALITY OF DESIGN PROJECTS

In 1991, *Engineering News Record* and the School of Building Construction at the University of Florida sent questionnaires about the quality of design specifications to 500 U.S. construction contractors*. Of the 120 that responded, the following conclusions were reached:

- 84% said specifications either sometimes, often, or generaly have major omissions.
- 55% said specifications often conflict with other contract documents.
- 75% called for specifications to be more extensive and comprehensive.

The traditional approach to improving the kinds of quality problems described above has been to increase quality control activities on each project. If plans and specifications are more carefully reviewed, corrections can be made before the documents are issued for bidding. Unfortunately, this additional level of reviews and corrections adds time and costs to the design. To make matters worse, clients don't want to wait any longer or pay any more than they do already! So we, as design professionals, resort to the old saw, "You can have it fast, good, or cheap—pick any two." To which our clients respond, "If you can't give me all three, I'll take my business to someone who can."

*Tuchman, Janice L., "Contractor Survey Finds that Specs Don't Measure Up," *Engineering News Record,* June 17, 1991.

Fortunately, Total Quality Project Management (TQPM) provides a solution to this dilemma. Most design firms spend 25–50% of design man-hours redoing work that had already been done once, redesigning details that have already been designed on other projects, and correcting errors caught during design reviews. *Through TQPM, quality is improved not by more checking but by eliminating the sources of these errors. By the time the design gets to the review stage, it has fewer errors so that less time (and money) is required for reviews and corrections. Also, fewer errors go undetected during the review.*

DEFINING REQUIREMENTS

In Chapter 3, we defined quality as "conformance with requirements." To achieve this definition of quality on a design project, *the requirements must be clearly defined at the beginning of the project and must be agreed to by both the client and the design team.* As obvious as this sounds, most design professionals and most owners fail to devote enough effort to early definition of requirements, only to discover major "disconnects" during construction and start-up. The more time and effort spent at the begining in defining requirements, the more smoothly the project will progress and the happier both the client and design firm will be when it's over.

Defining requirements on a design project must be viewed not as a task for the owner to do while preparing a request for proposal nor as an agenda item for a one-hour kick-off meeting. It should be an evolution that results from a dialog between the owner and the designer. The process requires a series of meetings and telephone conversations between the owner and design firm during which the requirements become clearly defined and understood by both parties.

The effectiveness of this dialog is dependent on the amount of preparation that is done *prior* to the meetings and telephone calls. The following tools can be used to help define requirements:

1. A pre-design questionnaire to determine the basic project requirements (see the example in Figure 4.1).
2. A list of questions that should be asked by the designer

1. What documents define the basis of design, e.g., programming documents, pilot plant reports, design criteria, preliminary design report, etc.? _____

_____

_____

_____

2. What codes, ordinances, and standards must be complied with?

_____

_____

_____

3. What is the schedule for completion?

   Submittal date for proposal: _____

   Authorization to proceed: _____

   Complete design development: _____

   Complete plans and specs: _____

   Award construction contract: _____

   Complete construction: _____

   Complete start-up: _____

   Other key dates: _____

   _____

4. What is the estimated construction cost? _____

5. How will construction be accomplished?

   General Contractor: _____

   Turnkey: _____

   Construction management by A/E: _____

   Construction management by owner: _____

   Construction management by other: _____

   Other: _____

   _____

6. Other comments: _____

   _____

Figure 4.1 Pre-design questionnaire to determine project requirements.

1. Are any regulatory approvals required? If so, how much assistance is desired from A/E? _____

_____

2. Are accurate as-built drawings available? If not, how much field verification will A/E need to perform? _____

_____

3. Who will hire surveyor? Geotechnical consultant? Other specialty consultants? _____

_____

_____

4. Are any interim submittals required? If so, describe: _____

_____

_____

5. Will separate bid packages be required for equipment procurement or construction activities? If so, describe: _____

_____

6. Will A/E prepare construction cost estimate? If so, at what points during the design? _____

_____

7. Does owner have any requirements to conform to standard drawings, specs, equipment types, etc.? If so, describe: _____

_____

8. Are there any unusual foundation, drainage, access, or other site problems? If so, describe: _____

_____

Figure 4.2 Pre-design questions to determine designer's scope of work.

to determine the scope of services desired by the client (see the example in Figure 4.2).

3. A checklist of typical services provided by the design firm for a particular type of project (see the example in Figure 4.3).

4. A drawing list (Figure 4.4) and specification index (Figure 4.5) to establish the scope and level of detail to be provided in the design.

I. Design Engineering
   A. Preliminary Design
      1. Prepare process and instrumentation diagrams
      2. Finalize site plans
      3. Prepare hydraulic profiles
      4. Finalize major equipment list
      5. Identify materials of construction
      6. Prepare equipment layout drawings
      7. Prepare major equipment specifications
      8. Obtain soils, foundation, and topographic information
      9. Develop final design criteria
         a. Process/mechanical
         b. Instrumentation/controls
         c. Electrical
         d. Civil/site/foundation
         e. Structural
         f. Architectural
      10. Prepare basis-of-design submittal
   B. Detailed Design
      1. Prepare mechanical plans
      2. Prepare instrumentation/control plans
      3. Prepare civil/site plans
      4. Prepare structural/architectural plans
      5. Prepare electrical plans
      6. Prepare minor equipment specifications
      7. Prepare bulk materials specifications
      8. Prepare construction specifications
II. Procurement of Equipment and Materials
   A. Prepare Bills of Material
   B. Prequalify Vendors
   C. Prepare Bid Documents and Assemble Bid Packages
   D. Evaluate Bids and Prepare Purchase Requisitions
   E. Expedite Delivery
   F. Review Shop Drawings
   G. Inspect Equipment
      1. Owner-furnished equipment/materials
      2. Contrator-furnished equipment/materials
   H. Assemble Equipment Data Books

III. Construction
   A. Prequalify Contractors
   B. Issue Bid Package
   C. Evaluate Bids
   D. Inspect Construction
   E. Prepare Field Orders and Change Orders
   F. Commission Equipment
   G. Prepare Record Drawings of Constructed Facilities
IV. Start-Up and Operator Training
   A. Prepare Operator Instructions Manual
   B. Start-Up Facility
   C. Train Operators
   D. Perform Periodic Operations Reviews
V. Project Management
   A. Project Planning
      1. Finalize responsibility assignments
      2. Prepare detailed project schedule (CPM diagram)
      3. Prepare cost estimates
         a. Construction costs
         b. O&M costs
      4. Prepare expenditure forecast
   B. Permitting Assistance
   C. Project Monitoring and Control
      1. Keep project schedule updated
      2. Keep expenditure forecast updated
      3. Prepare monthly status reports
         a. Equipment procurement status
         b. Overall schedule status
         c. Budget status
      4. Prepare final project cost report

Figure 4.3 Typical services provided by design firms for process facilities.

Sheet	Discipline	Title
1	General	Cover sheet/index to drawings/location map
2	Civil	Site plan
3	Civil	Paving/grading/storm sewers plan and details
4	Civil	Water/sanitation/power/phone/fire protection plan and details
5	Architectural	Floor plan
6	Architectural	Elevations
7	Architectural	Roof plan and roof details
8	Architectural	Reflected ceiling plan
9	Architectural	Wall sections and details
10	Architectural	Partial plans and interior elevations
11	Architectural	Door schedule and door details
12	Architectural	Finish schedules/notes/legend
13	Structural	Foundation plan/sections/details
14	Structural	Loading docks/containment bay plan/sections/details
15	Electrical	Legend and schedules
16	Electrical	Site plan and details
17	Electrical	Lighting plan and details
18	Electrical	Alarm/security/phone plan
19	Plumbing	Plumbing plan and details
20	Plumbing	Fire system plan and details
21	HVAC	HVAC plan
22	HVAC	HVAC section and details
23	HVAC	Schedules and details

Figure 4.4 Sample list of drawings.

THE BASIS OF DESIGN REPORT

During approximately the first 20 to 30 percent of all design projects, a detailed Basis of Design Report (BODR) should be prepared for internal review and subsequently to the client for review and approval. The BODR should then become the guide for all subsequent design activities. The BODR should include design criteria for each discipline such as civil, mechanical, architectural, electrical, instrumentation, etc. These should reflect all criteria, requirements, material selection, specialty design techniques, codes and all other pertinent items necessary to guide the designers. The BODR should also contain preliminary drawings such as process and instrumentation diagrams, floor plans and site plans.

There is also often a requirement to perform special stud-

BIDDING REQUIREMENTS

Invitation to Bid

Instructions to Bidders

Bid Proposal

Bid Security Form

Noncollusion Affidavit

CONTRACT REQUIREMENTS

Contract Agreement

Performance Bond

Payment Bond

Certificate of Owner's Attorney

CONDITIONS OF CONTRACT

General Conditions

Supplementary Conditions

DIVISION 1—GENERAL REQUIREMENTS

01010   Summary of the Work

01015   General Provisions

01030   Measurement and Payment

01035   Mobilization and Demobilization

01300   Submittals

01400   Quality Control

DIVISION 2—TECHNICAL SPECIFICATIONS

02220   Site Work

02221   Trenching, Backfilling, and Compacting

02300   Piping and Appurtenances

02605   Manholes and Fittings

02830   Chain Link Fencing and Gates

02900   Landscaping

Figure 4.5   Partial table of contents for construction specifications.

ies in order to determine the best solution to detailed problems or questions arising from the design. Such studies may include the technical evaluation of a new equipment, economic evaluation of alternative energy systems for a specific application or evaluation of special materials to be used in a design. Generally, these studies cover areas of innovative design or considerations not normally encountered in the preliminary engineering phase. When appropriate, these studies can be included in the BODR.

When completed, the BODR can serve the following functions:

- Provide a convenient review point for the owner to monitor the progress of the project and to determine whether the project is within the capital budget.
- Provide a guide for the conduct of the final design phase of the project.
- Define the scopes of work for engineering subconsultants (if any).
- Optimize communications between the various disciplines within the design team.
- Serve as a submittal to funding agencies for their review and or approval.
- Serve as a preliminary submittal application to agencies requiring permits.
- Define the project well enough to prepare a ± 15% construction cost estimate.

The Basis of Design Report need not follow a rigid format. Rather, the report should accommodate the special needs of each project. The objective is not to make sure that all of the blanks are filled in, but rather that sufficient information has been developed to fix all subsequent design production activities, as well as provide the basis for a Basis of Design cost estimate for the project. The Basis of Design approach can be applied to all facility designs. It is not difficult or complicated to apply; however, to be effective, it is necessary that all data relative to the project be gathered and applied to the report development.

The organization of a BODR should be flexible to permit inclusion of all information which is pertinent to subsequent design efforts. The report must be dynamic, lending itself to easy updating as a project proceeds. Even after approval of a BODR and commencement of design, changes wil occur. The BODR should continuously be updated to keep it current as the basic reference document for the project. This can be facilitated by issuing the report in a 3-ring binder with supplements and revisions issued as the design changes. A typical table of contents is presented in Figure 4.6.

Copies of the BODR should be distributed to the client as well as to each member of the design team. The distribution list should be well documented to assure that everyone receives each update as it is issued.

THE PROJECT MANAGEMENT PLAN

Just as the Basis of Design Report can be used to document the technical aspects of the design, the Project Management Plan can document the project management approach. An example table of contents for a Project Management Plan is presented in Figure 4.7. Some particularly important elements of the plan are described below.

Organizing the Team for Quality

In the ideal situation, only the most capable and experienced people are assigned to every project team and they are available precisely to the extent desired by the project manager. Unfortunately, this is not always possible. But having less than the perfect team does not relieve the design firm of the responsibility to produce a high quality design. To overcome the quality problems often associated with a less-than-ideal project team, the project manager should review the project team and identify the strengths and weakness of each individual.

The result of these evaluations can be tabulated confidentially in the form of a project team profile such as the example in Figure 4.8. This plan will enable the project manager to make the most effective use of each person's strengths while mitigating the quality impacts of their weaknesses. The result is a true team, which is capable of far more than the sum of the members' individual efforts.

1. Process
   A. Process flow diagram
   B. Material and energy balances
2. Mechanical Process
   A. Design Criteria and Calculations
   B. P&ID Development
   C. Hydraulic Profile
3. Process Equipment
   A. General
   B. Rotating Equipment
   C. Heat Transfer Equipment
   D. Vessels
4. Piping Design
   A. General Piping
   B. Pipe Sizes
   C. Fittings and Branch Connections
   D. Valves
   E. Control Valves
   F. Relief Valves
   G. Vents and Drains
   H. Line Blinds
   I. Utility Stations
   J. Vessels and Column Piping
   K. Heat Exchanger Piping
   L. Fired Equipment Piping
   M. Rotating Equipment Piping
   N. Reactor (heavy wall)
   O. Offsite Facilities
   P. Utility Systems
5. Materials Handling
6. Materials Application/Welding
   A. Materials Selection
   B. Cathodic Protection
   C. Coatings
   D. Welding and Fabrication
   E. Insulation

7. Mechanical Utilities
   A. General
   B. HVAC
   C. Fire Protection
   D. Noise Control
   E. Plumbing
8. Civil
   A. Engineering Design
   B. Civil Drawings
9. Architectural
   A. Design Criteria
   B. Drawings
   C. Specifications
   D. Special Features
   E. Construction Materials
10. Electrical
    A. Scope of Work
    B. Single-line Diagrams
    C. Power and Grounding
    D. Lighting
    E. Instrument
    F. Telecommunications
11. Instrumentation and Controls
12. Structural
    A. Design
    B. Drawings

Figure 4.6   Contents of a typical Basis of Design Report.

Anticipating Problems

Philip Crosby, the well-known expert in quality improvement, stresses the value of early recognition and solution to quality problems. A problem that costs $1 to prevent will cost $10 if it is caught by the firm's internal review system and

SECTION 1 PROJECT DEFINTION
A. Project Objectives
B. Scope of Services
C. List of Drawings
D. List of Specifications
E. Contracts/Bidding Packages

SECTION 2 ORGANIZATION AND RESPONSIBILITIES
A. Project Organization Chart
B. Names & Addresses of Key Personnel
C. Project Team Profile
D. Distribution of General Documents
E. Distribution of Engineering Documents

SECTION 3 SCHEDULE
A. Project Schedule
B. Project Milestones
C. CPM Schedule

SECTION 4 ESTIMATED COSTS
A. Task Cost Report
B. Project Expenditure Forecast
C. Project Expenditure Profile
D. Construction Cost Estimates
E. Task Budgeting Numbers

SECTION 5 QUALITY ASSURANCE
A. Crisis Prevention Plan
B. Quality Control Plan
C. Design Review Requirements
D. Constructability Review Responsibilities
E. Operability Review
F. QA Plan Approval Checklist
G. QA Audit Report Format
H. Certificate of Substantial Design Completion

SECTION 6 PROCEDURES
5.1 Administrative Procedures
5.2 Project Management Procedures
5.3 Design Management Procedures
5.4 Procurement Management Procedures
5.5 Construction Management Procedures
5.6 Controls Management Procedures

Figure 4.7 Example table of contents for a project management plan.

Name and Role on Team	Major Strengths	Ways to Utilize Strengths	Major Weaknesses	Ways to Compensate for Weaknesses
J. Stonewick, Project Manager	• Good with clients • Motivates team members • Good rapport with plan review agencies	Focus on regular communications with client, team members, review agency staff	• Tends to overcommit • Doesn't keep careful track of details	Assign S. Dalton to develop and maintain cost/schedule control system and document control system.
S. Dalton, Project Engineer	• Detail oriented • Good with computer	Serve as Assistant Project Manager to handle specified duties, e.g., cost/schedule control, document control	• Not creative • Does not communicate well	• J. Stonewick to handle most communications with client and in-house team. • V. Schwartz to take lead on layouts, schematics
V. Schwartz, Chief Designer	• Creative • Understands this kind of facility	Handle all layout work and review details developed by others	• Short attention span • Impatient with less experienced staff	S. Dalton to supervise staff of mechanical drafters
A. Cooper, Mechanical Engineer	• Pleasant personality • Dedicated • Hard working	Assist V. Schwartz in detailing layouts and concepts	• Inexperienced	Assure regular involvement of Mechanical Dept. Head and S. Dalton

Figure 4.8 Project team profile.

Potential Problems	Prevention Measures
1. Easements and rights-of-way (ROWs) may be difficult to obtain, especially from Railroad and State Dept. of Transportation (DOT). May cause delay in design schedule.	• Establish detailed listing of all easements and ROWs and update approval status every two weeks. • Set up early design review meetings with Railroad and DOT personnel responsible for granting ROWs.
2. Location of existing utilities may not be well-defined. Could generate excessive change orders during construction.	• Hire surveyor to "pot hole" congested areas to locate existing utilities. • Prepare bid documents on unit price (rather than lump sum) basis. • Include an allowance for utility relocation required during construction.
3. Older pipelines may not withstand pressure increase imposed when new system comes on line. May result in line breakage.	• Request engineering change order from client to test existing lines. • Owner should put all repair crews on 24-hour notice for one week after start-up of new system.

Figure 4.9 Crisis prevention plan for a water distribution system design.

$100 if it is caught by the contractor or client. How can this concept be used to reduce costs on design projects?

At the outset of the project, the project manager should assemble the team in a brainstorming meeting and ask, "What can go wrong that will hurt the quality of this project?" All the responses should be listed on an easel pad or blackboard. The project manager should then go back to each possible problem and ask for ideas that can prevent the problem or mitigate its impact. The results can be tabulated as shown in the example in Figure 4.9. This list is then incorporated into the project management plan and distributed to everyone on the team so that they can prevent these problems or solve them before they become severe. Preparing a crisis prevention plan takes only a few man-hours and can save many times that cost in reduced rework alone.

Preparing a Quality Control (QC) Plan

No matter how well planned, every design project will be plagued with errors and omissions. The purpose of quality control is to find and correct these errors before the design goes to the field. A good QC plan should define:

- Which documents should be reviewed.
- Who should review them.
- When they should be reviewed.
- What kinds of errors will be sought.
- The budget allotted for review.
- The schedule and budget allotted for corrections.

One of the most common mistakes made in quality control is for a reviewer to be given a set of documents and told, "Here, review these and mark any errors you find." Such vague instructions fail to provide explicit guidance as to *what kind of review* is expected. Following is a description of several different kinds of reviews typically conducted on design projects.

Conceptual Review. In the early stages of a project, basic concepts are developed that are implemented during the remainder of the design process. If these concepts are not sound, the facility will not function properly even if the details are totally correct. One or more independent reviewers should check these basic concepts to make sure that the facility will function properly, given the project's budget and schedule constraints.

Intradisciplinary Review. When dividing a project into various design disciplines, each discipline becomes responsible for its own quality. The structural engineer must design concrete that does not crack; the electrical engineer must select wire sizes that are large enough for the intended loads; the civil engineer must assure proper site drainage. An intradisciplinary review ensures that an independent, experienced person from each discipline checks the applicable calculations, drawings, and specifications produced by that discipline. Although the intradisciplinary review cannot be done by the person who performed the design, it can be done by another project team member. For example, if two experienced structural engineers are working on different portions of a design, one can easily check the work done by the other because they are already familiar with the project. This review approach tends to be more cost-effective than using independent reviewers who are not familiar with the project.

Interdiscipline Review. Even if the work of each discipline is flawless, problems may arise due to inconsistencies between disciplines. For example, the electrical engineer may have designed a suitable lighting system for an 8-foot ceiling; however, if the architect subsequently changes the drawings to show a 12-foot ceiling, the lighting design may be inadequate. To find these problems, one or more individuals should perform a detailed interdisciplinary review to assure consistency between disciplines.

Drawing-Specification Cross-Check. Just as there can be inconsistencies between drawings, there are often inconsistencies between the drawings and specifications. These can be identified by a checker who reviews the specifications page by page, identifying information that might also appear elsewhere on the drawings or specifications. For example, a specifications may call out a 10 horsepower pump. The checker knows that a single line diagram for the pump motor should be present in the electrical drawings. If the single line diagram is not consistent with the pump specification, the checker so notes.

Multifacility Cross-Check. Very large projects often involve multiple buildings or other related facilities, often designed by different project team members. A common source of design errors on such projects is the existence of inconsistencies between buildings located in the same complex. For example, a large wastewater treatment plant may consist of a dozen buildings or process facilities. If a pipe is shown leaving one building as an 8-inch line and arriving at another building as a 6-inch line, this is probably a design error.

Vendor Review. It is useful to obtain reviews from the manufacturers and suppliers who are expected to bid on major equipment and bulk materials. The vendors can identify equipment incompatibilities, out-of-date specifications, and inappropriate materials. They can also provide other requested information such as costs and delivery times. Vendors are usually happy to provide this review because it gives them a way to assure that their equipment and materials are properly described in the

Mr. William Duncan
Duncan Equipment Company
410 Seventh Avenue
Gotham, USA

Subject: Gotham Civic Center Project

Dear Mr. Duncan:

I am enclosing a copy of preliminary plans and specifications for the HVAC equipment for your review and comment. In order for your comments to be incorporated into the final documents, I will need your response no later than February 14.

In addition to reviewing the contract documents, I would also like you to provide the following support information:

- Approximate equipment costs (excluding sales taxes).
- Approximate freight costs to job site.
- Estimated installation costs and calendar time.
- Size and weight of each compressor unit.
- Estimated times for shop drawings preparation, equipment fabrication, and delivery.
- Catalog drawing showing principal dimensions and mounting arrangement.

If you have any questions or require additional information, please do not hesitate to call.

Sincerely,

Janet Roberts, P.E.
Project Engineer

Figure 4.10 An example of a letter requesting vendor review.

specifications. A sample letter requesting such a review is presented in Figure 4.10.

Constructability Review. Even if the drawings and specifications are technically correct and consistent, the design may be difficult or impossible for a contractor to bid or construct. Construction contractors often complain about designs for concrete that can only be placed by midgets, specifications for equipment that has not been manufactured for years, and construction sequencing that cannot be done without disrupting ongoing operations. These complaints often turn into costly change orders. The purpose of a constructability review is to identify these problems during design. The best person to perform this review is a construction contractor or former contractor. If there is no such person in the design firm, they are readily available as consultants, usually for a modest cost.

Operability Review. Perhaps the most serious quality problems occur when a facility is found to be difficult to operate or maintain. Unlike problems that occur during design and construction, operations and maintenance problems often plague the project for many years after the design firm has completed its work. The long-term effect can be devastating to a design firm's reputation. The best way to avoid these problems is to perform a thorough operability review during the design phase. The best person for this review is the individual responsible for operating and maintaining the completed facility (usually the owner's employee). For example, the building manager might identify valves located 12 feet high with no way of operating them or instrumentation whose maintenance requires an electronics engineer with a Ph.D. If the owner's operations/maintenance manager is not available, someone should be retained who has operated and maintained a similar facility.

The project manager must assess which of the above elements are required for a given design, and at what stages of completion the documents should be reviewed. For small, simple projects, one review at the end may be adequate. For large, complex designs, multiple reviews are essential in order to avoid extensive rework. Figure 4.11 presents a sample QC plan for a small project.

SEQUENCING THE WORK PROCESS

According to Dr. W. Edward Deming, all work is a process that can be represented by a flow chart. This is particularly true of design projects, which have a natural sequence of activities that lead to the most efficiently produced product. Deviations from this natural sequence introduce rework and errors, which cost time and money to correct. This natural se-

Reviewer	Documents to be Reviewed	Budget Man-Hours	Intradiscipline Review	Interdiscipline Cross-Check	Constructability	Operability
D. Fry	Civil drawings, specs, calculations	4	X	X	X	X
H. Richardson	HVAC drawings, specs, calculations	5	X	X		
R. Mayfield	Process drawings	3	X			
H. Richardson	Mechanical drawings, specs, calculations	4	X	X		
M. D'Alessandro	Instrument drawings, specs, calculations	4	X	X		
R. Liedtke	Electrical drawings, specs, calculations	4	X	X		
D. Fry	Structural and architectural drawings, specs, calculations	5	X	X		
C. Baylot	All drawings	3				X
K. Deagon	All drawings	3			X	
M. Yahya	All drawings and specs	4		X	X	
R. Lord	All drawings and specs	4				X
A. Lubell	Drawings prepared by all other disciplines	4		X		
J. Lugod	All drawings and specs	4	X			

Note: All reviews to be performed between August 7 and August 10.

Figure 4.11 An example of a quality control plan.

quence can be determined by preparing a task precedence diagram for each project, such as the example of Figure 4.12.

After determining the natural sequence of activities, the project manager can evaluate the impact of design changes throughout the project. Changes can be made at relatively low cost during the early stages of a project; however, once the size of the project team begins to increase, every minor change has the potential for generating many costly errors.

The cost of changes can be greatly reduced by a concept called "Lead Discipline Management." The objective of Lead Discipline Management is to plan and execute the project so that virutally all the design changes are made during the early stages. The following is an example of the application of this approach:

William, a project manager with ABC Consultants, has been assigned a project to design a new wastewater treatment plant for the town of Smallville. He has planned the project carefully so that all the key design decisions are made early in the project. These include the size of the facility, the unit processes to be used, the sizes of major tankage and equipment, general site plan, and design criteria for each discipline (structural, electrical, architectural, etc.)

William also assigns the process/mechanical discipline as the project lead. After defining all project criteria, only the process-mechanical staff works on the project. They lay out all the equipment, arrange the piping and valves, develop a detailed motor list, and prepare the mechanical drawings to about 80% completion. During this phase, input is solicited from the other disciplines regarding space allocations, interfaces, and so on. Periodic review prints are given to the other disciplines to assure that their requirements are being properly considered.

The 80% complete mechanical drawings are then given to each of the other disciplines for use as the basis for their drawings. Once this has been done, *the mechanical drawings cannot be changed unless an error has been found.* In this case, William must personally approve the change and immediately advise the other disciplines.

This approach allows the lead discipline (process/mechanical in this example) to direct the design process unimpeded by changes from other disciplines up to the 80% point. However, once the 80% point is reached and the other disciplines

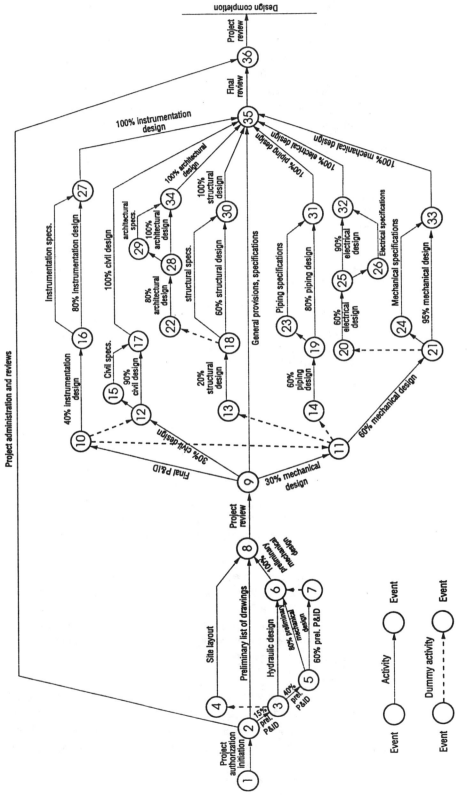

Figure 4.12 Design activity network for chemical process facilities.

begin work, nonessential changes in process/mechanical design can no longer be tolerated.

The concept of Lead Discipline Management is illustrated graphically in Figure 4.13. By delaying the increase in the size of the project team, the increase in the rate of expenditure is also delayed. This allows time to solidify the design concept while changes are relatively inexpensive. By the time the rate of expenditure (and cost of making changes) has increased, very few changes are required.

THE PRINCIPLE OF SINGLE STATEMENT

Mr. J. C. Reichenberger, a vice president with Engineering-Science, Inc., has described how the effective use of a simple concept can prevent many design errors. This concept is known as the "principle of single statement." Each dimension, coordinate, elevation, callout, and so on, must be shown *only once* in a set of drawings and specifications; it should be shown where it can be most easily found.

There is a tendency for design professionals to want to show dimensions, material callouts, coordinates, and other information at several places in a set of drawings, "just to make sure the construction contractor doesn't miss it." All too often such information changes during the course of the design and is not corrected on all of the drawings and specifications where it has been shown. Results: conflicts and potential contractor claims. If an item of information is called out only once and the contractor has to "dig" a little or read the plans and specs more thoroughly to find it, is this so bad? Even if a dimension is inadvertently left off completely, what would happen? The contractor would probably ask "where do I put this?" At that point the designer could either calculate the dimension or scale it from the drawings. Is that so bad? It is far more difficult for the contractor to file a claim for a missing dimension than for a conflicting one. Some specific examples of the application of the principle of single statement are illustrated in Figure 4.14.

In addition to creating potential construction problems, repeating dimensions and other information on the drawings takes extra design time. If a change becomes necessary and the designer is thorough (or lucky) enough to catch it in every place, it takes even more time. And if an error is not

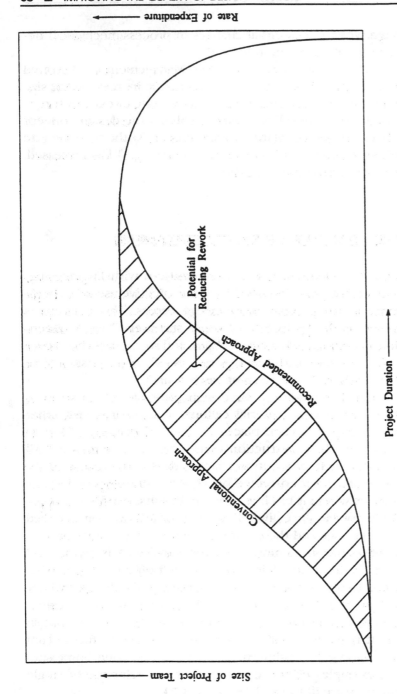

Figure 4.13 How proper planning can reduce rework.

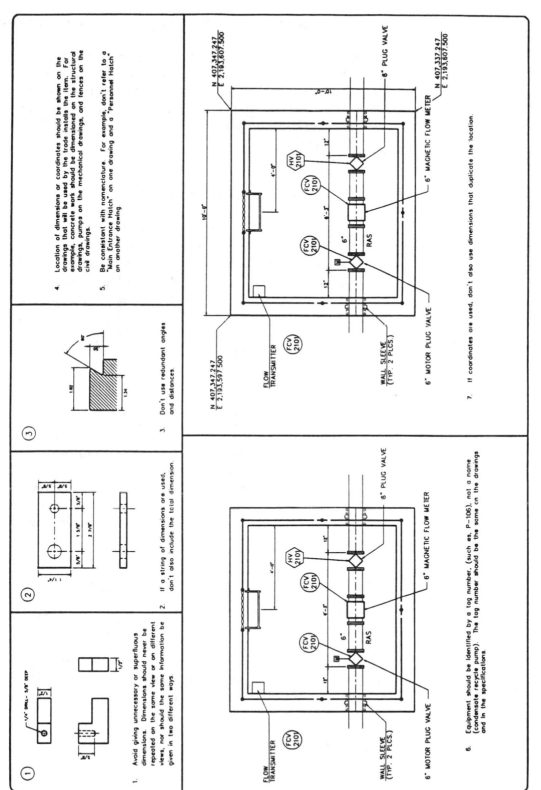

Figure 4.14 Examples of the application of the principle of single statement.

caught, it takes still more time during the construction phase to resolve.

It is not practical to achieve 100 percent compliance with the principle of single statement. However, this should be the goal that every project team member should strive for. As Mark Twain said, "Give a man a watch and he will always know what time it is; give him two watches and he will never be quite sure!"

QUALITY CONTROL WORKSHOPS

A commonly used approach for conducting design reviews is the QC workshop—a gathering of a multidisciplined team, *located in one place and protected from normal work load distractions*, for the purpose of reviewing contract documents. The QC workshop is external to the design team's normal internal reviews, but can be a vital part of the overall QC plan for the project. The following methodology was developed by Gary Nickerson, a principal project manager with Engineering-Science, Inc.

Number and Timing of Workshops

The number and timing of QC workshops should be planned in advance by the project manager. For major projects, at least two QC workshops are recommended. They can usually be conducted concurrently with scheduled owner reviews, for example at 30%, 60%, and 90% completion. The workshop should be held during a period of one to five consecutive days.

QC Team Makeup

The number of team members and their individual expertise is a function of the requirements of the project. However, each team member should have considerable experience in his or her field so that the owner and design team will respect their opinions. The team should *always* include at least one member with recent construction experience and one member with extensive experience in operating and maintaining similar facilities. Reviews conducted early in the project might include more individuals with conceptual design experience, while those conducted later in the project should in-

clude those with more detail design and construction expertise. The QC team members *must never* have been involved
in the project design prior to the workshop.

It is the responsibility of the team leader to: (1) be in
charge of the QC team and keep it on track to finish within
the allotted workshop time, and (2) convey the findings of
the review through written comments and presentations to
the design team and owner.

Pre-Workshop Activities

The project manager should perform the following activities:

1. Schedule the workshop and make the necessary logisti-
   cal arrangements for a spacious meeting room with
   plenty of tabletop area.
2. Send each QC team member a memo concerning all lo-
   gistical arrangements—where and when to report, appropriate charge number, and agenda for the workshop.
   This memo should also transmit project background information and authorization for charging a certain number of pre-workshop preparation hours if appropriate.
3. Arrange to provide appropriate document sets and
   project background data so that they are available in
   the workshop area at the beginning of the workshop. At
   least two sets of specifications and two sets of full-size
   drawings and half-size drawings are suggested for each
   design discipline.
4. Where appropriate, invite the owner's representa-
   tive(s) to be present for all or part of the workshop. The
   owner's representative(s) might also be invited to the
   QC team's presentation of comments to the design
   team.

Workshop Activities

As the first activities of the workshop, the QC team leader
should introduce the team members and describe the activity
plan and time schedule for the workshop. The project manager and design team members then brief the QC team on the
project, including the history of the design effort to date.
Project design schedule and budget constraints imposed by

the owner, regulatory agencies, and others should be high-lighted.

On major projects the review should be conducted in three phases. These are:

1. Development Phase
2. Evaluation Phase
3. Conclusion Phase

DEVELOPMENT PHASE

Under the Development Phase, the project is divided into elements in three different ways and organized as follows:

- Site/facilities
- Function (unit processes, etc.)
- Design discipline
  There will certainly be overlap in this approach which will aid in the review.

A creative session is then held to identify and express thoughts that each reviewer may have relative to any element of the project. For example, it would be appropriate to raise questions about:

- What was done or considered
- What has not been done
- What should or could be done

No evaluation of ideas is to take place at this time. It is intended for this phase to be a free exchange of whatever comes to mind. Some of the craziest ideas or comments can trigger the exposure of serious oversights.

EVALUATION PHASE

This phase considers each comment raised under the Development Phase and reduces them to significant comments which should be considered further.

CONCLUSION PHASE

This phase further considers comments singled out during the Evaluation Phase. From these deliberations, a list of comments will be prepared with recommendations for implementation or further evaluation. Also, each recommendation is evaluated as to the feasibility of its being carried out (because of monetary, schedule, client, or other constraints).

All significant comments are recorded on comment forms. Minor comments, reference errors, spelling errors, and so on, can be marked on the specifications and full-size drawing sets.

At the end, the QC team briefs the design team on the findings of the review to make sure that the written comments are properly interpreted. The QC team leader introduces the team members, summarizes the overall state of the documents, and briefly mentions several of the most significant comments. He or she then asks each team member to summarize their review comments, drawing by drawing. For small projects, time may allow addressing each comment listed.

Upon conclusion of the briefing, the QC team leader presents the project manager with the following:

1. The sets of specifications and full-size drawings marked up by the team.
2. The comment sheets, organized and numbered, and referenced to the team member making the comment.
3. A brief summary statement of the workshop indicating the dates of the workshop, team members, owner's representatives, and other interested parties present during all or part of the workshop, and some description of the most significant findings.

Post-Workshop Activities

After the workshop has been completed, the project manager assembles the materials produced by the QC team into a report. (The comment sheets need not by typed if they are legible.) The design team members then address each QC team comment on the review forms and indicate in the appropriate column what action has been taken on that comment. The QC team members should then review the design team's responses to their comments and provide further input to the design team, if appropriate, and sign off on each comment. A summary memo, along with the completed forms describing the design team's actions, constitute the design team's response report (see the example in Figure 4.15). The QC

Item Number	Drawing Number or Specification Page	Comment	Action
1	HV-8	Add a detail showing hinged base for exhaust and roof ventilator for access to damper.	Hinged base for roof exhaust fans are covered in specifications (see 15870-2).
2	HV-8	Add a detail for the fan guard or spec it.	Propeller fan specification (15870-3) covers fan guard.
3	HV-9	Fill in "Location" column or delete it.	"Location" column has been deleted from schedule.
4	HV-5	Remove the electrical design info on the HV drawings and put it on the electrical drawings (E-43).	Will not comply since design is near completion. Will reference HV drawing in electrical.
5	HV-6	Provide condensate drain routing.	Provided—see drawings P-2 and P-3.
6	HV-6	Provide diffuser mounting detail.	Not necessary because of lay-in panel.
7	P-3	Two way cleanout at grinder pump is needed.	Will provide two way cleanout detail on drawing.
8	15010-4	Specify number of shop drawing copies needed.	Will comply (8 copies).

I have reviewed the proposed action items and agree that they are appropriate.

Robert R. Blowhard   *8/19/92*
Signature of QC Reviewer   Date

Figure 4.15   Completed design review form.

team's report and the design team's report should then be filed in the project records and with the owner as documentation of the QC workshop effort.

THE REDICHECK METHOD*

During the late 1970s and early 1980s, William T. Nigro administered hundreds of U.S. Navy construction contracts designed by civilian architecture and engineering firms. He found that approximately one-half of the thousands of negotiated change orders were due to coordination errors that could have been avoided during design. The following are specific examples of some of the errors observed by Nigro:

- Civil site plans that have underground utilities (such as water, sewer, or storm lines) interfering with locations of electrical substations, power poles, or underground conduit, duct banks, or storage tanks.
- Landscape drawings with trees in the same locations as sewer lines, or in the middle of drainage swales shown on civil drawings.
- Structural drawings with column locations and grid lines that conflict with architectural locations.
- Architectural floor plans that do not match other discipline floor plans.
- Plumbing drawings with riser diagrams that do not match plumbing fixtures on architectural floor plans.
- Mechanical drawings that read "see structural drawings for additional roof supports" while the structural drawings do not indicate such supports.
- Electrical drawings that indicate items of equipment with horsepower ratings, voltages, and phases different from those shown on mechanical drawings and/or in specifications.
- Specification sections referring to other sections that do not exist or that say to install something "as indicated" or

*Nigro, William T., AIA, *REDICHECK Interdisciplinary Coordination*, The REDICHECK Firm, 109 Greensway, Peachtree City, GA 30269. Copyright © 1987.

"where indicated" when there is no indication of the item on the contract drawings.

A registered architect, Nigro applied his education and experience to find a way that these errors could be caught and corrected *before* the design was issued for construction. The result was REDICHECK, a simple yet comprehensive and effective method of conducting design reviews.

Starting in 1982, the REDICHECK system was put into place for all major military construction projects at the Trident Naval Submarine Base in Kings Bay, Georgia. Between 1982 and 1985, 29 projects with an estimated construction cost in excess of $400 million were subjected to the REDICHECK system. The cost was approximately $500,000, one-eighth of 1% of the estimated construction cost. As a result, from 1983 through 1986, the change order rate at the Trident base dropped from over 7% of construction cost to about 3%, the lowest rate of any major Navy command. During these four years at Kings Bay, REDICHECK appears to have saved 3 to 4% of all construction cost, a return on investment of approximately 30 to 1 (see Figure 4.16).

Basic Concepts

The first step in the REDICHECK system is to plan the design effort in a way that will minimize the opportunities for conflicts in the documents. Nigro identified the following basic concepts that should be understood and followed by the entire design firm:

- Draw all plans at the same scale so they can be overlaid on a light table.
- Show the right information the least number of times— preferably only once.
- Keep the same north-south orientation on all plans.
- Use consistent terminology between the plans and specifications.
- Avoid vague notes such as "see architectural" or "see structural."
- If possible, avoid match-lines.
- Show all wall sections at relative elevations to each other on the same sheet.
- Avoid the word "new."

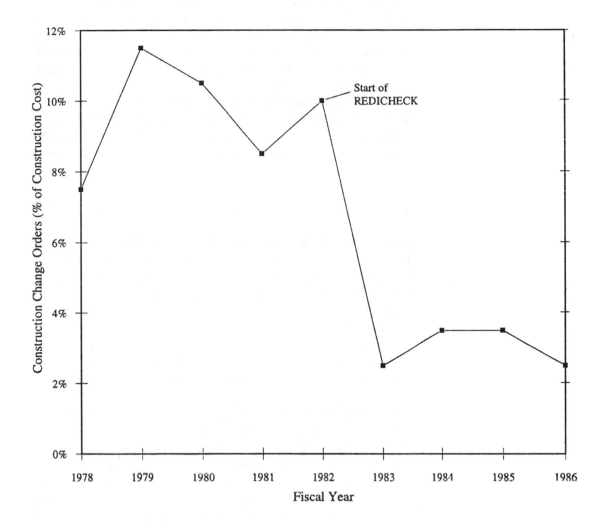

Figure 4.16 Change order history at Trident Submarine Base. Source: Nigro, William T., AIA, REDICHECK Interdisciplinary Coordination, The REDICHECK Firm, 109 Greensway, Peachtree City, GA 30209, Copyright © 1987.

Since REDICHECK was developed, the use of CAD has become virtually universal in design firms. This has greatly facilitated the application of the above concepts.

Spot-Check

After the plans and specifications have been prepared, the project manager or QC coordinator should perform a spot-check of the project. The spot-check, requiring only a few hours for most projects, is a means of determining how much effort will be required for the final review. The spot-check is performed by selecting a few items in the final review checklist. A good sampling for the spot-check would be the items shown on Figure 4.17.

If all 11 items are well coordinated, the project is in good shape. On the other hand, if 5 of the 11 items contain coordination problems, then considerable effort will probably be required to review the documents and make needed corrections.

Final Review

The last step in the REDICHECK process is the final review. The amount of time to allot for a final review is dependent upon the size and complexity of the project, the drawing size, and the number of people performing the review.

According to Bill Nigro, a typical project of average complexity requires about 45 minutes per sheet for a REDICHECK review. This is based on an average sheet size of 28 × 40 inches and one person performing the review. The matrix in Figure 4.18 is helpful in estimating the review time in minutes per sheet.

The final review should be conducted by people who have *not* worked on the documents. Someone who has been working on a project for a few months and hasn't yet spotted a particular problem will probably not do so during a final review. Also, human nature being what it is, most professionals have a tough time trying to find errors in their own work. It is much easier (and more fun) to find errors in someone else's work!

The physical setting for conducting the final review can have a major impact on its success. It is extremely important that a separate work area or room be provided. Typical architect/engineer cubicles or work stations do not have sufficient room for laying out multidiscipline drawings and making overlays. The space should be free of interruptions and have windows, light tables or other tables suitable for overlays. Most important is that the room *have no telephone.*

Equipment needed by each reviewer includes a red felt tip pen, colored highlighters, scales, a light table or window, and a complete set of plans and specifications. Each reviewer should also be given a preapproved checklist so that he or she can assure that this project benefits from lessons learned on

Documents	Checklist	Coordinated		
		Yes	No	N/A
Civil drawings	• New underground utilities (power, telephone, water, gas, storm drainage, fuel lines, grease traps, fuel tanks) have no interferences.	[ ]	[ ]	[ ]
	• Existing power/telephone poles, pole guys, street signs, drainage inlets, valve boxes, manhole covers, etc., do not interfere with new driveways, sidewalks, or other site improvements.	[ ]	[ ]	[ ]
Structural drawings	• Perimeter slab on structural matches architectural.	[ ]	[ ]	[ ]
	• Column grid lines and locations are the same on structural and architectural.	[ ]	[ ]	[ ]
Architectural drawings	• Building elevations match floor plans. In particular, check roof lines, window and door openings, louver openings, exterior light fixtures, and expansion joints.	[ ]	[ ]	[ ]
	• Reflected ceiling plans match architectural floor plans. Locations of electrical fixtures and mechanical registers/diffusers on electrical and mechanical plans do not conflict with reflected ceiling plans.	[ ]	[ ]	[ ]
Mechanical drawings	• Plumbing and HVAC floor plans match architectural floor plans.	[ ]	[ ]	[ ]
	• Openings for roof and wall penetrations (ducts, fans, etc.) are indicated on structural drawings.	[ ]	[ ]	[ ]
Electrical drawings	• Location of floor mounted electrical equipment is consistent with architectural and mechanical drawings.	[ ]	[ ]	[ ]
	• Major equipment has electrical connections, horsepower ratings, phases, and voltages consistent with other discipline schedules.	[ ]	[ ]	[ ]
Specifications	• Check specifications for phasing of construction.	[ ]	[ ]	[ ]

Figure 4.17 *Recommended REDICHECK spot-check. Source: Nigro, William T., AIA, REDICHECK Interdisciplinary Coordination, The REDICHECK Firm, 109 Greensway, Peachtree City, GA 30209, Copyright © 1987.*

| | Sheet Width (inches) | | | | | | |
Sheet Height (inches)	36	38	40	42	44	46	48
24	35	37	39	41	43	44	46
26	38	40	42	44	46	48	50
28	41	43	45	47	49	52	54
30	43	46	48	51	53	55	58
32	46	49	52	54	57	59	62
34	49	52	55	58	61	63	66
36	52	55	58	61	64	67	70

Note: Reduce above values by up to 33% for simple projects; increase them by up to 33% for complex projects. Add 5% per review if multiple reviewers are involved.

Figure 4.18 Estimated minutes per drawing for REDICHECK review. Source: Nigro, William T., AIA, REDICHECK Interdisciplinary Coordination, The REDICHECK Firm, 109 Greensway, Peachtree City, GA 30209, Copyright © 1987.

previous projects. Examples of such checklists are presented in Appendix B. The reviewer starts by removing the staples or post pins from the plans, then follows each item in the checklist and compiles the comments.

The reviewer should *not* provide direction as to how to correct an item. For example, if during a review it is discovered that the location of Column B3 on Structural Sheet S-4 conflicts with the same column on Architectural Sheet A-7, the reviewer should not attempt to indicate the correct column location. Rather, both details should be noted as being at variance with each other. The designer of record should then make the decision as to which is correct and what the impact may be on the rest of the contract documents.

When the checklist has been followed and the drawings and specifications have been marked in yellow and red, it is helpful to compile the comments on each drawing and refer to these numbers in the list. This makes it easy to distribute the comments to the various disciplines for review and correction. A sample list of REDICHECK review comments is shown in Figure 4.19.

One large U.S. Government agency set up an interesting team approach for final design reviews. A rotating review team with staggered temporary assignments was established. After the first review team was assembled and trained, additional members were rotated into the team as members rotated out every four months. Records were kept of avoided change orders, number of sheets checked, number of hours

SHEET C-3

1. *Building C6.* Transformer pad AVW fence on E-2.

2. *South of Building C421.* 24″ storm line AVW underground fuel tank on M-7.

SHEET A-3

1. *Office 102.* Location of HVAC supply and return registers AVW M-3.

2. *Conf. 104.* Number and location of light fixtures AVW E-3.

3. *Lounge 107.* "Acoustical tile" ceiling AVW A-10 "gypsum board."

4. *Men 109 and Women 111.* Floor plan AVW P-3.

SHEET S-4

1. *Mechanical Equipment Room 334.* Location of 8″ bearing wall AVW A-3.

2. *Stairs 44 and 152.* $18'\text{-}7\frac{1}{2}''$ AVW A-18 $19'\text{-}0''$.

SPECIFICATIONS

1. *Section 03300, Paragraph 2.1.* "4,000" PSI concrete AVW Drawing S-1 General Note 17 "3,000" PSI.

2. *Section 10201, Paragraph 1.2.* Verify reference to Section "15801," which is not in the specs.

3. *Section 11192, Paragraph 2.3.* Could not locate glass type "7" on the plans.

Note: AVW means "at variance with."

Figure 4.19 Sample REDICHECK review comments. Source: Nigro, William T., AIA, REDICHECK Interdisciplinary Coordination, The REDICHECK Firm, 109 Greensway, Peachtree City, GA 30209, Copyright © 1987.

spent checking, and estimated dollar amount of avoided change orders. The first four-person review team saved over $700,000 in avoidable change orders, for an estimated savings of over $1,300 for every hour of REDICHECK review. As personnel became more familiar with interdisciplinary coordination and review concepts, and as a documentation of savings was developed, a pride in quality construction documents soon spread throughout the organization.

RED-GREEN-YELLOW CHECKING TECHNIQUE

Mr. Scott Braley, a principal with Heery International and a recognized expert on project management, uses the "red-green-yellow" technique for checking contract documents. The basis of the approach is twofold: first, get the benefit of all disciplines' cooperation and collaboration and, second, complete the review and make corrections efficiently and effectively. Mr. Braley recommends the following procedure:

1. *Single Check Set.* A single set of complete documents (degree of completeness appropriate to the stage of the project) is made for review. All reviewers use the same set of documents. All comments are recorded on the same set of documents.

2. *Sequential Review.* The lead discipline reviews the documents first, then passes the check set on to the next discipline. One reviewer should be a person who has not worked directly on the project.

3. *All Notations Are Considered Recommendations.* All reviewers' comments are considered recommendations until approved by the review team leader.

4. *Potential Versus Definite Changes Recommendations.* Each reviewer makes notations that differentiate between potential and definite change recommendations. "Potential change recommendations" are made when a reviewer is not certain that a change must be made, has a question, or wants to recommend a design enhancement in a discipline other than his or her own. "Potential" changes are noted in *green*. "Definite change recommendations" are made when a reviewer is certain that a change must be made; they are noted in *red*.

5. *Reviewer Sign-Offs.* Each reviewer signs his or her name to the cover sheet of the check set, and notes the date the review was completed. Similarly, each reviewer puts his or her initials next to all comments made in the check set. It is also a good idea for each reviewer to initial every drawing, even if no comments were made, to ensure that no drawings were inadvertently missed.

6. *Consolidated Review of Change Recommendations.* After all reviewers have completed their review, key design team members meet to "walk through" the check set. Design team members who *must* participate in this consolidated review are:
   • Lead designer, design team leader (e.g., project manager).

- Lead architect (e.g., job captain).
- Lead engineer.
- Lead interior designer.
- Lead specifications writer.

During the consolidated review meeting, each question and change recommendation is reviewed and its impact discussed. This discussion includes impacts on design, cost, schedule, interdisciplinary coordination, constructability, and operability.

7. *Approval of Change Recommendations.* Based on these impacts, the review team leader either approves or rejects the change recommendation. The review team leader notes approval by putting his or her initials next to all approved change recommendations. It is also helpful to put a distinguishing mark such as a check mark or an "OK." These approval notations are made in *red.* No marks need be made regarding change recommendations that are not approved.

8. *Incorporation of Approved Changes.* After this final review, the check set is given to project team members who will incorporate the approved changes. If a change notation does not have the team leader's initials, it is not made on the working drawings.

9. *Final Verification.* The last step is independent verification that the comments have, in fact, been disposed of properly. This is done by an independent reviewer going through all the completed documents, backchecking by coloring each properly made correction in yellow. Corrections not made properly are noted in red. This backchecking process is repeated until no red marks are required.

MEETING DESIGN SCHEDULES AND BUDGETS

Many project managers believe that the goal of a high quality design is incompatible with the need to meet tight budgets and schedules. This old-fashioned thinking no longer works in today's highly competitive marketplace. Instead, project managers must recognize that design of high quality, on schedule and within budget, are *not* competing objectives; rather, they are the *results* of effective Total Quality Project Management. Properly managed projects are carried out efficiently, without extensive rework, making it possible to achieve high quality while meeting the tight schedules and budgets that owners are demanding.

To assure conformance with design schedules and budgets, the project manager must: (1) establish a baseline against which to measure progress, (2) know how much work is actually being accomplished throughout the project, (3) know the actual expenditures at all times, (4) be able to ascertain the true budget and schedule status, and (5) be prepared to take early corrective action if the project gets off course.

A graphical method known as the Integrated Budget and Schedule Monitoring (IBSM©) method, was developed by David Burstein in the early 1980s. This simple method, now in widespread use in hundreds of design firms, is described in the following.

Establishing a Baseline

The first step is to predict how fast the project team will spend the budget and how fast it can complete the work. This can be done by preparing an expenditure forecast, as shown in Figure 4.20. In order to perform these computations, the task outline must be the same for the scope of work, schedule, and budget. These elements must be agreed upon with the owner before work begins.

After completing the calculations, plot the results graphically, as shown in Figure 4.21. The left-hand y-axis is expressed as dollars of anticipated expenditures; the right-hand y-axis as anticipated progress.

If all goes as forecast, all the work will be completed at the same time as the budget has been expended. In other words, the "progress" of the work should be 100% complete when the budget has been 100% spent. This statement can be used to prepare a graphical forecast of progress as shown in Figure 4.21 by setting 100% progress equal to the project budget, then graphically scaling each 10% increment between 0% and 100%. Such a double-forecast of expenditures and progress will predict not only how much money the firm will spend throughout the project but, more importantly, how much progress the team expects to make. For example, at the end of June 1992, the project manager expects to have spent approximately $55,000 and have completed approximately 30% of the work.

Task Description	Task Budget ($/Task)	Unit Cost ($/Mo)	Jan	Feb	Mar	Apr	May	June	July	Aug	Sept	Oct	Nov	Dec	Jan	Feb	Mar	Apr	May	June	July	Aug	Sep
															1992 → → → → → → → → → → → →					1993 → → → → →				
A. Basis-of-Design Report																							
B. Drawings	13,140	2,170	2,190	2,190	2,190	2,190	2,190	2,190															
1. Civil	2,720	2,920			2,920																		
2. Architectural	2,960	987	987	987	987																		
3. Mechanical	7,650	2,550	2,550	2,550	2,550																		
4. Structural	19,700	3,283				3,283	3,283	3,283	3,283	3,283	3,283												
5. Electrical	17,500	2,917						2,917	2,917	2,917	2,917	2,917	2,917										
C. Specifications																							
1. Equipment	8,060	1,343	1,343	1,343	1,343	1,343	1,343	1,343															
2. Civil site	10,860	1,810						1,810	1,810	1,810	1,810	1,810	1,810										
3. Others	8,820	1,470							1,470	1,470	1,470	1,470	1,470	1,470									
D. Quality Control																							
1. In-progress review	4,420	316	316	316	316	316	316	316	316	316	316	316	316	316	316	316							
2. Final review	5,260	2,630													2,630	2,630							
3. Corrections	5,260	2,630													2,630	2,630							
4. Documentation	6,240	6,240															6,240						
E. Construction Inspection																							
1. Site work	8,940	4,470							4,470	4,470													
2. Concrete	8,940	4,470										4,470	4,470										
3. Equipment/piping	8,940	4,410												4,470	4,470								
4. Building	18,100	9,050																9,050	9,050				
5. Finishes	7,940	3,970																		3,970	3,970		
F. Project Management	173,790	638	638	638	638	638	638	638	638	638	638	638	638	638	638	638	638	638	638	638	638	638	638
Monthly Totals	173,900	8,276	8,024	8,024	10,944	7,770	7,770	12,491	14,904	14,904	10,434	11,621	11,621	6,874	8,854	3,584	6,878	9,688	9,688	4,608	4,608	636	638
Cumulative Totals			8,824	16,048	26,992	34,762	42,532	55,029	69,933	84,837	95,271	106,871	118,812	125,406	133,468	137,044	143,722	153,610	163,298	167,706	172,514	173,152	173,790

Figure 4.20 Calculation of projected expenditures.

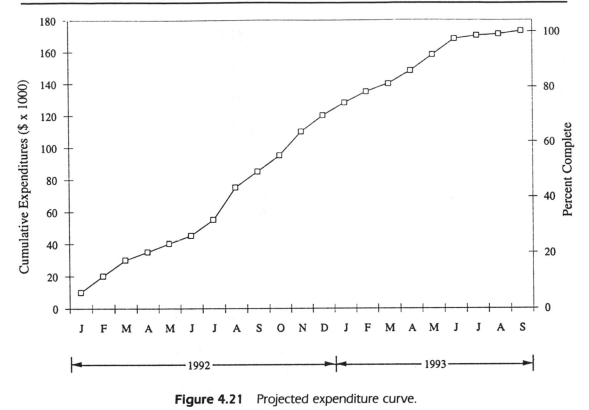

Figure 4.21 Projected expenditure curve.

The Concept of "Earned Value"

Almost every good monitoring system relies on the concept of "earned value," an estimate of how much progress has been made, expressed in dollars. Earned value is computed as follows:

$$\text{Earned value} = \%\ \text{complete} \times \text{budget}$$

For example, if a project consists of laying 1,000 floor tiles and 400 have already been laid, the project can be said to be 40% complete. If the original budget for laying the tiles was $5,000, the earned value is 40% of $5,000, or $2,000.

Of course, calculating progress and determining earned value are not usually as simple as in the above example. In fact, even in this simple project, our calculation of earned value may not be correct. Perhaps the entire sub-base had to be completed before any tile could be laid. In that case, if 400 of the 1,000 tiles have been laid, the project is really more than 40% complete and the earned value is more than $2,000.

To more accurately determine earned value, subdivide the project into its components, or tasks, as follows:

Project Task	Budget
Prepare floor	$ 500
Install sub-base	$1,500
Install tile	$2,500
Cleanup	$ 500
Total	$5,000

Now determine the earned value of each task and sum them to obtain the earned value of the total project, as illustrated below:

Project Task	Budget		% Complete		Earned Value
Prepare floor	$ 500	×	100%	=	$ 500
Install sub-base	$1,500	×	100%	=	$1,500
Install tile	$2,500	×	40%	=	$1,000
Cleanup	$ 500	×	0%	=	0
Total	$5,000				$3,000

It can be seen that the total project has an earned value of $3,000. In other words, it is 60% complete ($3,000 ÷ $5,000). Note that this determination has been made *independently* from any information regarding expenditures or elapsed time.

The above example is for a very simple project, but its methodology can be translated to estimate the progress (or earned value) of even the largest and most complex design projects. First, the person responsible for each major task should prepare a list of milestones and their corresponding percent completion. For example, the task of preparing civil/ site drawings can be broken into the following milestones:

Milestone	Value
1. Site survey	10%
2. Site layout	25%
3. Drainage calculations	15%
4. Site drawings details	20%
5. Grading/drainage details	10%
6. Review and corrections	20%
Total	100%

Standardized lists of milestones should be avoided. Each person has a unique way of approaching a task and that particular approach must be reflected in the milestones in order to assure reasonable accuracy.

When it is time to update the project's status, each person responsible for a major task should use the previously prepared milestones to determine the physical percent completion of that task. For the above sample, the civil engineer responsible for civil/site drawings might estimate progress of the task as follows:

Milestone	Value	Status	Progress
1. Site survey	10%	done	10%
2. Site layout	25%	done	25%
3. Drainage calculations	15%	done	15%
4. Site drawings details	20%	½ complete	10%
5. Grading/drainage details	10%	no progress	0%
6. Review and corrections	20%	no progress	0%
Total	100%		60%

The above analysis indicates that this task is approximately 60% complete. This percentage can then be multiplied by the budget for the civil/site drawings to determine the "earned value" for that task. Earned value for the entire project can then be determined by summing the earned values of each task, similar to the example in Figure 4.22. Dividing earned value by the total project budget provides an estimate of overall project progress as follows:

Overall progress = $32,387 ÷ $173,790 = 0.186 = 18.6%

Remember, the progress computation has nothing to do with how much money has been spent on the project.

Determining Overall Schedule and Budget Status

Using the projected expenditure curve of Figure 4.21 as a base, plot the actual project progress and project expenditures onto the same graph, as shown in Figure 4.23. The overall schedule status can be determined graphically by measuring the horizontal distance between the projected expenditure curve and the progress curve (distance A in Figure

Task Description	Task Budget		Percent Complete		Earned Value
A. Basis-of-design report	$ 13,140	×	65%	=	$ 8,541
B. Drawings					
1. Civil	2,920	×	100%	=	2,290
2. Architectural	2,960	×	100%	=	2,960
3. Mechanical	7,650	×	100%	=	7,650
4. Structural	19,700	×	20%	=	3,940
5. Electrical	17,500	×	0%	=	0
C. Specifications					
1. Equipment	8,060	×	10%	=	806
2. Civil/Site	10,860	×	0%	=	0
3. Others	8,820	×	0%	=	0
D. Quality control					
1. In-progress reviews	4,420	×	30%	=	1,326
2. Final review/corrections	5,260	×	0%	=	0
3. Documentation	6,240	×	0%	=	0
E. Construction inspection					
1. Site work	8,940	×	10%	=	894
2. Concrete	8,940	×	0%	=	0
3. Equipment/piping	8,940	×	0%	=	0
4. Building	18,100	×	0%	=	0
5. Project management	7,940	×	0%	=	0
F. Project management	13,400	×	25%	=	3,350
Totals	$173,790				$32,387

Total project progress = $32,387 ÷ $173,790 = 0.186 = 18.6%

Figure 4.22 Calculations of estimated progress and earned value.

4.23). The overall budget status can be determined by measuring the vertical distance between the project progress curve and the actual expenditure curve (distance B in Figure 4.23).

A common mistake is to compare the projected expenditures with the actual expenditures in an attempt to determine overall project status. If this comparison is made in the sample project (Figure 4.23), note that the actual expenditures are less than the projected expenditures. This comparison often leads to the wrong conclusion—that the project is under budget and thus on target—when in reality the opposite is the case. Comparing projected with actual expenditures is *not* a realistic way to determine either budget or schedule status, and may lull the project manager into a false sense of security. Projects often get so far behind schedule that they appear to be under budget!

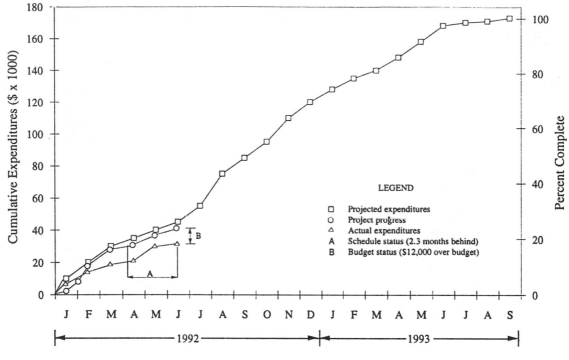

Figure 4.23 Computing overall schedule and budget status using the IBSM® method.

DEVELOPING A CORPORATE MEMORY

A powerful way of achieving long-term improvement in quality is through the use of feedback. The objective is to make a mistake only once, then learn from that mistake—and don't make it again. This "learning curve" concept works well for individuals, who usually remember all their mistakes. But it doesn't work well for organizations in which one person's mistakes are rarely learned by others doing similar work. How many times have you observed the same mistake being made over and over from project to project?

Breaking this cycle of repetitious errors requires the development of a "corporate memory" in which the mistakes of one person are learned by others in the organization. The first step is to develop a formal feedback system from the "customers" of the design team—the contractors who must use the documents to build a facility and the operations/ maintenance personnel who must make it perform its intended function. Such feedback can be solicited upon completion of each project by use of an evaluation form such as the one in Figure 4.24. The results can then be fed back into the firm's design procedures, training programs, design checklists, standard drawings, and specifications.

MEASURING LONG-TERM IMPROVEMENTS IN DESIGN QUALITY

Used properly, the techniques presented in this chapter will improve quality and lower design costs by reducing rework. But improving an occasional project on a hit-or-miss basis is not the road toward firmwide quality improvement. This objective requires measurements that will tell management how well the entire firm is doing over the long haul.

The first step in measuring long-term quality improvement is to select some parameters that are good indicators of how well the TQPM process is working. For design projects, the following parameters can be used.

1. Nonconformances, identified during final design reviews, expressed as the average number of design defects per sheet of drawings.
2. Efficiency of design, expressed as total man-hours required per sheet of drawings for each discipline.
3. Design cycle time, expressed as the number of calendar days required to complete designs of various sizes.
4. Variability in construction bids, expressed in terms of statistical process control parameters.
5. Costs of construction change orders resulting from design defects, expressed as a percentage of construction cost.

Nonconformances Identified During Design Reviews

"First pass yield" is a TQPM concept that measures quality *before* the organization's normal inspections. First pass yield measures the quality improvement that has been achieved through prevention rather than inspection.

Upon completion of the final design review, someone should tally the number of design errors that were detected, using forms such as those in Figure 4.25 and 4.26. Periodi-

Evaluation Criteria	Better Than Expected	Met Expectations	Needs to Improve	Serious Problem	No Opinion
Construction drawings and specs were complete	[ ]	[ ]	[ ]	[ ]	[ ]
Constructions drawings and specs were accurate	[ ]	[ ]	[ ]	[ ]	[ ]
Number of contractor questions and clarifications	[ ]	[ ]	[ ]	[ ]	[ ]
Impact of drawings and specs on contractor's ability to meet construction schedule	[ ]	[ ]	[ ]	[ ]	[ ]
Impact of drawings and specs on construction costs	[ ]	[ ]	[ ]	[ ]	[ ]
Ability of design to meet operations objectives	[ ]	[ ]	[ ]	[ ]	[ ]
Ease of maintenance	[ ]	[ ]	[ ]	[ ]	[ ]
Overall assessment of constructability	[ ]	[ ]	[ ]	[ ]	[ ]
Overall assessment of operability	[ ]	[ ]	[ ]	[ ]	[ ]

Other comments: _____

_____

_____

_____

_____

_____

_____

_____

_____

_____

The following information is optional:

Evaluator's Name: _____ Date: _____

Project: _____

Figure 4.24 Evaluation of constructability and operability quality.

Checker: _____*Arlene Washington*_____ Date: _____*5/29/91*_____

Job No.: ___*4629*___ Discipline: _*Electrical*_ No. of Days: ___*12*___

Category of Checker Red Marks	Number of Errors
1. Does not conform to client/discipline design criteria	2
2. Does not conform to code	10
3. Does not conform to calculations	3
4. Interdiscipline coordination problem	1
5. Operability/constructability problems	16
6. Does not conform to vendor data	0
7. Dimensional error	7
8. Callouts incorrect or missing	37
9. CAD-related problems	11
10. Incorrect notes	3
11. Additional views and details needed	7
12. Does not conform to drafting standards	2
13. Other	18
Total	117

Figure 4.25 An example of a drawing checking record.

cally, these data can be plotted using a bar chart to provide each discipline manager with the information needed to prioritize his or her quality improvement initiatives (see the example in Figure 4.27). Long-term trends can be determined by use of a run chart (see the example in Figure 4.28), which can be used to assess the overall effectiveness of the organization's quality improvement efforts.

Efficiency of Design

If TQPM is applied properly, the improvement in design quality will be accompanied by improved efficiency of the design process. This improvement in efficiency can be expressed as an increase in design productivity and measured as the average number of man-hours per sheet of drawings for various types of projects. (A word of caution: this method of measuring productivity works only for similar project types; com-

Checker: _____*Arlene Washington*_____ Date: _____*5/29/91*_____

Job No.: _____*4629*_____ Specification Division: _____*16-Electrical*_____

Category of Checker Red Marks	Number of Errors
1. Does not conform to client/discipline design criteria	___
2. Does not conform to latest codes	*4*
3. List of applicable publications incorrect	___
4. Codes and standards referenced incorrectly	___
5. Does not conform to calculations	___
6. Interdiscipline coordination problem	*1*
7. Operability/constructability problems	___
8. Inconsistent with industry practices	___
9. Contractual language incorrect......................................	___
10. Does not conform to format...	___
11. Cross-reference to other specifications and documents incorrect ...	*1*
12. Does not conform with the drawing	___
13. Spelling or grammatical errors	___
14. Other..	___
Totals...	*6*

Figure 4.26 An example of a specification checking record.

paring average hours/sheet for a refinery design to that for a water pipeline is simply not valid.) These data can be plotted as shown in Figure 4.29.

Design Cycle Time

One of the primary objectives of TQPM is to reduce the cycle time of every work process. In the case of design projects, this is the time required for preparation of a complete set of plans and specifications. This time is a function of several major factors, some of which (such as client input and regulatory reviews) are outside the direct control of the design team. To effectively reduce design cycle time, the design team must (1) reduce the time required for its own internal production efforts and (2) *influence* others outside the design team to reduce their time requirements. This second ob-

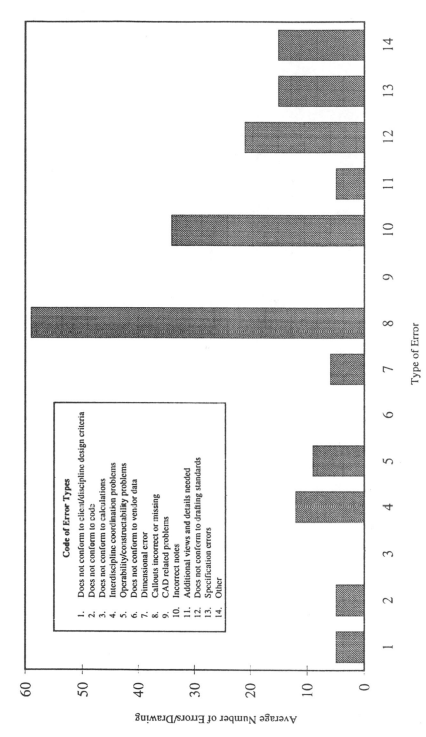

Code of Error Types

1. Docs not conform to client/discipline design criteria
2. Docs not conform to code
3. Docs not conform to calculations
4. Interdiscipline coordination problems
5. Operability/constructability problems
6. Docs not conform to vendor data
7. Dimensional error
8. Callouts incorrect or missing
9. CAD related problems
10. Incorrect notes
11. Additional views and details needed
12. Docs not conform to drafting standards
13. Specification errors
14. Other

Figure 4.27 Analysis of drawing/specification errors.

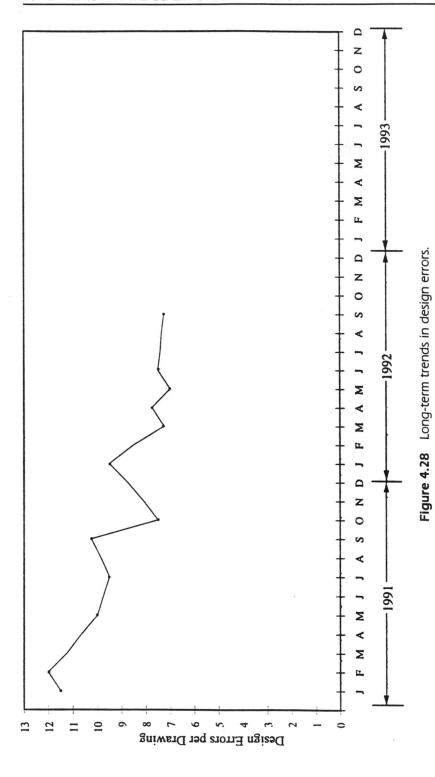

Figure 4.28 Long-term trends in design errors.

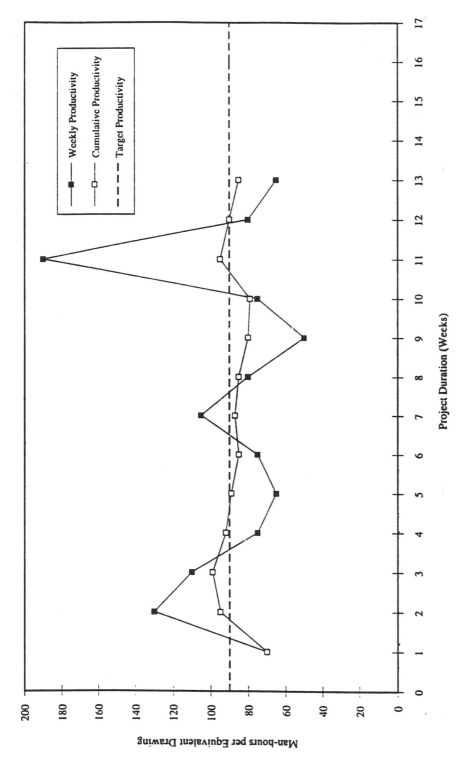

Figure 4.29 Productivity chart for structural drawings.

jective requires that these "outsiders" be brought into the design process from its initiation. To do this, they must be made to feel that their own interests are being served by cooperating with the design team.

Measuring design cycle time can be accomplished in a manner similar to that described above for measuring productivity improvements. However, measuring design cycle time is more complex because of the nonlinear relationship between calendar time and project size.

The first step is to develop background data on how long the firm has traditionally taken to produce various size designs. This information can be tabulated as shown in Figure 4.30 and plotted on a scatter chart as shown in Figure 4.31. Regression analysis can be used to develop the best fit for the data.

Once the historical baseline has been established, the firm can take advantage of improving design efficiency by continuously pushing down the cycle time of each project. If their efforts are successful, the cycle time line in Figure 4.31 will gradually move downward each time it is updated to include newly completed projects.

Variability in Construction Bids

Dr. W. Edward Deming's definition of quality—the degree of uniformity and dependability—can be measured using construction bid tabulations. If a set of plans and specifications properly defines the project requirements, the spread in construction bids should be small; if there are many ambiguities; the spread will be large. This spread can be expressed as the *standard deviation* using the following approach:

1. Determine the statistical mean (average) of all bids.
2. Compute the difference between each bid and the mean.
3. Sum the squares of the differences computed in Step 2.
4. Divide the results of Step 3 by the number of bids. This value is the *variance*.
5. Take the square root of the variance computed in Step 4.

(The above calculations can be performed very quickly using a hand-held calculator that has statistical functions.)

Job Number	Notice to Proceed	Issue for Bids	Calendar Days	Number of Drawings
2532	3/2/90	7/3/90	121	93
2604	9/6/90	10/14/90	38	8
2709	11/13/90	1/16/91	59	12
2714	12/16/90	4/3/91	102	46
2736	2/17/91	6/14/91	121	39
2813	6/21/91	10/18/91	120	72
2882	9/6/91	2/4/92	151	86
2886	11/3/91	6/2/92	214	122
2891	1/14/92	3/7/92	53	17
2912	2/6/92	4/12/92	67	22
2936	3/14/92	8/14/92	182	96

Figure 4.30 Tabulation of historical design cycle times.

The standard deviations from each group of construction bids can be expressed as a percentage of the mean and plotted onto a scatter chart, as shown in Figure 4.32. Periodic review of this chart will reveal trends in the uniformity of construction bids. Of course, there are many external factors that affect the spread of construction bids, so it will take a significant number of data points to establish real trends.

While analyzing construction bids, it is also useful to compare them with the designer's estimate to determine the quality of the firm's cost estimating process. A scatter chart such as Figure 4.33 can help management assess whether new estimated procedures are really producing more accurate cost estimates.

Costs of Construction Change Orders

Previously in this chapter, we described how Bill Nigro evaluated the effectiveness of his REDICHECK system by measuring the cost of construction change orders resulting from design defects (see Figure 4.16). This method can also be used to measure long-term improvement in the quality of designs performed by an organization. This requires a system of determining: (1) the cost of construction change orders for each project, and (2) how much of those costs were attributable to design defects.

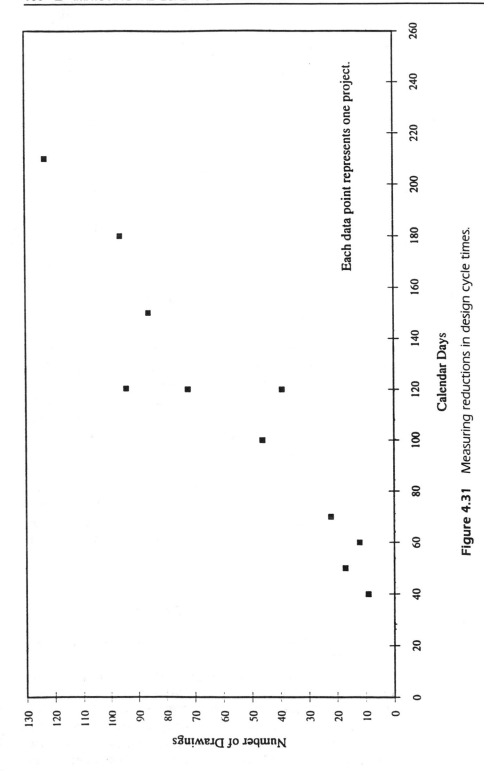

Figure 4.31 Measuring reductions in design cycle times.

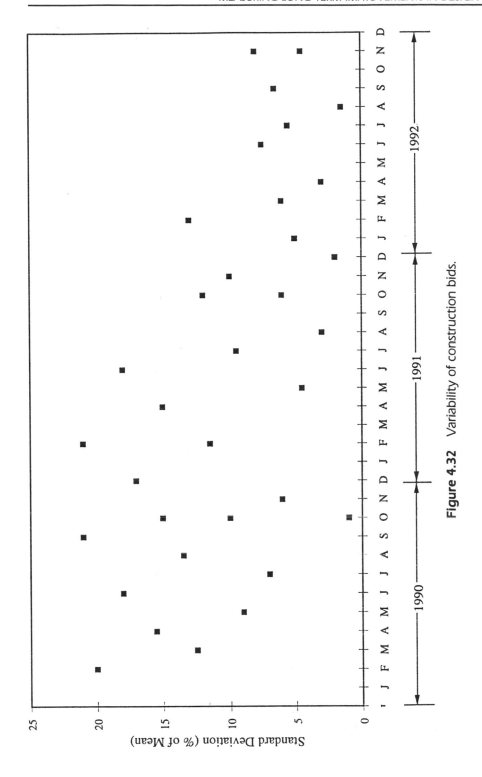

Figure 4.32 Variability of construction bids.

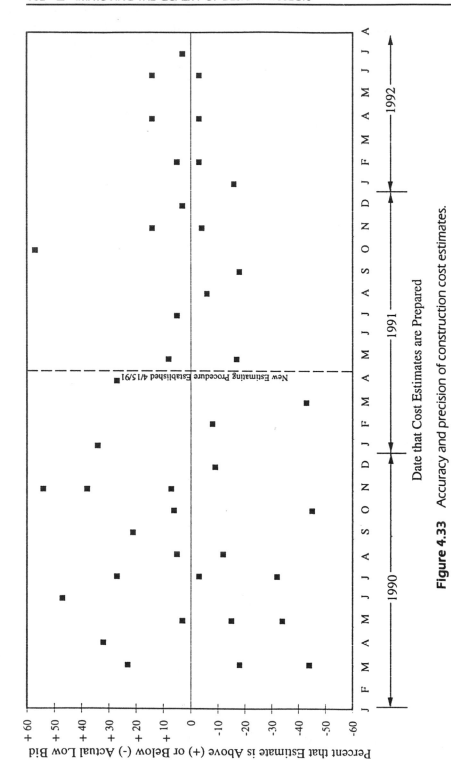

Figure 4.33 Accuracy and precision of construction cost estimates.

SUMMARY

This chapter has described how design quality can be improved through a combination of quality assurance, quality control, and quality improvement techniques. The next two chapters present recommendations as to how similar improvements can be made to studies and construction projects.

5 IMPROVING THE QUALITY OF STUDIES AND REPORTS

In Chapter 4 we described how the principles of TQPM can be used to improve the quality of designs while reducing design costs and accelerating design schedules. Many of the recommended techniques were based on the concept of "conformance to agreed-upon requirements." But professional service firms often are called upon to begin projects prior to the establishment of these requirements. For example, studies are often conducted by design firms when the client isn't quite sure of what (if anything) should be designed. Studies are also conducted for long-term planning purposes and to satisfy the requirements of legislators and regulatory officials. Although they tend to be very diverse, most studies share the following characteristics:

- Their scope is rather loosely defined and may be changed several times during the project.
- The product is some type of report.
- Compensation is generally on a reimbursable cost basis.
- A successful study can significantly enhance the client-consultant relationship.
- An unsuccessful study can terminate a budding client-consultant relationship.

This chapter describes how professional service firms can use TQPM to: (1) improve the quality of their studies, and (2) measure this improvement.

DEFINING PROJECT REQUIREMENTS

Because they tend to be ill-defined, studies require extra effort to properly establish requirements in a way that will be understood by everyone on the project team, including the client. Planning tools that work well on design and construction projects (critical path scheduling, multilevel cost accounting, etc.) have limited value for projects that don't have a well-defined scope. But there are tools available to help define requirements for studies. These include the work breakdown structure and detailed report outline, described below.

The Work Breakdown Structure

The work breakdown structure (WBS) is a method of defining how the scope, schedule, budget, and organization of the project are interrelated. In most studies, these elements tend to evolve during the project. Therefore, it is essential that the WBS be simple and easy to revise. Figure 5.1 illustrates how the requirements of a moderately large study can be presented on a single page WBS.

Detailed Report Outlines

Quality problems often result from ambiguity regarding the contents and presentation of the final report. To combat this problem, a detailed outline of the final report should be prepared *at the beginning of the project* in as much detail as possible. This initial outline should be reviewed and approved by the client (recognizing that it will probably change several times before the project is completed). An example of such a report outline is presented in Figure 5.2.

It is also desirable to incorporate a preliminary list of tables and figures in the report outline. For key tables and figures, the presentation format should be illustrated, even though the actual data have not yet been developed. For example, Figure 5.3 shows a sample format that can be used for presenting population data. Although the data have not yet been compiled, everyone on the project team (including the client) can easily see how these data will be presented in the report.

Of course, it will be necessary to modify the report outline, list of tables and figures, and example formats as the project progresses. Such revisions will take time. But the time saved

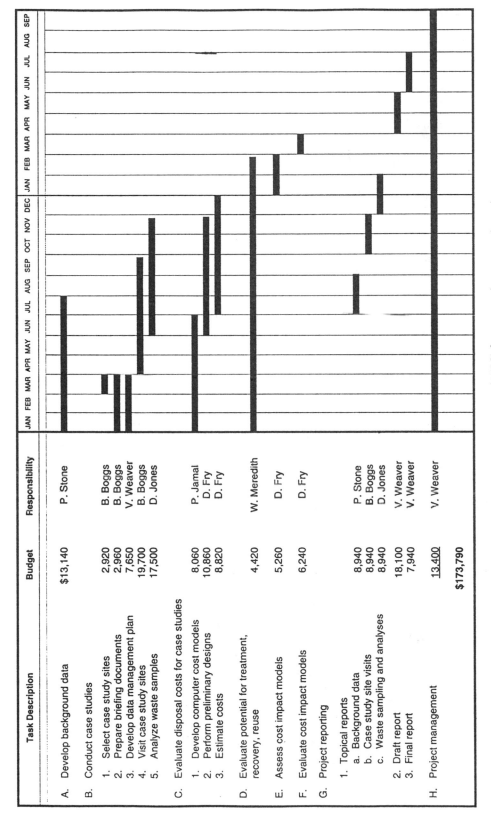

Task Description	Budget	Responsibility
A. Develop background data	$13,140	P. Stone
B. Conduct case studies		
1. Select case study sites	2,920	B. Boggs
2. Prepare briefing documents	2,960	B. Boggs
3. Develop data management plan	7,650	V. Weaver
4. Visit case study sites	19,700	B. Boggs
5. Analyze waste samples	17,500	D. Jones
C. Evaluate disposal costs for case studies		
1. Develop computer cost models	8,060	P. Jamal
2. Perform preliminary designs	10,860	D. Fry
3. Estimate costs	8,820	D. Fry
D. Evaluate potential for treatment, recovery, reuse	4,420	W. Meredith
E. Assess cost impact models	5,260	D. Fry
F. Evaluate cost impact models	6,240	D. Fry
G. Project reporting		
1. Topical reports		
a. Background data	8,940	P. Stone
b. Case study site visits	8,940	B. Boggs
c. Waste sampling and analyses	8,940	D. Jones
2. Draft report	18,100	V. Weaver
3. Final report	7,940	V. Weaver
H. Project management	13,400	V. Weaver
	$173,790	

Figure 5.1 Work breakdown structure (WBS) for an environmental study.

Synopsis of Key Assumptions and Impacts

Table of Contents

Notes on Report Arrangement

Acknowledgements

Executive Summary

SECTION I INTRODUCTION
Plan of Study
Content of Interim Report
Additional Studies

SECTION II FINDINGS AND RECOMMENDATIONS
Findings
Recommendations

SECTION III UTILITY SOLID WASTE ASSESSMENT
Introduction
Survey of Available State Information
State Survey Results
Coal Burn Projections
Ash Projections
Scrubber Sludge Projections
Coal Preparation Wastes
Other Wastes
Federal Energy Regulatory Commission (FERC) Data
By-Product Utilization

SECTION IV CASE STUDY DESCRIPTIONS
Approach Summary
Site Visit Information

SECTION V DEVELOPMENT OF DISPOSAL COST DATA
Introduction
Design Development Factors
Factors Used in Preparing Cost Estimates
Current Practice Disposal Methods
Nonhazardous Disposal
Hazardous Disposal
Mathematical Models
Costs for Facilities Located in Environmentally Sensitive Areas
Case Study Cost Summary

Figure 5.2 An example of a report outline.

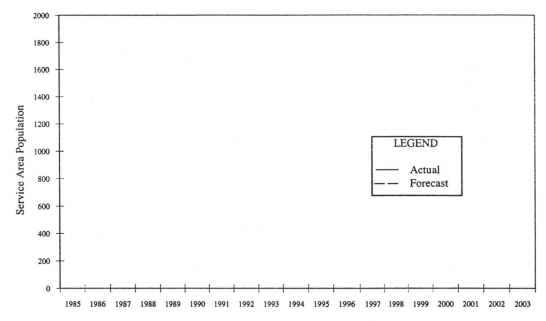

Figure 5.3 Sample format for forecast of population data.

in unnecessary rework resulting from unclear requirements will be far greater. It is a classic case in which the cost of preventing problems is much less than the cost of fixing them later.

ANTICIPATING CRISES

The planning effort for every study should include a structured approach to anticipating problems and avoiding rework. A good way to anticipate crises is to hold a "brainstorming" session with all the key members of the project team. The first discussion should identify a list of things that can go wrong. Once this list has been completed, the discussion should focus on ways these potential problems can be prevented. This list then becomes formalized into a *Crisis prevention plan* (as shown in Figure 5.4) and distributed to each project team member.

IMPROVING THE QUALITY OF FIELD WORK

Field work is often required to gather data and other information that will then be analyzed back at the office. These

Things That Might Go Wrong	How They Can be Controlled
1. Unable to get access to visit selected sites	• Select four alternate sites
2. Weather delays in collecting samples during site visits	• Schedule northern sites in summer, southern sites in winter
	• Plan for field team to work on data evaluation tasks in hotel room during inclement weather
3. Delays in developing and debugging computer program	• Programmer to prepare detailed plan for this task with periodic milestones
	• Project manager to closely monitor status of programming effort
	• Another programmer to meet weekly with principal programmer to provide input on how to break deadlocks

Figure 5.4 Crisis prevention plan for an environmental study.

field activities tend to be particularly problematic because: (1) field personnel do not have access to the normal support systems that exist at the office, and (2) field data that is incomplete or incorrect are often difficult or impossible to go back and collect. Therefore, the admonition to "do it right the first time" is particularly appropriate when it comes to field work.

The first step is to define all the requirements of the field team. This can be accomplished by:

- Use of checklists (such as Figures 5.5 and 5.6) to ensure thoroughness.
- Use of standardized forms (such as Figure 5.7) to insure consistency.
- Proper training of all field operation personnel.
- Thorough briefing with office personnel prior to mobilization.

When the field crew arrives on site and begins work, it is not unusual to find conditions substantially different than those that were envisioned in the original plan. A mechanism is therefore needed to make necessary changes quickly and properly. Such mechanisms for modifying the work plan should describe the reason for the change and the impacts on completed and ongoing work. The field change procedure

Prior to field mobilization, make sure the following applicable items have been completed:

☐   Work plan read by all field personnel.

☐   Discrepancies or questions with work plan discussed with project manager.

☐   Health and safety plan read by all field personnel and signed.

☐   Equipment and supplies gathered and shipped to site.

☐   Laboratory contacted and trip blanks ordered.

☐   Client informed of arrival and length of stay.

☐   Pre-field meeting with project manager.

☐   Travel arrangements made.

☐   Schedule of operations for field activities developed.

☐   Notebook and forms completed with pre-field information.

Field Team Leader: _____

Job Name: _____

Figure 5.5   Field readiness form.

should be worked out in advance and approved by the client prior to *beginning* the field work. An example of such a plan is presented in Figure 5.8.

The error prevention systems described above must be continuously measured to determine their effectiveness so that they can be continuously improved. A post-field checklist (see Figure 5.9) can be used by the field team leader to provide feedback regarding nonconformances that arose during the field effort so that they won't be repeated on future field projects. A job performance sheet similar to Figure 5.10 can be used to measure how well the field crew satisfied the needs of their internal "customer." Long-term trends in the performance of field work can be tracked by plotting the rating of each completed project on a run chart, similar to Figure 5.11.

TECHNICAL REVIEWS

Sound quality control procedures dictate that reports and other important documents be reviewed by someone other

Item	Item Needed (Yes or No)	Quantity Needed	Other Comments (size, length, type, etc.)
Steel toe boots	yes	2 pair	Size 11, 10
Safety glasses	yes	3 pair	
Hard hat	yes	3 pair	
Hearing protection	yes	3 pair	
HNu and calibration gas or	no		
OVA and hydrogen	yes	1	
Explosimeter and calibration gas	yes	1	
Draeger bellows	no		
Draeger tubes (list compounds)	no		
Respirator and cartridges	yes	3 sets	
Tyvek suits	yes	3	
Gloves (PVC, nitrile, butyl)	yes	3 pair	
Boot covers	yes	3 pair	
Face shield	yes	3	

Field Team Leader: _____R. U. Kidding_____   Date: _____6/14/92_____

Figure 5.6   Checklist for health and safety equipment.

than the author before being sent to the client. Many firms require that one or more knowledgeable, independent reviewers approve each report before it is finalized. Unfortunately, this traditional quality control method has yielded inconsistent results. In most firms, planning for reviews is a hit-or-miss proposition—some project managers plan well, others plan poorly or not at all. To assure consistency, every project should include a simple QC plan that defines:

- *Which* documents should be reviewed.
- *Who* should review each document.
- *When* each review is scheduled.
- *How much time* should be allocated for reviews and subsequent corrections

An example of a simple QC plan is presented in Figure 5.12.

Too often, the reviewers have not been involved with the project until the final draft is ready for review. Many review comments therefore question fundamental decisions made at the beginning of the project. The resulting changes can cause major rework, adding costs and delays in order to achieve acceptable quality. Because of these problems, many project

Project: _____ Project No.: _____

Location: _____

Well Identification: _____

Date/Time: _____ Sample #: _____

Well Secure [Y or N]? Comments: _____

_____

Sampler(s): _____

Organic Vapor Detector FEL No.: _____ Reading: _____

Weather: Wind: _____ Precipitation: _____ Air Temp.: _____

Water Level: FEL No.: _____ Measurement: _____

FEL No's: Conductivity: _____ pH/Temp.: _____ Redox: _____

SAMPLE DATA:

Cond. (Umhos/cm)	pH	Temp. (C)	Redox (mv)	Observations
_____	_____	_____	_____	_____
				_____

Sample Collection Device and FEL No.: _____

Sample Filtered for: _____ Filter Size: _____

	Bottles			Preservation Type			
Analyses	Number/Size	Bottle Media	HCL	NAOH	H_2SO4	NHO_3	Other
_____	_____	_____	___	___	___	___	___
_____	_____	_____	___	___	___	___	___
_____	_____	_____	___	___	___	___	___
_____	_____	_____	___	___	___	___	___
_____	_____	_____	___	___	___	___	___
_____	_____	_____	___	___	___	___	___
_____	_____	_____	___	___	___	___	___

Duplicate ID: _____

Trip Blanks ID: _____

Field Blanks ID: _____

Matrix Spikes ID: _____

Reviewed by: _____ Date/Time: _____

Form Complete [Y or N]? _____

Figure 5.7 Groundwater sampling form.

Field Change No.: _____

Page _____ of _____

Project: _____ Project No.: _____

Applicable Document: _____

Description: _____

_____

_____

Reason for Change: _____

_____

_____

_____

Recommended Disposition: _____

_____

_____

_____

Impact on Present and Completed Work: _____

_____

_____

_____

Final Disposition: _____

_____

_____

_____

Requested by:
Field/Project Manager: _____

Approvals:
Client's Project Manager: _____

Figure 5.8   Work plan variance form.

managers simply bypass their firm's review system, hoping
that no one will notice. The firm's principals are then faced
with a serious dilemma: do they insure that every report is
adequately reviewed (risking budget overruns, schedule slippages and demoralized project managers)? Or do they ignore
the problem and allow an ever-increasing number of reports

Job Name: _____ Project Manager: _____

A. Field readiness form complete prior to field activities? Yes   No

B. Job sheet completed?   Yes   No

C. Resample required?   Yes   No

Explain reason for resampling and percentage of resampling to be done:

_____

_____

_____

_____

_____

D. List any complications, observations, conflicts, or other information that will aid future site visits:

_____

_____

_____

_____

_____

_____

_____

Form completed by: _____

Figure 5.9 Post-field checklist.

to go to clients without adequate review—hoping that their project managers have done a good job?

There is a better way. Each study should be assigned a *technical director* who works with the project manager during the planning and execution of the project. The technical director's early and continuous involvement results in a final review process that is quick, inexpensive, and responsive to the needs of the project manager, the client and the firm's principals.

The key to making this technical direction system work is to monitor how well it is being implemented. When each final report has been completed, three documents should be prepared. The first is a certification that the report has been reviewed and meets the firm's quality standards (see Figure 5.13). This certification should be filed with the project files

Date: _____   Sampling Field Team Leader: _____

Job Number: _____   Evaluated by: _____

1. Was field team prepared to start work at desig-   Yes   No
   nated start time?   (1 point)

2. Was field effort completed on time?   Yes   No
                                                         (1 point)

3. Were any delays in work encountered due to   Yes   No
   inoperable field equipment?   (1 point)

4. Were field team members properly trained to   Yes   No
   perform work?   (1 point)

5. Was work performed in an efficient manner?   Yes   No
                                                         (1 point)

6. Return to site necessary due to sampling team   Yes   No
   inability to perform job successfully?   (2 points)

7. Did field team perform to project manager's   Yes   No
   satisfaction?   (3 points)

   If no, list problems below:

   _____

   _____

   _____

   _____

   _____

Total ranking (0 to 10): _____

Figure 5.10   Job performance sheet.

as documentation that adequate quality control has been provided.

The technical director and project manager should also complete evaluations (similar to Figures 5.14 and 5.15) of how well the technical direction process worked on that project. A scatter chart (such as Figure 5.16) can be used to track the results and establish firmwide trends over time. Once a year, a bar chart (such as Figure 5.17) can be prepared to identify which aspect(s) of the technical direction process need more attention.

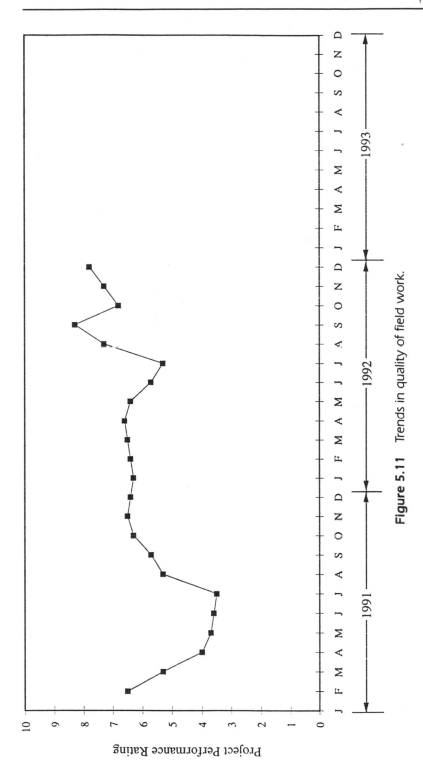

Figure 5.11   Trends in quality of field work.

Documents	Reviewers	Target Dates			Budget (Hours)	
		Begin Review	Complete Review	Corrections Made	Review	Corrections
1. List of study sites	V. Weaver, C. Mangan	3/22/90	3/26/90	3/31/90	16	8
2. Briefing documents	V. Weaver	3/22/90	3/26/90	3/31/90	12	8
3. Data management plan	D. Fry, C. Mangan	3/7/90	3/15/90	3/31/90	16	12
4. Computer cost model	D. Fry, F. Trinidad	6/1/90	6/15/90	6/30/90	40	80
5. Background data reports	V. Weaver, D. Fry	8/10/90	8/15/90	8/31/90	20	20
6. Case study site reports	V. Weaver, D. Fry	11/7/90	11/15/90	11/30/90	12	40
7. Waste analyses results	L. Jackson	1/7/91	1/15/91	1/31/91	16	16
8. Draft report	V. Weaver, C. Mangan, D. Fry	5/1/91	5/7/91	5/31/91	60	80

Figure 5.12 Quality control (QC) plan for an environmental study.

Client: _____*Green Acres Development Corp.*_____

Date: _*June 4, 1991*_

Project Short Title: _*Green Acres Master Plan*_   Project Number: _*2643*_

Document Title: _*Master Plan for Green Acres Retirement Village*_

Report Date: _____*May 29, 1991*_____

The report, manual, or permit document for this project has been completed and reviewed for technical and editorial quality. The report meets standards and is approved for submittal to the client.

_____*James Lofton*_____
Project Manager

_____*Nancy Barnes*_____
Technical Director

Figure 5.13   Report review certification.

REPORTS

The principle product of most studies is some type of report. The requirements for presentation and appearance, as well as content, must be agreed upon with the client prior to commencement of the project. For example, reports may be categorized as Types 1, 2, 3, or 4 in terms of presentation. The principal characteristics of each of the four report types are summarized below and in Figure 5.18.

Type 1 Reports. This type represents the top grade of reports. They are expensive due primarily to the use of phototypesetting, the extensive use of color, and the hard binding. A Type 1 report normally is prepared only if the client requires it (and approves the expenditures) or if it is considered necessary for marketing purposes.

Type 2 Reports. These are the standard type prepared by most firms. There is a wide latitude in the choice of format, typography, and graphics. (In some cases it may be desirable to prepare a report as a Type 2 report, but to hard bind a few copies for special purposes).

Type 3 Reports. This style can be used for short reports and for all drafts.

Job. No.:	2643	Project Name:	Green Acres Master Plan
Project Manager:	James Lofton	Report Date:	May 29, 1991
Technical Director:	Nancy Barnes		

Evaluation Criteria		Points
Project Planning (2 points maximum)		*1.5*
Adequate involvement of TD	= 2 points	
Inadequate involvement of TD	= 1 point	
No involvement of TD	= 0 points	
Project Execution (2 points maximum)		*1*
Consistent involvement of TD	= 2 points	
Sporadic involvement of TD	= 1 point	
No involvement of TD	= 0 points	
Project Review (6 points maximum)		*4*
Adequate time allowed for TD review	= 6 points	
Inadequate time allowed for TD review	= 3 points	
No TD review	= 0 points	
Total Rating (10 points maximum)		*6.5*

Comments: *Would have been helpful if technical director had attended key meetings with client.*

Evaluated by: *Nancy Barnes*   Date: *6/4/91*

Figure 5.14 Technical direction rating (by technical director).

Type 4 Reports. These can be prepared as "letter" reports.

Regardless of presentation, reports should be clear, concise, and easy to understand. One way to measure the clarity of report writing is Gunning's Fog Index. To use this method, select a few pages at random from various portions of the report. First, determine the average number of words per sentence. Then identify the number of difficult words per 100 words. ("Difficult" words are those which have more than two syllables and generally are not used during casual conversation. Proper nouns do not count.) Add these two values and multiply by 0.4 to determine the grade level to which the text is written. For example, this paragraph contains an average of 13.9 words per sentence and 16 difficult words out of a total of 140 words (11.5 difficult words per 100). The grade level is, therefore computed as follows:

Fog Index = 0.4 (13.9 + 11.5) = 10.2 or tenth grade

Job. No.: _____2634_____   Project Name: _Green Acres Master Plan_

Project Manager: _____James Lofton_____

Technical Director: _____Nancy Barnes_____

Evaluation Criteria		Points
Accessibility of TD when needed (2 points maximum)		_2_
Always	= 2 points	
Sometimes	= 1 point	
Never	= 0 points	
Quality of TD Contribution (3 points maximum)		_2_
Very useful	= 3 points	
Somewhat useful	= 1 point	
Not useful	= 0 points	
Cost-Effectiveness of Technical Direction (3 points maximum)		_0_
Very cost-effective	= 3 points	
Marginally cost-effective	= 1 point	
Not cost-effective	– 0 points	
Responsiveness of TD (2 points maximum)		_2_
Very responsive	= 2 points	
Somewhat responsive	= 1 point	
Generally unreponsive	= 0 points	
Total Rating (10 points maximum)		_6_

Comments: _Nancy did not adequately understand budget limitations of the project._

Evaluated by: _James Lofton_   Date: _6/12/91_

Figure 5.15 Technical direction rating (by project manager).

The appropriate Fox Index depends on the audience. If the report is intended for general distribution to the public, it should be written at 8th to 10th grade level. Even for highly technical reports written for specialists, the Fog Index should not exceed 14th grade level.

Another way to measure report quality is for the reviewer to fill out an evaluation form similar to the one in Figure 5.19. This information should be returned to the author(s) to help improve the quality of future writing assignments. Evaluation forms should also be kept on file and tallied at the end of each year to identify recurring weaknesses in the group's report

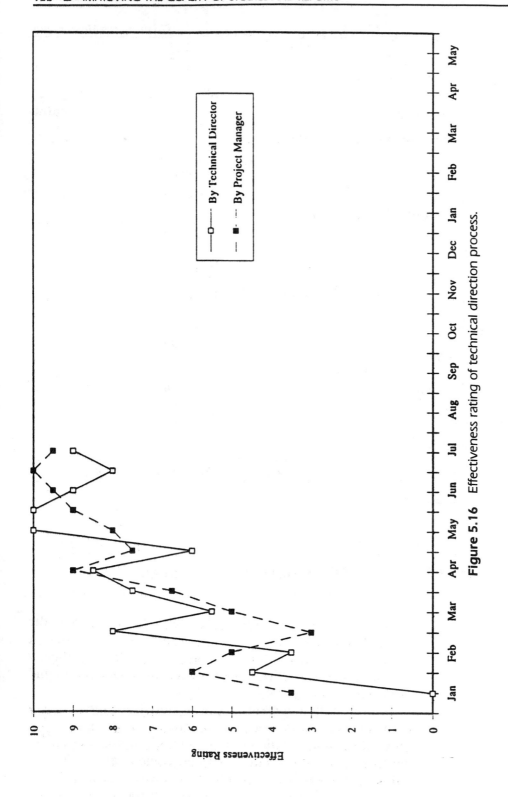

Figure 5.16 Effectiveness rating of technical direction process.

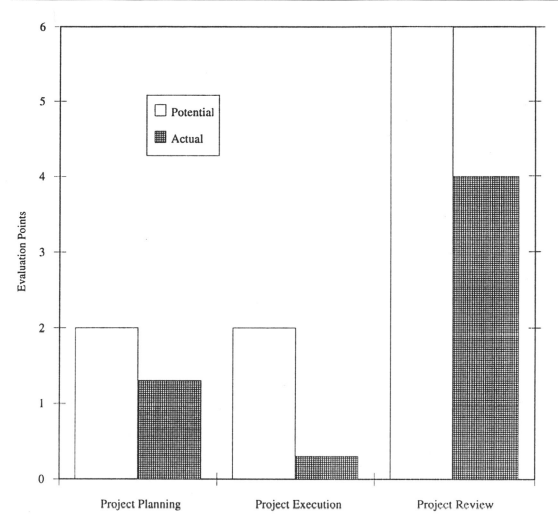

Figure 5.17 *Analysis of technical direction ratings.*

writing efforts (see example in Figure 5.20). This statistical information will provide management with the information needed to target a training program or other office-wide approach to improving writing quality.

CONTROLLING SCHEDULES AND BUDGETS

We have defined "quality" as conformance with requirements—*all requirements* including schedules and budgets. Frequent monitoring of schedule and budget performance is particularly important in studies projects since the scope and approach tends to evolve as the project progresses.

Report Type	Format	Typography	Graphics and Tables	Use of Color	Repro-duction	Binding	Applicability
1	One or two columns; right justified; printed two sides	Phototypeset with special headings	May be inset in columns	Liberal, as appropriate	Offset	Case	Major reports
2	One or two columns; may be right justified; may be printed two sides			As required		Perfect	
3	One column; not right justified; printed one side	Word processor	In text or on separate pages		Photocopy	Plastic comb	Short reports, drafts
4				None		Staple	Letter reports (20 pages or less)

Figure 5.18 Presentation and appearance of various types of reports.

Evaluation Criteria	Unsatisfactory		Acceptable		Outstanding
1. This document contains a concise, clear, complete and accurate abstract, executive summary, or introduction.	1	2	3	4	5
2. This document clearly and concisely explains its purpose and scope.	1	2	3	4	5
3. This document presents data on tables and figures that make the discussion easy to understand.	1	2	3	4	5
4. This document repeats key points to help the reader follow the discussion.	1	2	3	4	5
5. This document presents concepts in a logical manner, using an easy-to-understand vocabulary.	1	2	3	4	5
6. This document provides all the information necessary to justify and explain the conclusions/ recommendations presented.	1	2	3	4	5
7. This document contains conclusions and/or recommendations for action that are well-founded and clearly explained.	1	2	3	4	5
8. Were the results of review discussed with the project manager and primary author?		Yes		No	

9. Additional comments: _____

_____

_____

Technical Director/Reviewer: _____   Project No./Title of Document: _____

Project Manager: _____   _____

Primary Author: _____   Department: _____

Figure 5.19 Technical writing evaluation form.

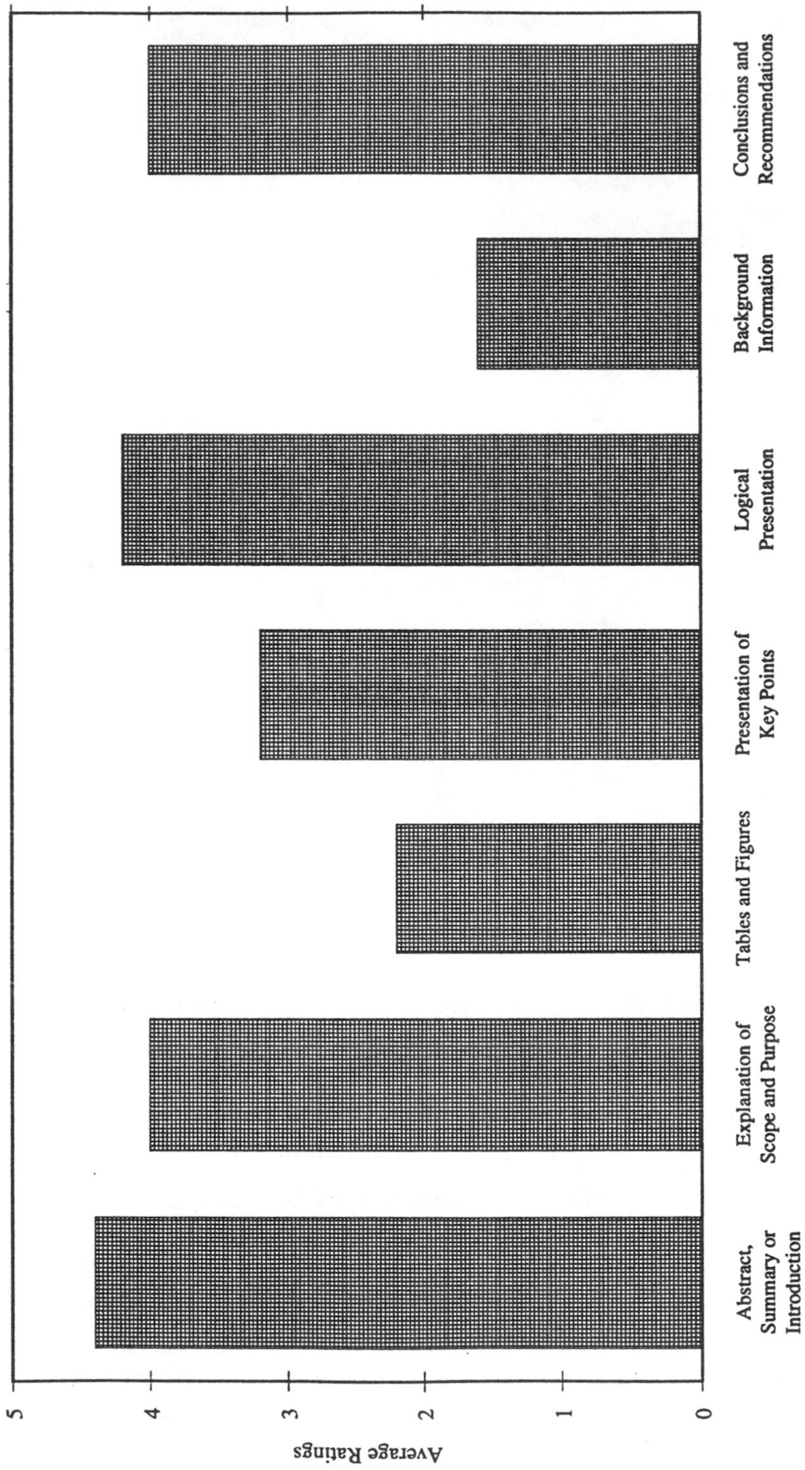

Figure 5.20 Analysis of technical writing evaluations.

The lack of a fixed baseline requires that the monitoring system be flexible and easy to modify.

Computing Budget Status

Having developed a thorough yet simple work breakdown structure (as shown in Figure 5.1), the next step is to periodically monitor budget status. To accomplish this, the project manager must estimate how much actual physical progress has been made on each task. This assessment must be based solely on *actual progress*, independent of how long it has taken or how much it has cost to achieve this progress. Each task's physical progress (expressed as percent completion) is then multiplied by the task budget to obtain "earned value"—the dollar equivalent of the work done to date. The budget status of that task can be determined by subtracting the task's actual costs from its earned value. A positive value indicates that the task is under budget; a negative value indicates it is over budget.

The earned value for the overall project can be computed by adding the earned values for each task. The overall project budget status can then be determined by subtracting the project's actual cost from its earned value. Again, a positive result indicates that the project is under budget; a negative result indicates it is over budget. Note that it is *not* necessary to track the actual costs of each task in order to compute the budget status of the overall project. An example of these calculations is presented in Figure 5.21.

Estimating Schedule Status

Schedule status can be estimated graphically, as shown in Figure 5.22, using the following steps:

1. Using the original schedule, fill in each bar based on the physical progress for the corresponding task. For example, a 5-month task which is 40% complete would have 2 months filled in.

2. Compare the end of the filled-in bar (indicating work completed) with the date of the update (June 1, 1991 in Figure 5.22). The difference is the schedule status of that task. (In Figure 5.22, Tasks A, B4, C1 and D are behind schedule).

Task Description	Budget	Physical % Complete 0 20 40 60 80 100	Earned Value	Actual Costs	Budget Status (+ = under)
A. Develop background data	$13,140		$8,541	$11,487	-$2,946
B. Conduct case studies					
1. Select case study sites	2,920		2,920	4,072	-1,152
2. Prepare briefing documents	2,960		2,960	2,526	+ 434
3. Develop data management plan	7,650		7,650	6,511	+1,139
4. Visit case study sites	19,700		3,940	7,086	-3,146
5. Analyze waste samples	17,500		0	0	--
C. Evaluate disposal costs					
1. Develop cost models	8,060		806	4,256	-3,450
2. Perform preliminary designs	10,860		0	0	--
3. Estimate costs	8,820		0	0	--
D. Evaluate treatment, recovery, reuse	4,420		1,326	2,625	-1,299
E. Assess cost impacts	5,260		0	0	--
F. Evaluate cost impact models	6,240		0	0	--
G. Project reporting					
1. Topical reports					
a. Background data	8,940		894	721	+ 173
b. Case study site visits	8,940		0	0	--
c. Waste sampling/analysis	8,940		0	0	--
2. Draft report	18,100		0	0	--
3. Final report	7,940		0	0	--
H. Project management	13,400		3,350	5,169	-1,819
	$123,790		$32,387	$44,453	-$12,066

Figure 5.21 An example of budget status for an environmental study.

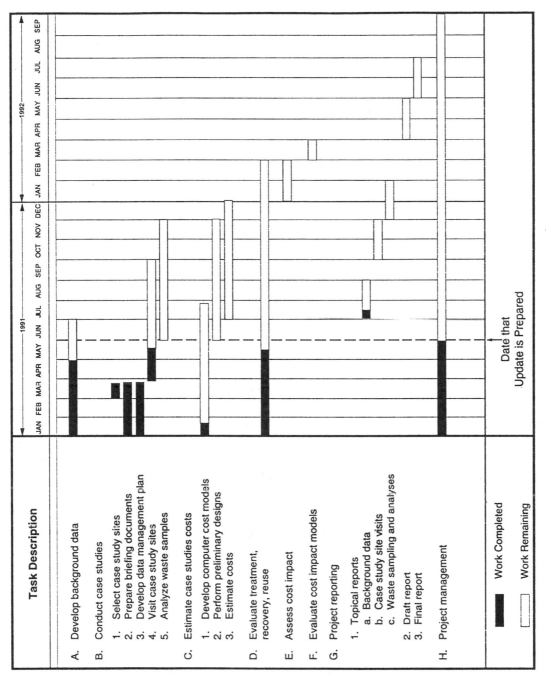

Figure 5.22 Determining the schedule status of each task.

Monitoring Small Studies

Monitoring the budget and schedule status of small studies is difficult because the project manager cannot afford to spend much time doing it. However, these jobs are generally of such short duration that failure to monitor them closely can quickly lead to irreparable schedule and budget problems.

Instead of breaking the project into tasks, a few milestones can be used to identify key points during the project. A percentage of the total budget can then be assigned to each milestone, as in the following example:

Milestone	Percent of Budget
1. Complete work plan	5%
2. Complete field work	50%
3. Reduce field data	10%
4. Prepare draft report	15%
5. Complete in-house review	10%
6. Issue final report	10%
Total	100%

When it comes time to determine job status, the project manager uses the milestones to estimate the total physical progress (percent complete) for the project. A single spreadsheet, as shown in Figure 5.23, can be used to track both the budget and schedule status of the project with a minimum of effort by the project manager.

LEARNING FROM YOUR MISTAKES

Everyone makes mistakes. TQPM requires these mistakes to be studied so that they will not happen again. Effective "postmortem" analysis and statistical tracking of results will result in prevention of recurrences by developing a "corporate memory." The objective is to prevent one person from repeating mistakes that another person made in a similar situation. For example, Figure 5.24 illustrates the kinds of preventive actions that can be taken as a result of previous problems experienced in performing hazardous waste remedial investigations. These measures can then be used in preparing a crisis prevention plan on future projects.

Milestone	Percent Of Budget	Target Completion	Status on June 15
1. Complete work plan	5%	4/26	Complete
2. Complete field work	50%	5/29	Complete
3. Reduce field data	10%	6/10	½ done
4. Prepare draft report	10%	6/20	Barely started
5. Complete in-house review	10%	6/27	No progress
6. Issue final report	10%	7/14	No progress
7. Close out report	5%	7/30	No progress

Project budget = $7,600

Overall Budget =   60% Complete

Earned Value = $0.6 \times \$7,600 = \$4,600$

Expenditures to Date = $4,200

Results: The project is about a week behind schedule; $400 under budget

Figure 5.23 Determining budget and schedule status of small projects.

Potential Problems	Prevention Measures
1. Delays in getting clearances to move drill rigs onto site	Hand-carry clearance documents through each person who requires approval
2. Difficulties in finding adequate locations to dispose of spoils from drilling	Define in drilling specs location of spoils disposal area and requirements for use of that area
3. Sample bottles getting broken during shipping	Train sampling technicians on bottle packing procedures prior to their taking samples
4. Field personnel charging overtime without prior authorization	Describe overtime approval procedures during project kick-off meeting
5. Critical equipment breaking down during field work	Take a spare unit to the field

Figure 5.24 Problem prevention measures for hazardous waste remedial investigations.

SUMMARY

This chapter has described some techniques that will improve the quality of studies and reports while reducing time and costs by eliminating unnecessary rework. The next chapter describes how TQPM can be uscd to improve the quality of construction services often provided by design firms.

6

IMPROVING THE QUALITY OF CONSTRUCTION SERVICES

During the construction phase of a project, design firms are often retained to keep an eye on the constructor to be sure that the work is being performed in accordance with the plans and specifications. Many excellent books and manuals have been written describing how design professionals should perform these services. This chapter neither repeats nor attempts to embellish on these fine works. Rather, it describes how construction phase services can fit into a design firm's overall strategy for improving quality.

DEFINING REQUIREMENTS

The first step, as always, is to define the requirements of the project. This begins with an agreement with the owner as to the responsibilities of the design firm during construction. Should the design firm's role be confined to that of a consultant, providing assistance only on an "as requested" basis? Or should the design firm be totally responsible for all aspects of construction including cost, schedule, and quality? Or does the owner want something in between?

Do *not* rely on commonly used terms to define the design firm's role. For example, to one person the term "construction management" might refer to oversight of a general contractor. To another person, the same term might refer to the oversight and coordination of multiple trade contractors.

Such differences in definitions can create disastrous misunderstandings between the design firm and the client. Instead, define *precisely* what services should be performed and, insofar as possible, how they will be performed. Let's look at some examples of poorly defined requirements and how their definition can be improved.

> *Preconstruction Activities.* Most contracts contain vague provisions requiring the design firm to "assist the owner during the bidding process." A more precisely defined requirement would be to specify that the design firm "shall conduct a prebid conference at the job site, answer questions from contractors and vendors, issue clarifications and addends to all planholders, evaluate bids and make recommendations for award."
>
> *Shop Drawing Review.* Instead of vaguely requiring that the A/E "shall review and approve shop drawings," the contract should specify the specific duties of the design firm. For example, it might state that "the A/E shall, within five working days of receipt, advise the construction contractor if submittals cannot be reviewed because of incompleteness. If submittals are complete, the A/E shall, within 15 working days' of receipt, return submittals to the contractor as 'approved,' 'approved with exceptions noted' or 'disapproved' with reasons cited for disapproval."
>
> *Progress Payments.* Instead of merely stating that the A/E "shall review and approve contractor's requests for progress payments," the contract should specify the requirements in detail. For example, it might state that, "the A/E shall, together with the contractor, establish a mutually agreeable schedule of values. Each month, the A/E shall review contractors' estimate of percent completion for each line item, compute the overall progress, and recommend to the owner the proper amount of progress payments."

All construction phase activities should be discussed between the owner and the design firm. The answer to each question should be mutually agreed upon and documented so that there is no ambiguity.

- Who will expedite equipment deliveries?
- Who will prepare operations and maintenance manuals?

- Who will collate manufacturer's maintenance manuals?
- Who will provide resident inspection?
- Who will prepare record drawings?
- Who will review shop and mill drawings?
- Who will conduct periodic site visits?
- Who will perform final inspection?
- Who will review contractor's payment schedule?
- Who will review construction bids?
- Who will prepare change orders?

The following guides provide excellent lists of construction phase services that can be performed by design firms. It is highly recommended that these texts be consulted as an aid to defining requirements.

Project Checklist, ASA Document 2000, American Institute of Architects, 1735 New York Avenue, Washington, D.C. 20006.

Consulting Engineering—A Guide for the Engagement of Engineering Services, Manual No. 45, American Society of Civil Engineers, 345 East 47th Street, New York, N.Y. 10017.

Quality in the Constructed Project—A Guide for Owners, Designers, and Constructors, Manual No. 73, American Society of Civil Engineers, 345 East 47th Street, New York, N.Y. 10017.

Each member of the project team must also understand the requirements and know how his or her duties will satisfy them. Shop drawing reviewers must understand that their job is to compare the submittals with the contract documents and note any deficiencies or discrepancies. It is *not* their job to change the design for the convenience of the contractor or because the project is running behind schedule. Field inspectors must understand the contract documents and enforce them—not bargain with the contractor about which deviations can be traded for other concessions.

THE CUSTOMER-SUPPLIER RELATIONSHIP

All parties involved in a construction project have their own interests, and each approaches the project in pursuit of two different agendas—one open, the other hidden. Consider the following example:

Owner. The owner is a city agency that is responsible for construction of a new library. The owner's project manager is Robert Grey, a lifelong bureaucrat who has worked for the city for 22 years. His open agenda is to build an attractive, high quality facility on time and within budget. His hidden agenda is to make sure that any problems that arise are blamed on someone else.

Contractor. The contractor is a small local construction company that has been affected by a slowdown in its normal business—residential construction. In order to pay its overhead costs, the owner, Sam Green, has decided to bid on the construction of the library (even though he has never built a library before). In his zeal to be competitive, his bid was 8% less than the next lowest bidder. Sam's open agenda is to build an attractive, high quality facility on time and within his budget. His hidden agenda is to: (1) "front-end load" his progress payments to develop a positive cash flow that can be used to pay his creditors, and (2) seek every opportunity to make up for anticipated losses by filing claims and change orders.

Design Firm. The design firm is a large A/E firm that recently established a branch office in the city where the new library is to be built. It is represented by Ellen Brown, an architect who graduated at the top of her class five years earlier and recently became registered. The library project is her first assignment as project architect. Her open agenda is to build an attractive, high quality facility on time and within budget. Her hidden agenda is to prove to the partners of the firm that she is capable of managing major projects. Her boss has made it clear that Ellen must: (1) protect the firm from liability claims, and (2) obtain additional work from the client.

Construction Manager. The owner has decided to retain a construction management firm to provide cost/schedule control and field inspection services. The construction manager is Walter White, whose open agenda is to build an attractive, high quality facility on time and within budget. His hidden agenda is to demonstrate to the owner that he knows more about construction than the contractor and more about design than the architect.

The first time a problem arises on the project, each party will *act* in pursuit of his or her hidden agenda, while giving *lip service* to the need to build an attractive, high quality facility on time and within budget. Such duplicity is highly destructive, with the final result being that none of the parties achieve their objectives.

Is there a better way? Let's examine one of the principles of TQPM—the customer-supplier relationship. Under this concept, anyone who provides input to the work process is a *supplier* and anyone who uses the output of the work process is a *customer*. As shown in Figure 6.1, construction projects require an interwoven web in which each party serves as performer, supplier, or customer depending upon the nature of the specific work process. This built-in interdependence can be used to direct each party's efforts toward a common goal. This is done by a process of mutually defined requirements for each supplier-customer interface based on a two-way flow of information, as illustrated in Figure 6.2. Let's look at an example of how this can be accomplished.

An important element of the city library project is the *computerized document inventory system.* The design firm must prepare a specification defining the requirements of the system so that the constructor can arrange for a subcontractor to furnish and install it.

The suppliers to the design firm's activity include: (1) the owner (represented by Robert Grey), who must tell the design firm what kind of system is desired, and (2) system vendors who can provide information regarding various options that are available. The customers of this activity include: (1) the system vendor, which has a subcontract to furnish and install the document inventory system, and (2) the construction manager (represented by Walter White), who must oversee the installation of the system.

During the preparation of the specifications, there must be a dialog among the performer (the design firm), the suppliers, and the customers to assure that all important requirements are well defined. However, there is a problem: at the time that the specifications are being prepared, the design firm does not know which system vendor will be successful in being awarded the contract. Therefore, a dialog must be established with several vendors whose systems could satisfy

Work Process	Performer	Suppliers	Customers
Preparation of product specifications	Design firm	Owner Product sales representatives	Product manufacturers Construction contractor
Preparation of equipment shop drawings	Equipment manufacturers	Construction contractor	Design firm
Construction of building foundation	Construction contractor	Design firm Material suppliers Equipment leasing company	Owner
Processing of contractor's progress payments	Owner	Design firm Construction manager	Construction contractor
Preparation of project schedule	Construction manager	Design firm Construction contractor Equipment manufacturers	Owner Construction contractor

Figure 6.1 Suppliers and customers for work processes on a construction project.

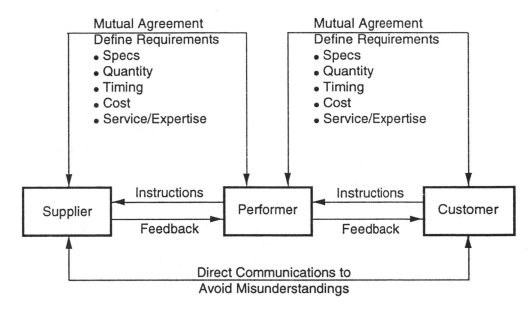

Figure 6.2 Flow of information in customer/supplier relationships.

the owner's needs. This will allow the design firm to prepare a specification that can: (1) assure that the selected system will meet the owner's needs, and (2) eliminate vendors whose systems will not meet the owner's needs.

Holding regularly scheduled, well planned meetings during the construction phase can also assure the ongoing dialog that is essential to healthy supplier-customer relationships among all the parties. This should begin with a preconstruction meeting whose agenda might include such items as the following:

- Introductions
- Lines of communications and submittals, including correspondence
- Site rules and regulations
- Procedures for issuing and revising design information and authorizing changes
- Survey information
- Contractor's designated areas and coordinating procedures
- Shop drawing and submittal requirements
- Methods of payment
- Certificates of insurance
- Procedures for overtime and shift-work
- Labor agreements (if applicable)
- Labor availability
- Security
- Cleanup
- Safety and first aid
- Temporary facilities and services
- Project-schedule program
- Project-cost program

- Material handling
- The Equal Employment Opportunity (EEO) Act
- Environmental procedures
- The role and responsibilities of the owner, designer, and construction manager
- Specific state and local laws or regulations
- Requests for information
- Claims, disputes procedures
- Subcontractor approval
- Community relations
- Critical specifications clarification
- Quality control testing

During construction, meetings should be scheduled on a regular basis, say weekly, biweekly, or monthly. It is best to schedule all meetings at the same time, day, and location, for example, every Tuesday at 10:30 A.M. at the contractor's construction trailer. The agenda should also be standardized and should include:

- Old business.
- Correspondence.
- Progress of the work since the last meeting.
- Interfaces, critical items, current and potential problems.
- Action items, due dates, responsible parties.
- Outstanding proposals, amendments, claims.
- Purchase and submittal schedules.
- New business.

These meetings should be chaired by the owner's representative (usually the design firm or construction manager), who should issue clear and concise minutes of each meeting (see example in Figure 6.3). Tape recording is not essential, but can be useful in resolving disagreements about what was said during a meeting.

Let's look at how the customer-supplier relationship can be fostered during the shop drawing process. As shown in Figure 6.1, equipment shop drawings are usually prepared by the manufacturers based on the requirements supplied by the construction contractor and are submitted to the design firm for review. Delays often occur when shop drawings are rejected by the design firm, sometimes requiring several resubmittals before finally being accepted. This problem can be largely prevented by the following measures:

Subject: Construction Progress Meeting #005 Filtration Plant Improvement Projects	**File:** 0800.30 **Job:** 029.04

Time: 10:00 A.M.   **Place:** Filtration Plant   **Date:** 2/1/90

Originated by: XYZ Consultants, Inc.   **Recorded by:** Xavier Y. Zimmer

Participants	Organization/Title	Phone #
Jamal Washington	City Engineering Manager	533-5125
James Olson	ABC Constructors	452-3737
Xavier Zimmer	XYZ Cons.	461-4626

Description of Subject Matter/Action	Action Party
Old Business and Action Items XYZ Consultants stated to ABC Constructors that proposal for the Preliminary Change Order (PCO) #3, 8″ water relocated main installation, was unacceptable due to insufficient backup. ABC Constructors stated they would fax this information today in order to avoid doing the work on time-and-material.	James Olson
Progess of Work (Updated Schedule) Connection #2 was completed 1/25/90 as scheduled. XYZ Consultants had the two welded connections near Station 5 + 93 x-rayed by TSI. One weld was acceptable and the second weld was rejected. ABC Constructors cut out the defective weld area and acceptably repaired.	None
Interfaces, Critical Items, or Problems It was necessary to install an additional 3-foot section of 42″ pipe due to a layout error by City surveyors. XYZ Consultants and the City have recognized this change and ABC Constructors will be compensated at the contract unit price for the extra pipe.	Jamal Washington
New Business Mr. Zimmer has received approval to dispose of all extra fill material in the area of the pumping facilities north of ABC's temporary field office. ABC Constructors has been informed accordingly.	None

Distribution:
   Original—File
   Copy—William Leonard, City Manager
   Copy—Each Meeting Participant

Figure 6.3 Example of a construction progress meeting summary.

1. During the design phase, the design firm should send draft copies of the relevant design documents to various potential equipment vendors. Their comments can then be incorporated into the design, significantly reducing the requirements for resubmittals during the construction phase.

2. The design firm should include in the specifications a complete description of the shop drawing review process including required contents, number of copies, days allowed for turnaround, and so forth.

3. The design firm should specify that, within 30 days of contract award, the contractor must submit a schedule for all shop drawings and other approval documents that the contractor plans to submit, including the names of all vendors, fabricators, and subcontractors who will prepare these submittals.

Similar techniques can be applied to foster a constructive customer-supplier relationship among the various parties involved during construction. Such relationships will not eliminate "hidden agendas." The idea is to mutually define requirements so explicity that the destructive influences of "hidden agendas" are avoided.

REDUCING CONTRACTOR CLAIMS

Contractor claims are, by definition, nonconformances. They reveal a breakdown in the desired customer-supplier relationships among the designer, constructor, and owner. Yet, like design errors, they are a fact of life in virtually every significant construction project.

The first step in producing nonconformances is to quantify the magnitude of the problem. This can be done for each project by tallying the number and size of all contractor claims. The data can be displayed in the form of a run chart, as shown in Figure 6.4.

After compiling the claims experience of several projects, the next step is to define these claims by category and plot their relative frequency (as shown in Figure 6.5). This graph shows which categories are the most serious and deserve the highest priorities.

An excellent way to reduce the number and size of con-

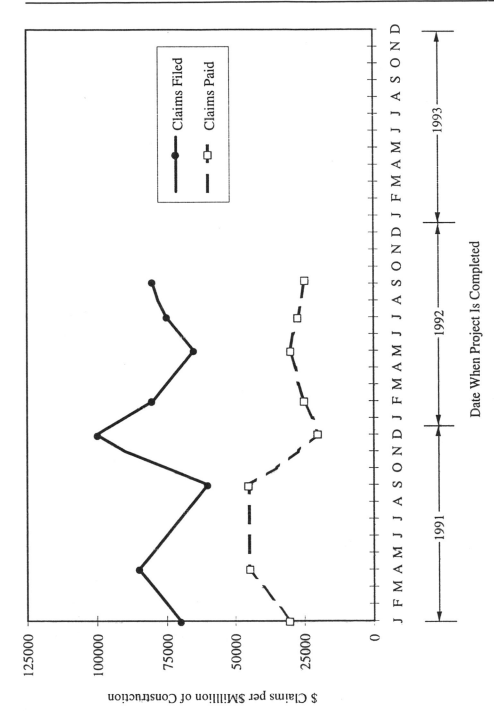

Figure 6.4 Record of contractor claims.

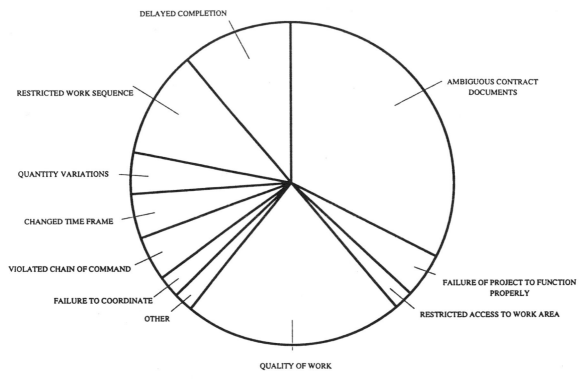

Figure 6.5 Categories of contractor claims.

tractor claims is by conducting a "claims discovery review." This review should be performed on a 90 + % complete set of drawings and specifications; it should be performed by someone who is or has recently been a construction contractor. The reviewer should put himself or herself in the position of a contractor who is seeking out every possible opportunity for a claim. The findings can be used to "tighten up" the contract documents prior to bidding. A checklist for conducting claims discovery reviews is presented in Appendix C.

These claims which cannot be prevented must be given the highest priority for early resolution. Contractor claims are not like wine—they don't get better with age!

REVIEWING CONTRACTOR SUBMITTALS

Most design professionals view the task of reviewing contractor submittals as a way of confirming that the design intent will indeed be carried out during construction. But contractor submittals also tell the design professional how effectively he or she has communicated the project's requirements to the contractor, equipment vendors, fabrication shops, and other "customers" of the design effort.

The Submittal Plan

Most design firms begin each construction project with only a vague idea of how many contractor submittals there will be, what they will contain, or when they will arrive for review. Worse yet, many constructors enter such projects with an equally vague plan for making these submittals. As a result, each submittal tends to be handled as an unanticipated interruption to the design firm's workload rather than as a planned part of that workload.

This problem can be resolved simply by requiring the constructor to prepare a submittal plan indicating the content and timing for each shop drawing and other submittal which requires the designer's approval. An example of such a plan is presented in Figure 6.6. The constructor should (1) obtain the designer's approval for the plan and (2) update the plan monthly. This will provide the designers with an opportunity to schedule the appropriate personnel for thorough and timely reviews.

Defining the Review Process

One common mistake made by design firms is to find the most available person in the office and give him or her a set of shop drawings with instructions to "review these right away." More often than not, the reviewer has little idea of what is required during the review, turning the review process into a hit-or-miss situation. Then when it turns out later that a submittal had been incorrectly approved, a three-way battle ensues as to who should pay for fixing the problem in the field. The contractor says, "The design firm approved the shop drawings, so I should be paid for the change." The design firm replies, "Approval of the shop drawings does not relieve the contractor of responsibility to conform to the drawings and specs." The owner's position is, "All I know is that it wasn't *my* fault and I don't expect to pay for it."

This ugly (but all too familiar) scenario can be avoided by assuring that the reviewer knows exactly what is to be reviewed. Standard checklists, such as the one in Appendix D,

Submittal Number/ Spec. No.	Activity	Contractor's Initial Submittal	Engineer's Approval (or Comments)	Contractor's Resubmittal (If Required)	Engineer's Final Approval
001/01310	Contractor Submittal Plan	2/5/92	3/2/92		3/2/92
002/01500	Site Utilization Plan	2/5/92	3/2/92	3/13/93	3/29/92
003/02125	Sediment and Erosion Control Product Data	2/11/92	3/9/92		3/9/92
004/02200	Soil Test Reports	3/30/92	4/28/92		4/28/92
005/02555	Water Pipe Product Data	2/11/92	3/10/92	3/20/92	3/31/92
006/02612	Asphalt Concrete Test Reports	6/29/92	7/7/92		7/7/92
007/02710	Chain Link Fence Product Data	2/11/92	3/5/92		3/5/92
008/02821	Seed Material Certification	7/3/92	7/31/92		7/31/92
009/03100	Formwork Drawings	3/30/92	9/27/92		4/27/92
010/03200	Reinforcing Bar Product Data	2/11/92	3/10/92		3/10/92
011/03200	Reinforcing Bar Shop Drawings	5/1/92	5/22/92	6/3/92	6/19/92
012/03300	Concrete Mix Design	5/15/92	6/2/92		6/2/92

Figure 6.6 Contractor submittal plan.

can be very useful. It is even better to begin with such standard checklists and customize them to the needs of the particular project, prior to beginning the actual reviews.

Shop Drawing Rejections

Rejected shop drawings and other contractor submittals constitute a classic type of nonconformance. Regardless of who was at fault, such rejections are very damaging to all parties—vendor, constructor, designer, and owner. Everyone will certainly agree on the desirability of reducing the frequency of such rejections.

The first step in reducing shop drawing resubmittals is to measure their magnitude. As part of its Quality Improvement Process, the Ralph M. Parsons Company has developed a vendor data analysis sheet, which is used to identify the types of errors found on vendor data (see the example in Figure 6.7). When vendor data are received, the reviewer identifies the errors in the vendor data and counts the number of marks corresponding to the appropriate headings shown on the vendor data analysis sheet. The reviewer also notes his or her opinion of the major cause(s) of the errors.

On major construction projects, it is useful for the constructor and designer to agree upon such a checklist as a way of tracking the number and type of resubmittals. The completed form can then be returned to the contractor to provide valuable feedback that should help to reduce future nonconformances. The success of this approach can be determined from a bar chart showing the reduction in rejections during the construction period (see the example in Figure 6.8).

The above approach might benefit an individual large project, but can it help reduce resubmittals on the many small construction projects in which most design firms are involved? It can, but the data must be charted somewhat differently. A run chart (as shown in Figure 6.9) can be used to determine long-term trends in the nonconformances of shop drawings. Each time a project is completed, two data points are plotted on the date corresponding to the completion of the project. One data point is determined by dividing the total number of resubmittals by the total number of shop drawing packages received from the contractor. The other data point is computed by dividing the total man-hours required for shop drawing review by the total number of submittals.

EXAMPLE OF
VENDOR DATA ANALYSIS

Job No. ___*4579.62.05*___   Job Name ___*Antarctica Oil Refinery*___

Purchase Order Number ___*PE 216*___

Vendor Data Control Number ___*4.3*___   Equipment Tag Number ___*T-104*___

Type of Vendor Data (e.g., Electrical, Arrangement Drawing, etc.) ___*Tank Fabrication Details*___

Reviewer ___*I.M. Thoreau*___   Date ___*April 12, 1991*___

Category of Reviewer Comments   **Number of Errors**

1. Does not conform with the specification... _2_

2. Does not conform to code... ___

3. Poor quality drawing.. _

4. Equipment weights and center of gravity not shown...................................... _____

5. Operability/constructibility problems... _____

6. Equipment and/or instrument tag numbers not listed................................... _18_

7. Dimensional errors or dimensioning incomplete.. _____

8. Incomplete notes ....

9. Additional views and/or details needed... _2_

10. Prior comments not incorporated .... _1_

11. Calculations incorrect.. _

12. Requirements on requisition and specification incorrect
    (Vendor has not received latest requirements).. _____

13. Other...

    Total .... _____

Manhours spent by reviewer .... _6_

Reviewer Opinion on Cause(s) of Errors

6. *Vendor did not read specification requiring tag numbers to be noted on shop drawings for each nozzle.*

Figure 6.7 An example of vendor data analysis.

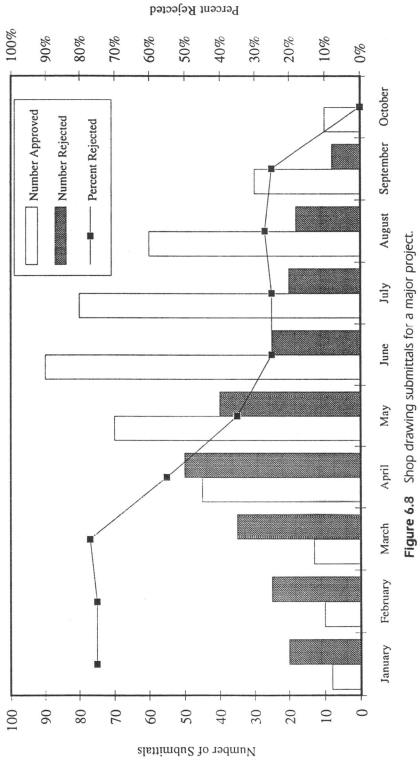

Figure 6.8 Shop drawing submittals for a major project.

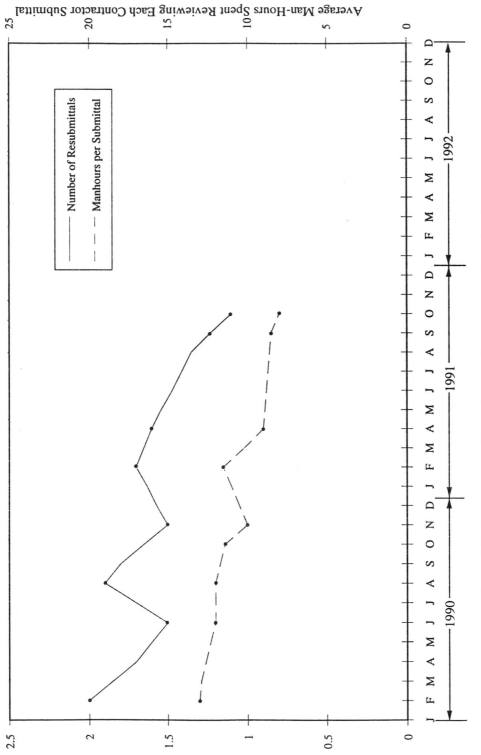

Figure 6.9 Long-term tracking of nonconformances on shop drawings.

Delays in the Shop Drawing Approval Process

The techniques described above and illustrated in Figures 6.8 and 6.9 can also be applied to measuring delays in the shop drawing approval process. Each month, the design firm can identify the percentage of late submittals received from the contractor on all its active construction phase projects. The percentage of missed turnaround times by the design firm can also be computed each month. These data can be charted on a graph similar to Figure 6.10. This measurement will identify how serious the problem really is, and will allow management to begin the search for causes and solutions.

CONTRACTOR CORRESPONDENCE

When contractors write to describe a field problem or request information, they are issuing the first warning of a possible claim. Every day's delay in responding to such correspondence increases both the probability that the problem will become a claim and the ultimate amount of such a claim. Each item of contractor correspondence should be logged in the same way as shop drawings and other submittals are logged. Responses should be made, in writing, within three working days of receipt. Conformance with this requirement can be measured on the same chart as used for tracking turnaround time on shop drawings (see Figure 6.10).

FIELD INSPECTION

Total Quality Project Management of construction consists of the following distinct components:

Quality Control. The constructor's activities to insure that all materials and workmanship conform to the contract documents and satisfy the needs of the project.

Quality Assurance. The activities of the owner's representative to inspect the contractor's quality in order to assure that quality control is adequate.

Quality Improvement. Transmission of knowledge gained in the field back to the design staff as a way of preventing problems from recurring on future projects.

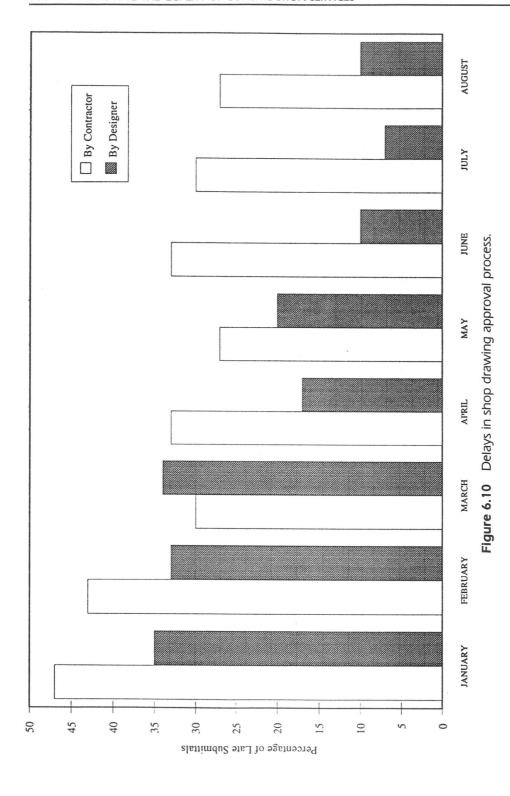

Figure 6.10 Delays in shop drawing approval process.

Quality Control

Everyone (constructor, designer, and owner) must clearly understand that quality control is *solely* the constructor's responsibility. The constructor has been hired to build a facility that conforms to specified requirements. Even if the owner's representative inspects the work, the constructor is still responsible for making sure it conforms to these requirements. Inspection by the owner does *not* reduce the constructor's responsibility for quality control.

Quality Assurance

The designer's role during construction is generally that of quality assurance, that is, auditing certain critical elements to be sure that they conform to specified requirements. The extent of this audit may range from occasional site visits to full time on-site observation of every construction crew. The audit should determine not only if the constructor is conforming to the requirement of the drawings and specifications, but also to generally recognized standards of quality such as those issued by the organizations listed in Figure 6.11.

Daily field reports (similar to the example in Figure 6.12) provide a means of recording the contractor's day-to-day operations and reflect the total quality of the work. The report should cover all important aspects affecting job conditions and progress. It can be used as a basic reference to determine the history and progress of the work at any time. Daily field reports are especially useful in resolving claims and disputes and verifying progress payment requests. The report should be concise, detailing only the facts, not opinions. It should always be prepared on the same day as the performance of the work (or no later than the following morning). Notation should be made when the contractor has complied with instructions for corrective action. When the resident inspector observes that the contractor is doing work (or has done work) which is *not* in compliance with the contract, the owner's representative should promptly notify the contractor's representative verbally and note such action in the daily field report.

In addition to the daily field report, each inspector should maintain a bound diary. This diary can contain more detailed information pertaining to the project. As with the daily field report, the diary should only contain facts, not opinions. However, it may contain sensitive material that would not be appropriate for contractor review.

Item	Source of Information
Earthwork	American Society of Foundation Engineers The American Concrete Institute Portland Cement Association American Society for Testing and Materials American Association of State Highway and Transportation Officials
Masonry	American Society for Testing and Materials American National Standards Institute National Bureau of Standards Masonry Society Brick Institute of America National Concrete Masonry Association
Timber	American Institute for Timber Construction National Forest Products Association
Structural steel	American Institute for Steel Construction American Iron and Steel Institute
Reinforcing steel	Concrete Reinforcing Steel Institute Wire Reinforcing Institute
Asphalt	American Association of State Highway and Transportation Officials Asphalt Institute
Painting (of metals)	Steel Structures Painting Council
Electrical installations	Institute of Electrical and Electronic Engineers National Electrical Manufacturers Association National Electrical Code National Fire Protection Agency
Mechanical installations	American Society of Mechanical Engineers American Petroleum Institute American Water Works Association
Welding	American Welding Society Lincoln Welding Foundation American Society of Mechanical Engineers
Skid resistance	American Society for Testing and Materials

Figure 6.11   Sources of information on acceptance standards.

If the contractor, after being notified of a problem, continues to do work contrary to the terms of the contract, or starts to cover up unacceptable work, the inspector or resident designer should immediately prepare a warning of noncompliance (see Figure 6.13) and hand a copy to the contractor's representative at the job site. Within 24 hours, a copy of the

JOB NAME _Oakwood Estates_   **DATE** _9/14/91_

REPORT NO. _23_   **JOB NO.** _2398_

LOCATION _Suburbia, Ohio_   **WEATHER** _Sunny_

CLIENT _Fastbuck Developers, Inc._   **TEMP** _66°_   **AT** _8:30_   **AM/PM**

CONTRACTOR: _Centerville Construction Co._

Work Activity	Equipment	Qty	Work Force	Qty
Item No. 1: _Sect. 03100 & 0200_	_Paver_	_1_	_Supt._	_1_
Formwork & Excavation	_Dump Trucks_	_2_	_Foreman_	_1_
	Grader	_1_	_Surveyors_	_3_
Item No. 2: _Sect. 0220 Backfill_	_Drill Rig_	_3_	_Carpenters_	_4_
	Cranes	_1_	_Electrician_	_3_
	Backhoes	_3_	_Pipelayers_	_2_
Item No. 3: _Sect. 02200 & 15060_	_Dozers_	_1_	_Equip. Oper._	_3_
Excavation & Plumbing	_Loaders_	_1_	_Sheet Metals_	_4_

WORK PERFORMANCE SUMMARY, INCLUDING SUBCONTRACTORS

1) Blake Const. Co. - Continued excavation of footing @ line A. Installed inside forms for retaining wall @ gridline 15 from 10' east of G proceeding west. Clean up of footings in progress.

2) Price Equip. Rental - Started backhoe of trench for 6" storm drain from existing catch basin @ Westside proceeding east to 5' of administrative bldg.

3) Cooke Mech. - Continued excavation of trench for 3" acid waste lines between E & F lines from GMP line 3 to 10. Working on assembly of pipe fittings.

REMARKS: _1) Mike Gardner inspected & approved rein. steel in place @ retaining wall gridline 15 & rein. steel @ elev. pit footing. 2) As per R. Bundy, control joint should be located @ midpoint of wall & before or after a column (Ref. Report 5/21)_

ACCIDENTS REPORTED TODAY _0_   _L. C. Branchlee_
                                                 Construction Inspector

Figure 6.12 An example of a daily field report.

warning should be mailed to the contractor's office unless the warning has previously been lifted due to compliance. Once a warning of noncompliance has been written, no money should be paid for the item(s) listed until corrective action has been taken and signed off by the owner's representative.

File _____ NC #1 _____

Project: _____ _Pump Station P-3 Replacement Project__

No. _____ _NC246_ _____

Contractor: _____ _D. C. Constructors_ _____

Engineer: _____ _Centerville Engineering Co._ _____ **Owner:** _____ _Centerville Community Services District_ _____

Reference _____ _Spec 14300 - Travelling Crane Assembly_ _____

Location _____ _Contractor's construction storage yard near intersection of Spyglass Hill Rd_ _____

Description _____ _Submittal for travelling crane assembly is not approved, but equipment has been_ _____ _delivered. Also, manufacturer's instructions for storage have not yet been provided._ _____

Noncomplying work may be required to be removed and replaced at no cost to Owner.

It shall be your responsibility to determine the corrective action necessary, and to determine whether you wish to discontinue operations until additional investigations by the owner's representative confirm or refute the initial findings.

Photos Taken By: _____ _L. L. Weiner_ _____ **Date** _____ _3/5/91_ _____

Warning Issued By:

Inspector _____ _L. L. Weiner_ _____ **Time** _10:15 P.M._ **Date** _____ _3/21/91 Letter_ _____

Warning Received:

Contractor _Dan Carter_ _____ **Time** _3:20 P.M._ **Date** _____ _3/25/91_ _____

Owner/Client _H. L. Meyers_ _____ **Time** _3:20 P.M._ **Date** _____ _3/25/91_ _____

Notice Lifted _L. L. Weiner_ _____ **Date** _____ _4/12/91_ _____

Distribution:
Original - Contractor
Copy - Inspector
Copy - Project Manager
Copy - Owner/Client
Copy - File

Figure 6.13 An example of a warning of noncompliance.

In cases of continued noncompliance, appropriate action should be taken by the owner's representative in agreement with the provisions of the contract. The notice of suspension or resumption of work (see Figure 6.14) may be used by the owner's representative to direct the contractor to stop work on the project. This form should not be issued except in cases of serious quality problems or safety violations and only as allowed by the contract.

When the resident inspector observes that the contractor, one of the subcontractors, or other party has damaged an underground or overhead utility facility, structures, or private property, the resident inspector should prepare a construction damage report (see Figure 6.15). The incident should be added to the project punch list.

Quality Improvement

The purpose of quality improvement is to take the lessons learned during construction back to the designers in the office so that future designs can avoid these problems. There should be a formal procedure in place to assure that this invaluable feedback is provided and acted upon.

The Quality Improvement Process begins with documentation of a problem by the field inspector (see the example in Figure 6.16). This information is then reviewed by the project manager and, if appropriate, is used to modify the firm's standard specifications, drawings, or design approaches.

RECORD DRAWINGS

One of the last activities in most construction projects is updating the drawings and specifications to reflect changes made during construction and to add details from approved shop drawings and other submittals. This activity is normally initiated by someone (usually the constructor's and/or designer's field representative) who keeps a marked up set(s) of documents on which any changes or additions are noted. These marked up documents are then brought back to the designer's office where they are used to update the originals into what is usually termed "record drawings." (The term "as built" should be avoided since it connotes a degree of accuracy which is rarely achieved in the field.)

Project   _Hidden Hills Water Line_

Contractor _ABC Contracting_

Engineer _XYZ Engineers_

Owner/Client   _City of Hidden Hills_

Reference (Regulation and/or Specification) _Section 01150_

[X] You are hereby notified to suspend operations on the above project because

of   _Trenches Not Shored In Accordance With Shoring Plan_

Effective   _5/29_   19_91_   until further notice.

Areas where work shall be suspended   _All Trenches Areas_

[   ] You are hereby notified to resume operations which were suspended _____

_____, 19 _____

Notice issued By: _____ _C. U. Encort_

Title _Inspector_

Date _5/29/91_

Distribution:

Original	-	Contractor
Copy	-	Inspector
Copy	-	Project Manager
Copy	-	Owner/Client
Copy	-	File

Figure 6.14 An example of a notice of suspension or resumption of work.

Date: _7/5/91_

Project: *Pump Station P-3 Replacement Project*

File: _Construction Damage Rpt_

Location: *Centerville, KS*

Time: _9:40 AM_

Reference Drawing No. _C-1 & C-2_

Type of Utility or Structure Damaged: (indicate by check mark)

Gas _____, Water ____, Telephone _____, Sanitary __X__, Other ____, Mainline __X__
Service line _____. If other, describe: _____

Utility/Agency involved: _PBCSD_ _____

Name of Contractor/party causing damage: _B. C. Constructors_ _____

Address of Contractor/party: _202 Lewis Road_ _____

Centerville, KS _____

Was utility or structure shown on construction drawings? Yes__X__ , No____. If yes, was it
shown correctly? Yes____, No._X_ If no, explain _Force main (14") was shown 10 ft from pavement edge._
Contractor's Drilling Hole @ 6 ft from pavement _____

Was utility or structure field marked? Yes____, No._X_ If yes, was it shown correctly?
Yes____, No____. If no explain_____

Did Contractor call Underground Service Alert prior to excavation? Yes____, No__X__
If yes, indicate by USA Ticket No._____ and date_____

Did Contractor verify depth, location and alignment of utilities or structures shown on construction drawing and as
field marked? Yes____, No_X_ If no, explain_Contractor field measured approximate location of new structure_
and added 4 Ft. This distance is within the clearance shown on C-1 _____

Was customer out of service? Yes____, No_X__ If yes, how long?_____

Did damage require repair by a Local Utility Agency? Yes____, No_X_ If yes, what was the cost?_____
Emergency Repair Work Order No._____? If no, who made repairs?_Dan Kasper Co. - Contractor_ _____

If damage to private property, provide parties name, address and nature of damage_____

Based on above information, who is responsible for claim?_Not yet determined_ _____

Additional information on back ____. Inspector _Charles Weeks_ Date _7/5/91_

Disposition:
Original - Project Manager
Copy - Project File

Figure 6.15 An example of a construction damage report.

To: *Chief, Specification Section*

From: *M. Richardson*   **Job No.:** *2698*

Project: *Century Tower*

Inspector: *H. Gunaji*   **Project Manager:** *L. Gibbons*

Division: *11*   *Equipment*   **Section:** *11221*   *Mechanical Mixers*
          (No.)   (Title)   (No.)   (Title)

Problem: *Shop drawings were reviewed and approved, but when unit was installed, the propeller did not fit inside the opening provided.*

Recommended Solution: *Add propeller size to the information required for vendor to submit with shop drawings.*

To: Chief Engineer

From: Chief, Specification Section

I have reviewed the subject Problem and Recommended Solution and recommend as follows:

    [ ] Specification is satisfactory as written.

    [X] Revised Division and Section is enclosed.

Remarks: *Project managers on all existing design projects should be sent a copy of revised spec.*

To: Design Managers

From: Chief Engineer

I approve of the recommendations of the Chief, Specifications Section, and request that they be implemented in the future.

Howard Taylor   *October 2, 1991*
   (Signature)   (Date)

cc: Chief, Specifications Section (after Chief Engineer approval)

Figure 6.16 An example of a design improvement form.

Although the accuracy of such documents is very important for future use by the owner, this activity occurs at a bad time. During construction, both the constructor's and designer's representatives are concerned with field problems, schedule problems, budget problems, and other issues that take on greater urgency than keeping the marked-up drawings up to date. By the time the construction is completed, everyone is tired of dealing with the project, so it is hard to build enthusiasm for the unglamorous task of completing the

Job No.: _____4126_____

Project Name: _____Smallville Hospital_____

Client: _____City of Smallville_____   **Location:** _____Smallville, Ohio_____

Construction Period: _____2/14/90 to 10/11/90_____

Type of Information	Conforming	Nonconforming
Equipment descriptions	5	1
Tag Numbers	1	1
Dimensions	2	6
Elevations	1	0
Sizes	1	0
Finishes	5	0
Totals	12	8

_____A. N. Walters_____   _____November 16, 1990_____
Auditor   **Date**

Figure 6.17   An example of a record drawing field audit.

record drawings. Too often, the result is a large number of discrepancies between the record drawings and actual field conditions.

This problem can be solved by applying the principles of TQPM. The first step (as usual) is measurement of the problem. This can be done during a one-day field audit to determine nonconformances. The auditor should randomly select 20 information items that were changed in the field during construction. He or she should then note any significant discrepancies between what is shown on the drawings and specs versus what actually exists in the field. The results can be tabulated as shown in the example in Figure 6.17.

After compiling these data for several projects, the results can be plotted on a bar chart similar to Figure 6.18 to show which problems are the most serious. A run chart similar to Figure 6.19 can be used to see if the overall problem is getting better or worse.

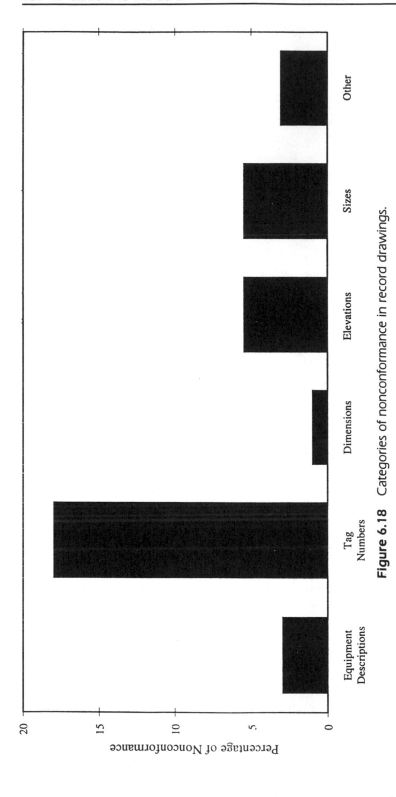

Figure 6.18 Categories of nonconformance in record drawings.

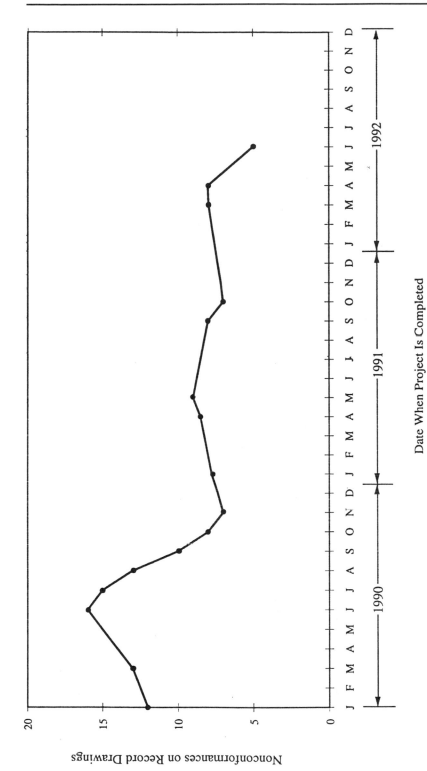

Figure 6.19 Trends in nonconformances on record drawings.

COMPLETION, ACCEPTANCE, AND FINAL PAYMENT

Completion of construction projects is usually a three-part process involving substantial completion, final acceptance, and close-out.

Substantial completion occurs when the facility is ready for the intended use, despite some defects to be corrected or minor incomplete aspects of the work. Generally, the owner's representative is required to issue a certificate that: (1) establishes the date of substantial completion, (2) defines the responsibilities of the owner and the contractor for security, maintenance, heat, utilities, damage to the facilities and insurance; and (3) fixes the time within which the contractor will complete any unfinished items (see example in Figure 6.20). The unfinished items are listed on a construction punch list.

After final inspection and determination that the work has been fully completed, the resident engineer issues a certification of completion and final acceptance (see Figure 6.21). Upon *final completion*, payment is then made to the contractor; this ordinarily amounts to a waiver of further claims by each party against the other, subject to stated exceptions on the part of the owner. Exceptions may include unsettled liens, faulty or defective work appearing after substantial completion, special guarantees running in the owner's favor (such as manufacturer's warranties), failure of portion of the work to comply with the contract documents, and so on.

The last step is *close-out,* when all records are gathered, organized, reviewed, and stored. It is at this point that all the data required to evaluate nonconformances are compiled and evaluated.

MEETING BUDGET REQUIREMENTS

"Quality" construction services include the need for keeping the design firm's costs within the requirements agreed upon with the owner. To accomplish this goal, the design firm's construction services budgets should be established using the following separate components:

1. One-time costs such as mailing of bid packages, running pre-bid conferences, and establishing project procedures.
2. Calendar-based costs, which are proportional to the du-

Project: _Secluded Beach Manhole Replacement_

Job No. _4654_

Project or Specified Part Shall Include: _Replacement of all manholes_

Date of Substantial Completion: _8/26/91_   Contract Date _8/30/91_

The Work performed under this Contract has been inspected by authorized representatives of the Owner, Contractor, and Consultant. The Project (or specified part of the Project, as indicated above) can be utilized for the purpose for which it was intended. All items that affect operational integrity and function of the facility must be capable of continuous use.

A tentative list of items to be completed or corrected is appended hereto. This list may not be exhaustive, and the failure to include an item on it does not alter the responsibility of the Contractor to complete all the Work in accordance with the Contract Documents.

| _ABC Engineering_ | **By** | _Alex B. Crawford_ | _8/26/91_ |
| **Consultant** | | **Authorized Representative** | **Date** |

The Contractor accepts the above Certificate of Substantial Completion and agrees to complete and correct the items on the tentative list within the time indicated.

| _XYZ Constructors_ | **By** | _Xavier Y. Zolsky_ | _8/26/91_ |
| **Contractor** | | **Authorized Representative** | **Date** |

The Owner accepts the Project or specified area of the Project as Substantially Complete and will assume full possession of the Project or specified area of the Project at _8:00 A.M._, on _8/27/91_. The responsibility for utilities, security, and insurance under the Contract Documents shall be as set forth under "Remarks" below.

| _Secluded Beach Township_ | **By** | _Andrew Richards_ | _8/26/91_ |
| **Owner** | | **Authorized Representative** | **Date** |

Figure 6.20 An example of a certificate of substantial completion.

ration of construction. These include preparing monthly progress reports, providing periodic or full-time on-site inspection, and attending weekly contractor meetings.

3. Contractor-controlled costs for such items as shop drawing reviews and witnessing of final testing. The better job the contractor has done, the less it will cost the design firm to do its job.

The first component is amenable to establishing a reasonably accurate budget if the requirements are well defined and agreed upon between the owner and designer. The second component can be budgeted with reasonable accuracy on a

Date of Completion: *26 October 1991*

File No.:   *NC014.15*

Specification No.:   *G. C. 20.7*

To: *ABC Constructors*

Project Title: *Secluded Beach Community Services District*

Manhole Replacement Project

The work performed under this Contract has been inspected by the Owner's Representative and the Project was completed on the above date.

Contractor has fulfilled its obligations under the Contract and this Certificate shall constitute Final Acceptance.

This Certificate is issued with the understanding by both Contractor and Owner that said Final Acceptance shall not operate as a bar to a claim against Contractor under the terms of the guarantee provisions of the Contract.

The Owner's Representative will prepare and record a Notice of Completion after Owner has received the Release and Certificate of Final Payment, Executed by Contractor.

By: *Andrew Richards*   **Date:**   *11/16/91*
            General Manager

Distribution:

    Original   –   Contractor

    Copy   –   Project File

Figure 6.21   An example of a certificate of completion and final acceptance.

cost per unit of calendar time, such as dollars per month. The third component must be budgeted with respect to the contractor's performance. For example, a budget can be prepared for review of shop drawings with a unit price supplement for each required shop drawing resubmittal due to an initial rejection.

This three-component approach to budgeting construction services will greatly reduce budget overruns that often plague design firms and owners. To apply this approach successfully, it is helpful to track the results of previously completed projects to aid in budgeting future projects. Because the requirements differ greatly from job to job, it is not realistic to plot the data on a time-scale and look for trends. Rather, results should be plotted by project, as shown in Figure 6.22. This will permit the design firm's project managers to select data from the most similar past projects in order to predict budgetary needs for a particular new project.

SAFETY IS QUALITY TOO

One cannot discuss quality on construction projects without discussing safety. While safety is the responsibility of the construction contractor, the design firm is often involved whenever it provides resident inspection services. Since 1988, The Business Roundtable has recognized 11 owners and 32 contractors in the U.S. through its Construction Industry Safety Excellence Awards Program.* Although The Business Roundtable recognizes that contractors have the primary responsibility for execution of jobsite safety, it recommends that owners using construction contractors should:

- Understand the total workers' compensation insurance premium concept and how it is affected by work site accidents.
- Require contractors to provide their state workers' compensation insurance rate sheet and OSHA 200 Logs for the three most recent years at the time of inquiry.
- Set numerical Experience Modification, Total Recordable Incidence, and Total Lost Workday Incidence "Hurdle Rates" as targets of acceptability for prequalifying contractors, and allow only prequalified contractors to bid.
- Ensure that contractors bidding work have well planned on-site safety performance improvement programs and

*Source: "The Workers' Compensation Crisis ... Safety Excellence Will Make a Difference," *The Business Roundtable*, January 1991.

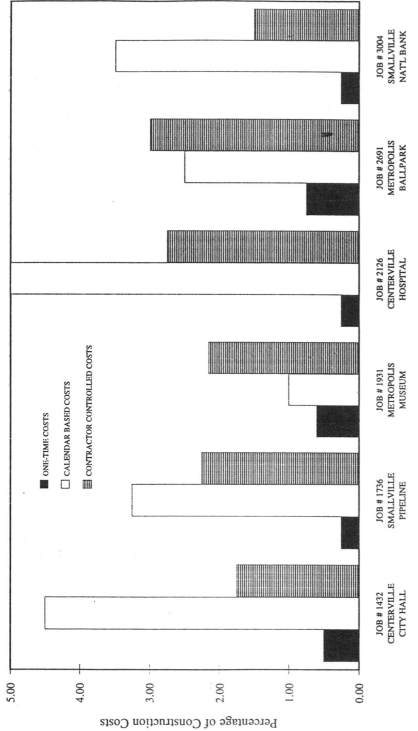

Figure 6.22 Cost tracking for construction oversight activities.

that contractors on the work site effectively implement those safety improvement programs.

- Encourage a commitment to the Zero Injury concept at the top management level in the owner company and at the top management level in the construction contractor company. Routine and frequent reports of contractor safety performance status must be given to the Chief Executive Officer.

- Insist that a jobsite visit by senior level executives of both contractor and owner occur no later than the day following a lost time accident to review what occurred and plan steps to prevent further deterioration of safety performance.

- Develop routine means of recognition of safety performance. Recognition of Zero Injury achievement must be given the highest level of management attention.

- Maintain a contractor accident statistic record keeping program for all contractors working on owner sites.

- By helping the owner accomplish these objectives, design firms can provide a valuable service in reducing construction injury rates.

SUMMARY

This chapter concludes the portion of the book that describes how TQPM can improve the quality of technical services provided to clients. In the next chapter, we look into the internal management of the professional service firm to see how TQPM can make it more effective.

7 IMPROVING MANAGEMENT, ADMINISTRATION, AND MARKETING

Many managers believe that TQPM is not well suited for management, administrative, and marketing activities because they cannot be measured in the same way as manufacturing processes. This notion is *totally false.* This chapter describes how administrative and marketing activities can be measured and improved using TQPM techniques.

WHO ARE THE CUSTOMERS?

Virtually every new design firm is started by one or more technical professionals. In the beginning, they handle all management, administration, and marketing activities themselves with assistance from hourly personnel (such as secretaries) and outside specialists (such as accounting firms). These functions support the firm's mission of providing technical services to its clients. The personnel involved in these activities understand that their job is to support the technical staff who serve the clients.

As the firm grows, this relationship undergoes a subtle transformation. Specialists are brought in with expertise in human resources, marketing, accounting, contracts, and other non-technical fields. As the administrative workload increases, each of these areas becomes a department headed by a highly paid professional manager. The firm's senior managers, who are almost all technical profesionals, begin to spend more of their time with these non-technical managers than with the project managers or their clients.

The administrative managers, who rarely deal with clients, view the firm's technical personnel as being irresponsible and in need of tight control lest they create serious problems for the firm. The administrative managers view their own role as guardians of the company jewels and overseers of the un-trustworthy technical staff. Because they tend to monopolize the time of the firm's senior managers, the administrative managers become increasingly powerful in formulating poli-cies and procedures.

The firm's technical personnel (including project manag-ers) tend to view this relationship very differently. They view themselves as the source of the firm's revenue and profits. The firm's administrative managers are viewed as empire-building bureaucrats who don't understand the business and get in the way of progress. The technical personnel are also jealous that they have less access to senior managers than the administrative managers.

Not only are both of these views wrong, they lead to an adversarial relationship that increases overhead costs, hurts morale, and encourage destructive office politics.

How Can This Situation Be Avoided?

The answer requires everyone to understand the relationship from a customer/supplier viewpoint. Each administrative function has two objectives: (1) to support the firm's techni-cal personnel so that they can better serve their clients and (2) to protect the firm (and its owners) from large financial losses. In the first objective, the technical staff are the cus-tomers; in the second objective, the administrative groups are the customers. In both cases, there must be mutually agreed requirements. This means that a project manager can-not simply demand faster response from the accounting de-partment without first understanding what constraints might prevent such improvements. It also means that the contracts manager cannot demand compliance with an elaborate con-tract review process unless he understands its impacts on cli-ent relations. This chapter describes some techniques for de-veloping effective customer-supplier relationships.

MAKING THE OFFICE RUN SMOOTHLY

Every firm has a variety of administrative procedures designed to make the office run smoothly. These include such activities as:

- Filling out time cards.
- Preparing expense reports.
- Obtaining travel authorization.
- Notifying management of vacation and travel time.
- Logging long distance calls.
- Purchasing office supplies.
- Using office equipment.
- Logging computer time to projects.

Administrative managers are routinely frustrated because of frequent and habitual failures of many employees to abide by the firm's administrative procedures. Under traditional management approaches, such failures are dealt with by issuing nasty memos, threatening the offenders, and complaining to their supervisors. These tactics usually yield limited, temporary results and tend to alienate the employees from the firm's administrative managers.

TQPM offers a better way to deal with the problem of complying with office procedures. First, let's distinguish between "policies," "guidelines," and "procedures."

A *policy* is a description of the philosophy of the organization with respect to a specific topic. For example, there may be a policy that all hiring and promotion will be done in accordance with all state and federal laws and regulations. Each policy is implemented through a combination of guidelines and procedures.

A *guideline* is a good idea that generally benefits the user if it is followed, but is not mandatory. For example, a design firm may have a guideline specification for reinforced concrete. The structural engineers will usually save time by using this guideline specification, but they may deviate if project conditions warrant. Issuing guidelines is a good way to let everyone learn from previous mistakes and develop a "corporate memory."

A *procedure* is a requirement established by management; conformance is not optional and any exceptions must be ap-

To: _____ *N. L. Sun* _____

Date: _____ *5/1/91* _____

Subject: Itineraries

No itinerary was left at the reception desk on this date: _____ *4/29/91* _____.

Please make it a priority, before leaving the office, to leave an itinerary in your message box. If you are not coming into the office, notify Betty by 9:00 A.M.

Thank you,

_____ *Betty* _____

Figure 7.1 Nonconformance advisory for missing itineraries.

proved in advance. Procedures describe in detail how a policy is to be implemented. Issuing procedures and ensuring they are followed is a way of maintaining discipline in an organization.

From a management viewpoint, the key difference between guidelines and procedures is enforcement. Guidelines must be made available to all those concerned and some training in their use is usually beneficial. This is also true of procedures, but there must *also* be a mechanism to assure that procedures are followed. Enforcement of procedures is time-consuming, frustrating, and costly. Therefore, procedures should be replaced with guidelines for all but most critical administrative matters.

Where procedures are required, enforcement measures should emphasize future compliance rather than placing blame for past transgressions. A successful approach is the "nonconformance notice," a nonthreatening handwritten note sent by the "customer" to the offender notifying him or her of the type of nonconformance and asking that it not be repeated in the future.

For example, let's say that a firm has established a procedure that all employees must leave an itinerary with the receptionist whenever they are out of the office. In this case the "customer" is the receptionist who is expected to know each employee's whereabouts at all times. An employee's failure to submit an itinerary will prevent the receptionist from knowing where the employee may be. To resolve this problem the receptionist can send a nonconformance notice (similar to Figure 7.1) to each employee who fails to leave an itinerary. In order to avoid the appearance of placing blame, the employee's supervisor should *not* be advised of this nonconformance. If, after repeated notifications, an employee still fails to leave an itinerary, the receptionist should have a confidential conversation with the employee's supervisor to enlist his or her support in resolving the problem. The success of such a system for achieving compliance can be monitored using a run chart. If, as in Figure 7.2, the nonconformances are continuously being reduced, it is clear that the system is working. If such improvement is not apparent, other means must be employed,

This same nonconformance advisory system can yield similar results on a variety of administrative policies such as:

- Filling out time cards.
- Opening project numbers.
- Logging computer charges.
- Logging long distance telephone calls.
- Arriving on time to meetings.
- Preparing expense reports.
- Reviewing/approving invoices promptly.

OPTIMIZING INTERNAL SUPPORT SERVICES

Virtually every professional service organization with more than 20 to 30 employees has some internal support services, such as a word processing pool, drafting group, accounting department, and so on. Technical professionals regularly complain about the high error rate, long turnaround times, high costs, and inefficiencies of these services. Personnel within these support services organizations have their own complaints about the technical professionals; these include unrealistic deadlines, failure to advise them of upcoming work, inadequate budgets, and so on.

Must the energy of a professional services firm always be consumed with these internal disputes? To answer this question, let's look at how successful U.S. and Japanese manufacturers handle their internal service organizations. A strong trend among both U.S. and Japanese companies is to "outsource" many of these activities, that is, subcontract them to firms specializing in these services. For example, in the past most U.S. manufacturers used their own employees for janitorial services. Virtually all large manufacturers now subcon-

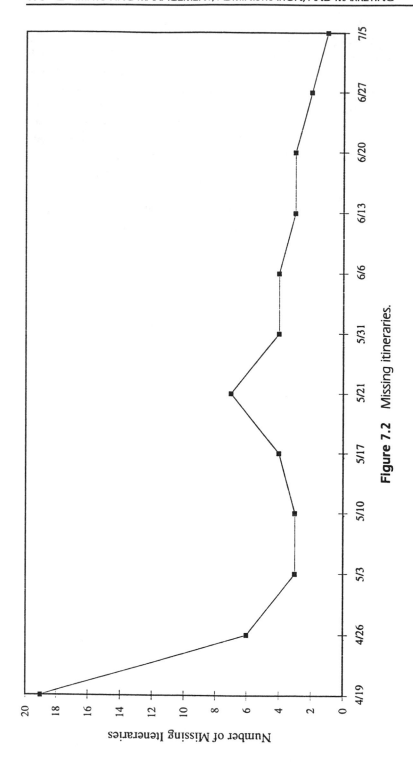

Figure 7.2 Missing itineraries.

tract these activities to firms that specialize in such services and, as a result, are far more efficient than the manufacturers could ever be. Most manufacturers are also reducing the size and scope of their in-house engineering organizations, instead contracting more design work to outside firms.

What kinds of internal support services can a design firm "farm out" to an outside specialist? Let's look at some actual examples.

1. At a 200-person A/E firm in the Southeast, project managers were always complaining about how much time was charged by the Electrical Department for their portion of each design project. To determine the validity of this complaint, a local electrical engineering firm was asked to propose on the electrical design for a typical project. When the outside firm's estimate was compared with the estimate from the in-house Electrical Department, it was found that the in-house estimate was *three times* that of the outside firm!

2. A medium sized engineering firm in Boston discovered it could get better and more timely results by buying accounting services three days a week from a local accountant than by maintaining a two-person staff plus computers.

3. A California firm in the civil engineering business does *no* drafting. Instead, they "farm out" all drafting to a CADD drafting firm that performs faster than their former staff at a controlled contract price. One further benefit: the CADD firm "shares" some of the liability for delivering on schedule in their contract, due to penalties for late delivery.

While outsourcing may solve some problems, not all internal service organizations can be eliminated. The key to their effectiveness lies in the supplier-customer relationship discussed previously. When these support organizations are put in the role of suppliers, their objective becomes that of meeting the agreed-upon requirements. This first step, of course, is to agree upon a set of requirements for each assignment *before* the work begins. For a CADD assignment, this might include a discussion of the layering system to be used, drawing scale, sheet numbering system, and so on. There also needs to be a feedback mechanism for the internal customers to advise the suppliers of how well the requirements were met. This might also include a measurement system to track overall performance.

To illustrate how this can work, let's take an example of a word processing pool that provides services to an office of a design firm. A work request form can be used by an engineer to establish the requirements of a particular assignment. If these requirements cannot be met, the head of the word processing department must consult with the engineer to modify the requirements, revise priorities, or find suitable alternatives. When the typing has been completed, the document is returned along with an indication of turnaround time and hours charged. The engineer then prepares an evaluation of how well the product conformed to the agreed-upon requirements. All of this information can be documented in a single requisition form, such as the one shown in Figure 7.3. These data can be used to track responsiveness (using a probability chart similar to the example in Figure 7.4), quality (using a run chart such as Figure 7.5), and cost-effectiveness (using a run chart such as Figure 7.6).

An alternative way of measuring the quality of internal support departments is by an annual or semi-annual evaluation by the department's customers. For example, each customer of the CADD department might be requested to fill out a form similar to Figure 7.7. Tracking this information will help determine if customer service is improving. Narrative comments can be a source of ideas on how to improve internal customer service.

MANPOWER PLANNING

Manpower planning can be among the most difficult and frustrating activities in the management of design firms. The most detailed and accurate plans can be made obsolete without warning by a client who has an emergency or one who suddenly cancels a project. It is because of these uncertainties that manpower planning should be performed as a two-stage process.

The purpose of the first stage is to allocate the short-term work load among the individuals in the office. This can best be accomplished in a 30 to 60 minute meeting held weekly or biweekly. In an office of five or six persons, it is most convenient to invite everyone to these meetings so that work as-

WORD PROCESSING REQUISITION FORM

THIS SECTION TO BE FILLED OUT BY CUSTOMER

AUTHOR:_____ EXT:_____   SECRETARY:_____ EXT:_____

JOB NAME_____ JOB #_____   CLIENT NAME:_____

S U B M I T T O R

Submittal	Date/time Submitted	Date/time Desired	No Later Than
☐ 1st DRAFT	_____/_____	_____/_____	_____/_____
☐ 2nd DRAFT	_____/_____	_____/_____	_____/_____
☐ 3rd DRAFT	_____/_____	_____/_____	_____/_____
☐ FINAL	_____/_____	_____/_____	_____/_____

Note: 1st Draft Is <u>Not</u> Double Checked   Final Submittal Includes TOC and Final Format

WORD PROCESSING SHOULD: (Include Log Numbers)

☐   ASSIGN NEW LOG NO. FOR PROJECT TITLED:_____

☐   EDIT OR ADD ATTACHED TO LOG NO.:_____

☐   COPY TEXT FROM LOG NO.:_____

☐   USE ES STANDARD FORMAT

SPECIAL INSTRUCTIONS PLEASE BE SPECIFIC_____
_____
_____

THIS SECTION FOR WP USE ONLY

S U P P L I E R

TOTAL QC RESULTS	1st Draft	2nd Draft	3rd Draft	Final
TURNAROUND TIME (HOURS):_____	_____	_____	_____	_____
TOTAL TYPING TIME (HOURS):_____	_____	_____	_____	_____
NO. OF PAGES PRODUCED:_____	_____	_____	_____	_____
NO. OF ERRORS PER DOCUMENT [BY CHECKER] ☐ Edits ___ ☐ Spelling ___ ☐ Format ___	_____	_____	_____	_____
DESCRIPTION OF DOCUMENT: ☐ Text ☐ TOC ☐ Table				

WP RECOMMENDATIONS/COMMENTS_____
_____
_____

THIS SECTION FOR CUSTOMER EVALUATIONS WHEN JOB COMPLETED

C U S T O M E R

	1st Draft	2nd Draft	3rd Draft	Final
1. DID "TOTAL" RETURN TIME MEET YOUR NEEDS:	_____	_____	_____	_____
2. QUALITY OF WORK: Overall Document Rating 0 = Poor, 10 = Excellent	_____	_____	_____	_____

3. SPECIFIC RECOMMENDATIONS/COMMENTS:_____
_____
_____

Please return this form to WORDPROCESSING SECTION

Figure 7.3   Word processing requisition form.

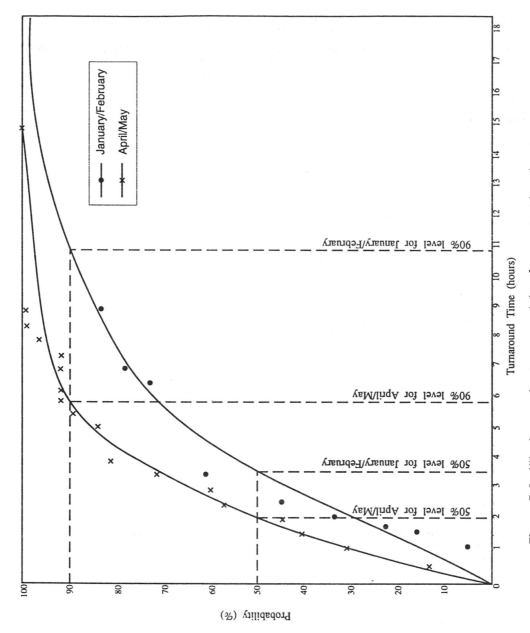

Figure 7.4 Word processing turnaround time for new text less than ten pages.

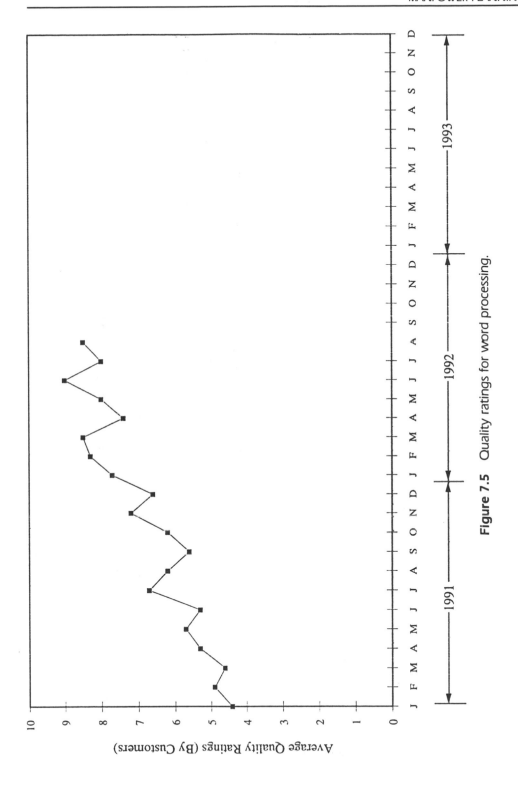

Figure 7.5 Quality ratings for word processing.

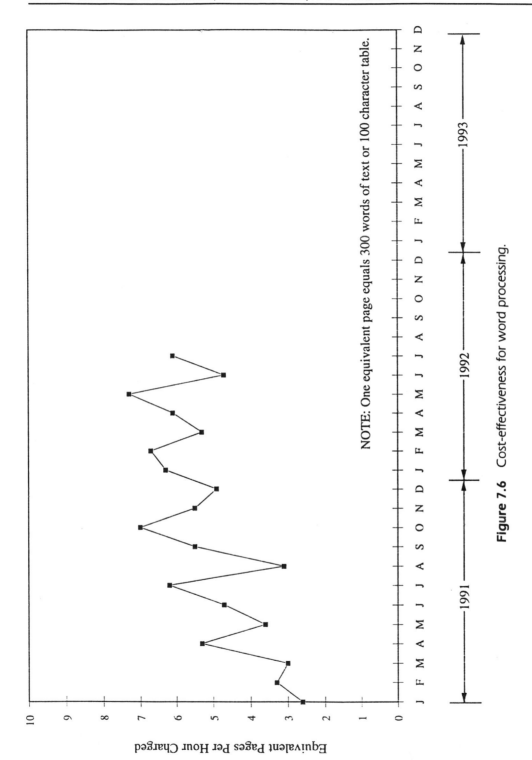

NOTE: One equivalent page equals 300 words of text or 100 character table.

Figure 7.6   Cost-effectiveness for word processing.

Questions	Strongly Agree (4)	Agree (3)	Sometimes Agree/ Disagree (2)	Disagree (1)	Strongly Disagree (0)	Undecided/ Don't Know
1. When I provide reasonable lead-time, CADD regularly meets my schedules and the turnaround time is reasonably prompt.	SA	A	AD	D	SD	U
2. CADD lets me know in advance when a schedule looks to be a problem.	SA	A	AD	D	SD	U
3. When I submit something on a very tight schedule that can't be met in regular working hours, CADD lets me know that overtime will be needed to accomplish the work or makes arrangements to get the work done in another office.	SA	A	AD	D	SD	U
4. Work returned to me matches the markup I submitted and rarely needs correcting.	SA	A	AD	D	SD	U
5. CADD provides me with constructive advice for improving drawing layouts or figures for reports/proposals.	SA	A	AD	D	SD	U
6. CADD provides advice to me on how I could reduce rework and other CADD costs on my jobs.	SA	A	AD	D	SD	U
7. When I inform CADD and Graphics personnel of their joint report/proposal preparation effort, I can be assured coordination will take place and the presentations will appear similar.	SA	A	AD	D	SD	U
8. Time charged to jobs/proposals for CADD-produced drawings and/or figures is reasonable.	SA	A	AD	D	SD	U
9. When I provide CADD with something that needs to be increased or decreased in size, I can always be assured the new scale will be calculated correctly and it will be useful for obtaining dimensions.	SA	A	AD	D	SD	U
10. The lettering size, style, and placement for figure titles, figure numbers, and legends are all done consistently in a report/ proposal so I don't have to make significant corrections.	SA	A	AD	D	SD	U
11. CADD does an effective job of drawing organization and layout to minimize the number of drawings and produce an understandable document for construction.	SA	A	AD	D	SD	U
12. CADD drawings/figures from jobs done in the past several years can be readily retrieved.	SA	A	AD	D	SD	U
13. The CADD staff is cooperative and treats me like an internal "client" or "customer."	SA	A	AD	D	SD	U
14. CADD support services have improved during the past six months.	SA	A	AD	D	SD	U

Please attach any additional comments concerning the manner in which CADD Support Services meets or does not meet your needs.

_____

Name (Optional)

Figure 7.7 CADD support services survey.

signments can be communicated directly. In a large office, it may be more practical to invite only project managers. In an even larger office, it may be necessary for each department to hold its own meetings with minutes distributed to other department managers.

The second stage of the manpower planning process is a longer range view necessary for making decisions regarding hiring, borrowing/loaning people, and possible layoffs. Here, a statistical approach is best to make such an analysis. Each project manager must forecast the total manpower requirements for each project. These can then be tabulated into a manpower forccast, as shown in Figure 7.8. In a multidisciplinary or multidepartmental office, a similar forecast should be made for each group. Note that the forecast includes both jobs in hand and anticipated projects (those with a 90% or greater probability of capture). This separation is made because of the uncertain start dates for jobs that are anticipated but not yet in hand. Delays in start dates (which occur frequently) can produce overly optimistic workload projections in the short term.

Manpower forecasts can be illustrated graphically using bar charts as shown in Figures 7.9 and 7.10. These graphs (often referred to with tongue in cheek as "going out of business curves") define the rate at which the backlog is being exhausted. This amount of new work must be booked in order to maintain the current staffing level. If such analyses are performed regularly (every two to three months), a frame of reference will emerge that will advise management of whether the rate of decline is abnormally shallow or steep.

Long-term trend analysis can be done by plotting the total backlog each time a forecast is made. (This value should include only the next 12 months to avoid distortions caused by a few large multiyear projects.) With experience, upper and lower control limits can be drawn as shown in Figure 7.11. If the backlog is above the upper control limit, plans should be made for hiring additional staff. If the backlog is below the lower control limit, plans should be made for increasing marketing efforts and/or reducing staff size.

JUST-IN-TIME INVENTORY PLANNING

During the 1970s, Japanese manufacturers developed a system that keeps their inventories of supplies low while still

Department Name: Enviromental Studies and Permitting

People Available= 9
Percent OH & Proposals= 17%

JOBS IN HAND

Projected Professional Man-days by month

Job No.	PM	Job Name	Total Man Days	Sept	Oct	Nov	Dec	Jan	Feb	March	April	May	June	July	Aug
AT513	SER	Chanute AFB	2,230	200	200	250	300	160	160	160	160	160	160	160	160
AT518	LW	AF Spill Plan	78	39	39										
AT608	JM	Eglin PAs	92	14	50	28									
AT668	LW	ANG Spill	360	40	40	40	40	40	40	40	40	40			
AT685	BB	Grant Co. EAs	55				5	10	10	10	10	10			
AT727	JM	Kimberly Clark	17	7	10										
AT735	BB	Roswell Rec. Plan	7	3	4										
AT741	BB	Grant Co. - P.D.	2	2											
AT747	SER	Monroe Assessment	10	6	4										
AT787	SER	Colonial Assessment	14	10	4										
AT792	AG	MARTA - MLK	22	22											
AT796	SER	U.S. Can	2	2											

TOTAL BACKLOG: 2,889

	Total	Sept	Oct	Nov	Dec	Jan	Feb	March	April	May	June	July	Aug
(Monthly totals)		345	351	318	345	210	210	210	210	210	160	160	160
TOTAL AVAILABLE MAN-DAYS	196	196	196	196	196	196	196	196	196	196	196	196	196
ESTIMATED OH & PROMO DAYS	33	33	33	33	33	33	33	33	33	33	33	33	33
SURPLUS (DEFICIT) FOR BACKLOG	(182)	(182)	(188)	(155)	(182)	(47)	(47)	(47)	(47)	(47)	3	3	3
NET 2-MONTH BORROW (LOAN)	105	(182)	182										
ADJUSTED SURPLUS (DEFICIT) FOR BACKLOG	(77)	(77)	(6)										

JOBS ANTICIPATED

Projected Professional Man-days by month

Job No.	PM	Job Name	Total Man Days	Sept	Oct	Nov	Dec	Jan	Feb	March	April	May	June	July	Aug
AT608	JM	Eglin Mod #1 PA	516		86	86	86	86	86	86					
	AG	MARTA East Point	47	27	20										
	SER	CHWMEG	158		30	30	30	30	30	8					
	SER	AFCEE/Thermal Desort	300			30	30	30	30	30	30	30	30	30	30

TOTAL ANTICIPATED: 1,021

	Total	Sept	Oct	Nov	Dec	Jan	Feb	March	April	May	June	July	Aug
TOTAL ANTICIPATED	1,021	27	136	146	146	146	146	124	30	30	30	30	30
TOTAL BACKLOG & ANTICIPATED	3,910	372	487	464	491	356	356	334	240	240	190	190	190
TOTAL AVAILABLE MAN-DAYS	196	196	196	196	196	196	196	196	196	196	196	196	196
ESTIMATED OH & PROMO DAYS	33	33	33	33	33	33	33	33	33	33	33	33	33
NET MANPOWER SURPLUS (DEFICIT)	(209)	(209)	(324)	(301)	(328)	(193)	(193)	(171)	(77)	(77)	(27)	(27)	(27)

Figure 7.8 Department manpower summary.

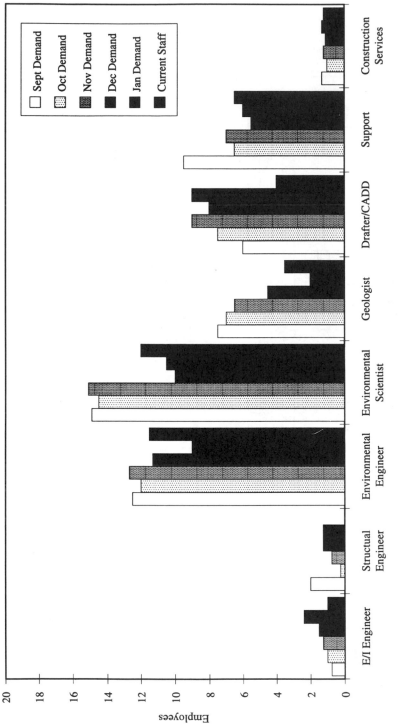

Figure 7.9 Manpower projection, September–January 1992–1993.

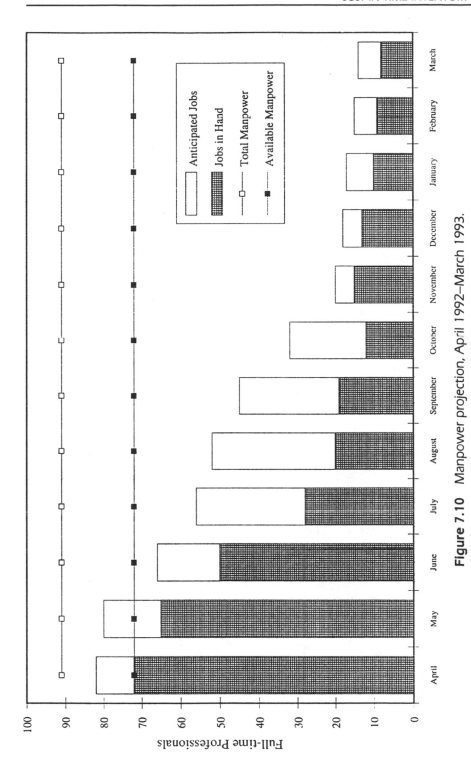

Figure 7.10 Manpower projection, April 1992–March 1993.

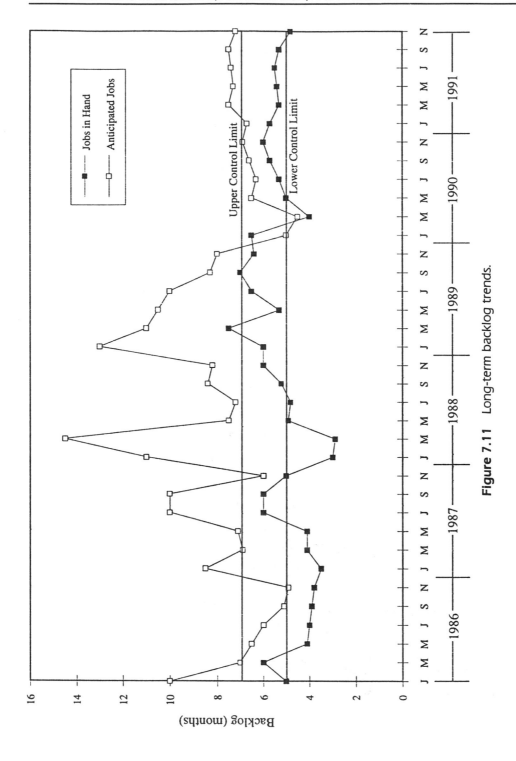

Figure 7.11 Long-term backlog trends.

maintaining high production rates. This system, known as just-in-time (JIT) inventory planning, is now being successfully adopted by American manufacturers. Can it be used in a professional service firm?

JIT in an automobile plant means that the supply of engines arrive just in time for them to be installed in the cars as they are going onto the assembly line; the inventory of engines is kept as low as possible.

The "products" of design firms include drawings, reports, specifications, and so on. These products are produced using the firm's "inventory" of personnel and equipment. This "inventory" should be as small as possible. The "inventory" of personnel can be measured by the "labor utilization rate," which is computed as follows:

$$\text{Labor utilization rate} \quad = \quad \frac{\text{Hours charged to projects}}{\text{Total hours charged}}$$

The target rate should be established by subtracting from 100% reasonable allowances for: (1) employee benefits such as holidays, vacation, sick leave, jury duty, and military leave; (2) normal office administrative time; and (3) time spent on marketing and proposals. For example, a design firm might establish a target as follows:

Holidays, vacation, sick leave	=	9%
Administration	=	7%
Marketing/sales	=	7%
Total overhead time	=	23%
Target utilization rate	=	100% − 23% = 77%

The firm's ability to achieve this target can have a dramatic impact on its profitability. As shown in the example in Figure 7.12, the firm can double or even triple its total profits by increasing its labor utilization rate (assuming that all other factors remain constant).

Because of its importance, managers should not only strive to achieve their labor utilization targets, they should examine these targets regularly with the objective of maximizing them. For example, a firm might invest $3,000 in an optical disk computer backup system and save eight man-hours per week of administrative time required to manually back up the

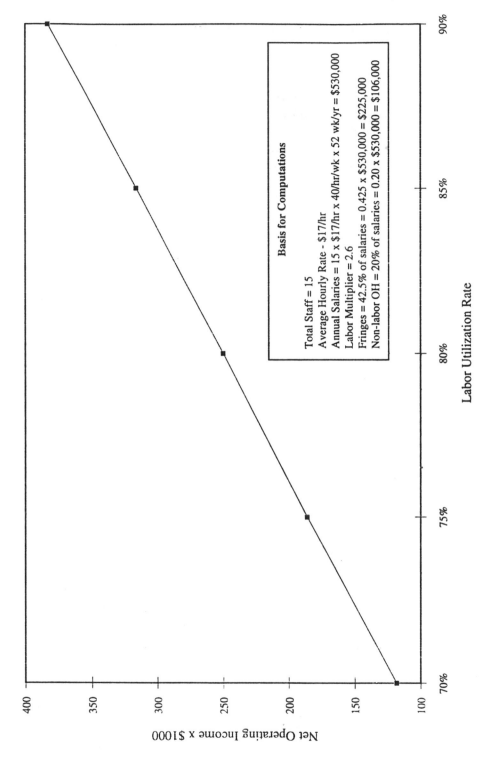

Figure 7.12 Effect of labor utilization rate on profits.

system. It may hire more part-time employees, reducing the overhead allocation required for holidays, vacation time, sick leave, and so on. (Of course, increasing this target too much may have negative repercussions such as poor employee morale or inadequate marketing efforts.)

In today's design firms, equipment utilization is becoming increasingly important as CADD and other computer uses continue to proliferate. The same kind of JIT analysis can be used to assure that the "inventory" of equipment time is kept to a minimum. For example, the computer utilization rate can be determined as follows:

$$\text{Computer utilization rate} = \frac{\text{Hours of productive usage}}{\text{Total hours available}}$$

The "hours of productive usage" refers to the time in which computers are used on projects or on overhead activities in which their usage significantly reduces labor costs. The "total hours available" can be computed as 168 hours per week multiplied by the number of computers. Thus, if a design firm had 10 computers and averaged 330 hours per week of productive computer usage, its computer utilization rate would be $330 \times (10 \div 168)$ or 19.6 percent. Like the labor utilization rate, managers should continuously seek ways to increase this value. Such increases might be obtained by working a second shift, making computers more accessible to potential users, or increasing the activities that computers can productively perform.

Long-term trends in "inventories" of labor and equipment can be monitored using a run chart similar to Figure 7.13. Upper and lower control limits are shown to highlight nonconformances with planned targets. In this example, the labor utilization rate has remained within the control limits with only minor deviations; the computer utilization rate began very low and took a year to consistently achieve compliance with desired control limits.

RECRUITING AND HIRING QUALITY EMPLOYEES

The following ingredients are needed to formulate an effective and efficient system for recruiting and hiring new employees:

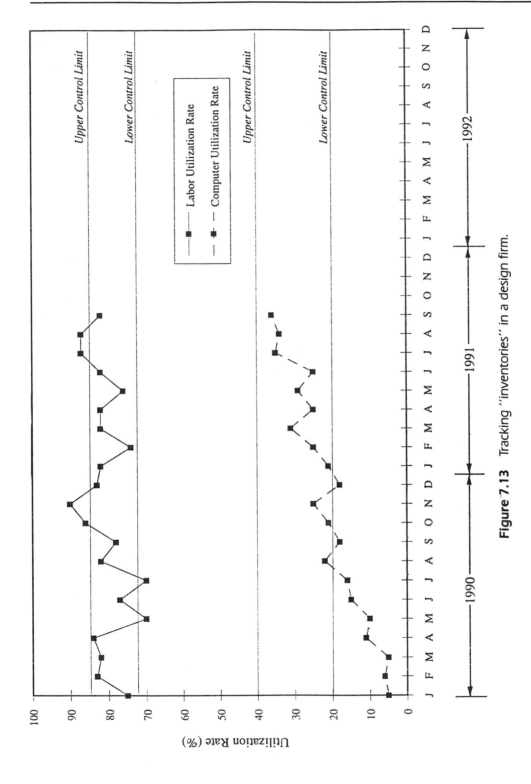

Figure 7.13 Tracking "inventories" in a design firm.

1. The firm must receive a large number of resumes from qualified personnel so that there are plenty to choose from.

2. The resume screening process should insure that only the most qualified candidates are invited for interviews.

3. The interview process must include a "selling" element so that candidates will accept offers of employment.

4. A feedback system should measure the effectiveness of the hiring process and the quality of employees that are being hired.

Each of the above elements can be monitored to measure the success of a design firm's recruiting and hiring program. The first step is to measure the raw data; a bar chart similar to Figure 7.14 can be used for this purpose. The first analysis of these data determines the firm's success in attracting resumes. This can be done by measuring the total number of resumes received and the number surviving the initial screening. These values can be compared to the firm's expenditures for advertising, campus visits, and other recruiting costs to determine cost-effectiveness. For example, let's say that ABC Architects spends $2,000 for an employment ad in the local newspaper and receives a total of 43 resumes, 16 of which survive the initial screening. The cost-effectiveness of this ad is $46.51 per resume and $125.00 per screened resume. This second value is the important one since only the resumes that survive initial screening are candidates for employment. Such tracking of various recruiting methods will quickly identify which are the most cost-effective.

Personal interviews can be costly, time-consuming, and disruptive to the firm's day-to-day activities. Therefore, there should be a high probability of making an offer to any candidate who is invited for a personal interview. This goal can be achieved by an additional screening step to weed out all but those candidates who will probably be made an offer. This step can usually be accomplished by a telephone interview combined with reference checks.

The success of the final screening step can be measured to determine what percentage of interviewed candidates receive job offers. An analysis of the recruiting data in Figure 7.14 reveals the following:

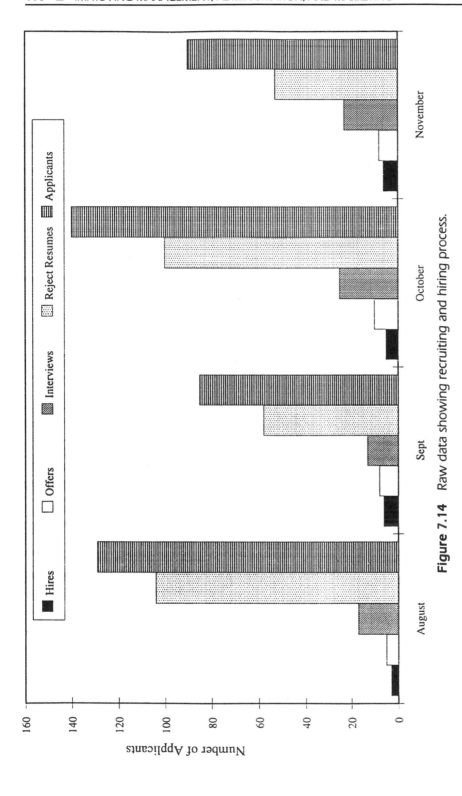

Figure 7.14 Raw data showing recruiting and hiring process.

Month	Interviews	Offers	Percentage
August	17	5	29%
September	13	8	62%
October	25	10	40%
November	23	8	35%
Totals	78	31	40%

The above data indicate that most candidates who were interviewed were *not* given job offers. The screening process may not have been thorough enough.

If a low percentage of job offers are accepted, it probably means that most of the interview time is spent "grilling" the employees to determine if they should be given a job offer. Inadequate time is being spent "selling" the candidate on the advantages of working for the firm. The following evaluation can be made from the data in Figure 7.14:

Month	Offers	Hires	Percentage
August	5	3	60%
September	8	6	75%
October	10	5	50%
November	8	6	75%
Totals	31	20	65%

Most of the offers in this database are being accepted; the firm is probably doing a good job of "selling" itself to prospective employees.

Perhaps the single most important factor in the long-term success of a professional service firm is the quality of people that it hires. Yet, in large firms, this is generally overlooked when Human Resources departments evaluate the performance of the recruiting and hiring process. They tend to play a "numbers game," tracking numbers of applicants, interviews, job offers, and hires rather than focusing on the *quality* of the employees that are eventually hired.

The true measure of employee quality can only be revealed after employees have been on the job for enough time to demonstrate how they can contribute to the goals of the firm and its clients. One way to measure the quality of new employees is to track the results of their performance evaluations one year after they were hired. This can be done using a bar chart similar to Figure 7.15.

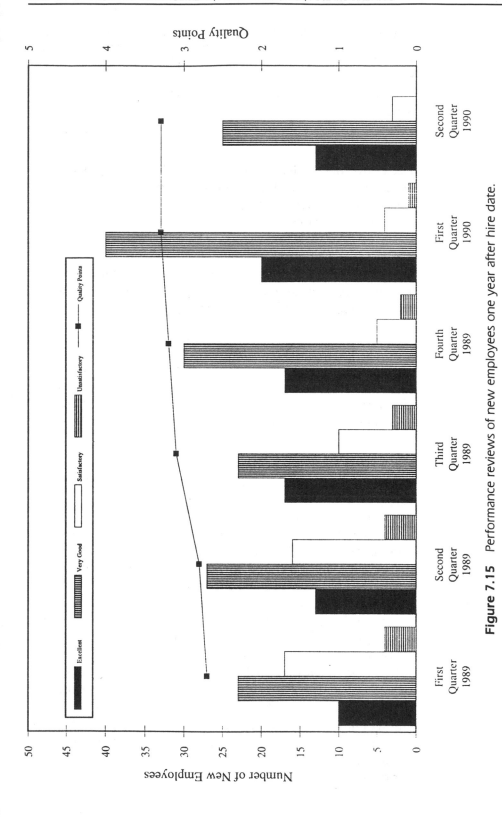

Figure 7.15 Performance reviews of new employees one year after hire date.

Trends can be identified by assigning rating points corresponding to the evaluations. For example, "excellent" can be worth 4 points, "very good" 3 points, "satisfactory" 2 points, and "unsatisfactory" worth 1 point. The data from Figure 7.15 can thus be analyzed as follows:

Time Period	Quality Points
1st quarter; 1989	2.75
2nd quarter, 1989	2.80
3rd quarter, 1989	3.06
4th quarter, 1989	3.14
1st quarter, 1990	3.23
2nd quarter, 1990	3.28

It can be seen that this firm has had steady improvement in its goal of hiring top quality personnel.

INTEGRATING NEW EMPLOYEES INTO THE FIRM

Starting a new job is a traumatic experience. Whether it is the employee's first job out of school or a change from a previous employer, the first few days and weeks can determine the level of loyalty and dedication that the employee will feel toward the firm. Most firms have new employee procedures that include administrative activities such as filling out the proper insurance forms. These routine procedures should be expanded to include assignment of a "sponsor" — generally a co-worker from the same department who can introduce the new employee to other key personnel and provide advice as to how to get around within the office structure. Assistance can be provided for such seemingly mundane issues as telephone usage, office supplies, use of support services, and so on. For new employees who have relocated from another city, the sponsor can also provide invaluable assistance in getting acclimated to a new place to live.

It may also be desirable to assign a "mentor" to help assimilate new employees into the workings and culture of the firm. The goal is to initiate a relationship between the new employee and a senior level staff member who has been with the firm for some time. By applying their knowledge and skills, an effective mentor can provide a valuable interface between the new employee and the company. Specific duties might include the following:

1. Meet with the new employee on at least a bimonthly basis for one year. (The mentor should be responsible for initiation of the meetings.) Establish a schedule for regular meetings with the employee at the first meeting. Discuss any issues related to the employee's indoctrination period and focus on the following:
   - Be sure the new employee understands the organization's mission and values.
   - Help the new employee understand policies and procedures—not just "what" but also "why."
   - Answer questions and resolve problems (professional or personal) that, for whatever reason, the employee feels cannot be brought to his or her direct supervisor.
   - Provide career guidance and counseling to the employee.
2. Continue to provide counseling on an as-needed basis after the first year.
3. Maintain mentoring conversations in strict confidence if desired by the employee. Obtain employee's approval before divulging any discussions with others.

To work effectively, the mentor program must comply with the basic principles of TQPM, that is, requirements must be defined, there must be a system of measurement, and feedback must be used to continuously improve the program. A sample flow diagram (Figure 7.16) illustrates how such a program might be structured. Figure 7.17 is a form that can be used to track whether mentoring sessions have actually taken place. After a prearranged time—usually one year—the effectiveness of the program can be measured by an evaluation form (similar to Figure 7.18), which is prepared by the new employee.

PERFORMANCE EVALUATIONS

In almost all design firms, performance evaluations are made by each employee's direct supervisor. The drafters are evaluated by the head of the drafting department, the structural

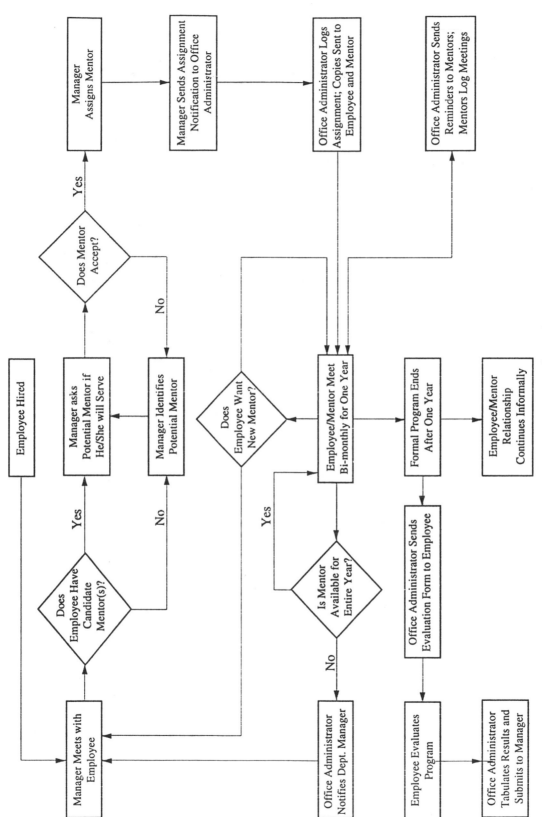

Figure 7.16 Mentor program flow diagram.

To: _____   Date: _____

You are listed as the Mentor for _____ . One of
the requirements of this program is a bimonthly meeting away from the office. Please
provide an appropriate answer for any of the items below and return the form to the
Office Administrator within one week.

Meeting occurred on: _____ .

No meeting. Reason: _____

_____

_____

_____

_____

Date of next meeting: _____

If you have not had a meeting, please set a meeting as soon as possible so that you
can help our new employees get better integrated into the company.

_____   _____
Mentor   Date

Figure 7.17   Mentor program meeting notice.

---

engineers by the head of the structural department, and so
on. The basic principles of TQPM force us to rethink this traditional approach and question its results.

When employees are evaluated by their supervisor, the
employees will tend to do the things they believe will make
them look good to their boss. Their boss's desires (or *perceived* desires) therefore become the employee's highest priorities. To illustrate this point, let's take a common situation
in a design firm: a secretary (let's call her Ann) handles the
work of a ten-person department and reports to the head of
that department (let's call him Bob). If Ann is given more
work than she can handle, whose work will *definitely* be
done on time? Bob's, of course. Is this because Bob's work is
more critical than that of the other nine people in the department? Is it because of an objective evaluation in which Bob
decided that the other people's work was not as important as
his? Probably not. The decision to put Bob's work at the "top
of the pile" was probably made unilaterally by Ann—after all,
Bob *is* the one who gives Ann her performance evaluations.
Because this mode of operation is so common, no one in the
department thinks much about it. However, Bob is a bit puz-

	Yes	No			
1. Was written information about the mentor program disseminated to you when you began work?	( )		( )		
2. Were you assigned a mentor within the first week on the job?	( )		( )		
3. Did your mentor initiate contact with you?	( )		( )		

	Always	Usually	Sometimes	Rarely	Never
4. My mentor and I met bimonthly at a minimum during my first year.	( )	( )	( )	( )	( )
5. My mentor has been available for consultation when I needed assistance.	( )	( )	( )	( )	( )
6. My association with my mentor was helpful in my understanding of the company's values and mission.	( )	( )	( )	( )	( )
7. My mentor helped me understand the company's policies and procedures.	( )	( )	( )	( )	( )
8. I was provided valuable career guidance and direction by my mentor.	( )	( )	( )	( )	( )
9. My mentor was helpful in answering questions and resolving problems whether personal or professional.	( )	( )	( )	( )	( )
10. Conversations with my mentor were held in strict confidence unless we agreed otherwise.	( )	( )	( )	( )	( )

	Strongly Agree	Agree	Neutral	Disagree	Strongly Disagree
11. The mentor program has been a worthwhile experience, helping me to get well grounded with the company and helping establish a future career course.	( )	( )	( )	( )	( )
12. A formal mentor program should be continued.	( )	( )	( )	( )	( )

Please provide any comments or suggestions from your experience that can be used to improve the mentor program.

_____

_____

_____

_____

Figure 7.18 Mentor program evaluation form.

zled about all the complaints from his staff about inadequate secretarial support—after all, *his* work always gets out on time.

The escape from this trap lies in a TQPM concept known as NOAC: "next operation as customer." This means that, in any work process, the "customer" is the person who relies on the work product of another person (a "supplier") to perform his or her own activities. In the above example, *everyone* in the department is Ann's customer. The NOAC concept requires that performance be evaluated by an employee's *customers*, not necessarily the boss.

If Bob wants to solve the problem of lack of secretarial support—and it may be a bigger problem than he thinks—he should have *everyone* in the department evaluate Ann's performance. Bob will no doubt find that he doesn't get nearly the personal attention he used to, but he will also get a much better assessment of Ann's performance. More importantly, he will be able to assess whether everyone's complaints about inadequate secretarial support are due to Ann's poor performance, improper prioritization of Ann's time, or the need for additional support staff.

Can customer-based performance evaluations be done with technical personnel? Certainly. The first step is to identify the most frequent "customer" that the employee served during the period of performance being evaluated. For designers and drafters, it may be the engineers and architects. For engineers, it could be the project managers. In the quest for customers, don't overlook people in a "lower" position than the employee being evaluated. For example, a mechanical engineer's customers may include a designer who takes the calculations and sketches and converts them to working drawings. The designer probably has a better idea of the engineer's performance than the head of the mechanical department!

Project managers should be evaluated by their principal customers—the firm's clients. (Methods for obtaining client evaluations are described in Chapter 8.) Technical staff who are temporarily assigned to work for a project manager should be evaluated by that project manager using a form similar to Figure 7.19.

Line supervisors can also be evaluated by their customers—their subordinates as well as their bosses. The idea of subordinates evaluating supervisors strikes fear into

EMPLOYEE NAME	ASSIGNMENT DATE	REVIEW PERIOD
Wanda Snodgrass	3 / 1 / 92	FROM 3 / 1 / 92 TO 7 / 14 / 92

CLASSIFICATION	PROJECT NAME	PROJECT NUMBER
Senior Engineer	Centerville Civic Center	2604

OVERALL PERFORMANCE ASSESSMENT: (PLEASE COMMENT BRIEFLY ON EMPLOYEE'S PERFORMANCE IN REGARD TO ASSIGNED PROJECT RESPONSIBILITIES. INCLUDE PERFORMANCE ON SUCH THINGS AS BUDGET, SCHEDULE, QUANITY/QUALITY OF WORK, ETC.)

Work was well done and well received by client. Interfacing with other disciplines was generally good, but a few lapses occurred due to miscommunication of requirements.

STRENGTHS/WEAKNESSES: (PLEASE COMMENT BRIEFLY ON EMPLOYEE'S STRONG POINTS AND ANY AREAS NEEDING IMPROVEMENT. BE SPECIFIC. SUGGEST CORRECTIVE ACTION AS APPROPRIATE.)

Wanda's strongest assets are her technical knowledge of structural engineering and her dedication to the project. She needs to work on communications skills, particularly with other disciplines.

PROJECT MANAGER/SUPERVISOR Alice Warcinski   DATE: 7 / 21 / 92

FORWARD TO THE APPROPRIATE COST CENTER.

Figure 7.19 Project performance survey.

the hearts of almost every manager. But this information, collected properly, can help supervisors do a better job of satisfying some very important customers—the subordinates who look to their boss to meet their needs as employees. A form similar to Figure 7.20 can be used for this purpose. The effectiveness of each supervisor or group of supervisors can be measured by assigning points to each rating as follows:

> 4 points — always
> 3 points — usually
> 2 points — sometimes
> 1 point — rarely
> 0 points — never

The points can be totalled and the average ranking plotted on a run chart similar to Figure 7.21, which can, over time, indicate if a supervisor is improving his or her service to subordinates. A histogram similar to Figure 7.22 can be used to determine which areas are most in need of improvement, so that management training can be focused in these areas.

EMPLOYEE TRAINING

When problems have arisen, traditional management approaches have tackled them by: (1) searching for the guilty persons; (2) punishing them to discourage repetition of the problem; and (3) firing them if the problem persists in spite of such punishment. The result of these techniques has been to develop an almost paranoid fear of failure among the employees. In seeking to protect themselves from retribution (or even losing their jobs), employees have stopped looking for creative new approaches and have resorted to a variety of techniques to "cover their tail" in case something goes wrong. Such behavior has led to the built-in mediocrity that can be seen in many old-line organizations.

To break out of this downward spiral, enlightened managers must stop blaming employees for the firm's problems. Where it appears that an employee's work is unsatisfactory, the manager must ask why. Often the answer lies in a lack of the skills required to do the job. Such skills may be technical (such as knowledge of the firm's CADD system) or they may be interpersonal (such as the inability of an engineer to comunicate effectively with the designers). The solution to

1. Does your supervisor encourage you to prepare quality work within the cost and scope constraints of our clients?

   Always _____   Usually _____   Sometimes _____   Rarely _____   Never _____

2. Does your supervisor provide adequate support or assist you in finding resources for your work?

   Always _____   Usually _____   Sometimes _____   Rarely _____   Never _____

3. Does your supervisor exercise a consistent leadership style that allows you to know your strengths and areas for growth?

   Always _____   Usually _____   Sometimes _____   Rarely _____   Never _____

4. Does your supervisor show a willingness to try out new ideas?

   Always _____   Usually _____   Sometimes _____   Rarely _____   Never _____

5. Does your supervisor encourage you to take outside or company-provided seminars and training to further your capabilities?

   Always _____   Usually _____   Sometimes _____   Rarely _____   Never _____

6. Please list two actions that would make your department and your firm a better place to work:

   A. _____

   _____

   B. _____

   _____

7. What two aspects of working here do you enjoy the most?

   A. _____

   _____

   B. _____

   _____

8. Place additional comments or explanations in the space provided below:

   _____

   _____

   _____

Figure 7.20 Supervisor evaluation form.

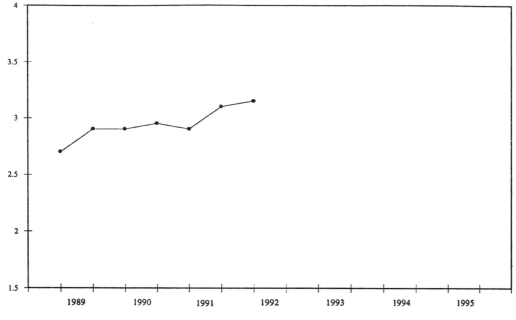

Figure 7.21 Supervisor evaluations.

these problems might include more training. This realization has resulted in a dramatic increase in training programs sponsored by design firms.

But *more* training isn't necessarily *better* training. The *quality* of all company-sponsored training programs (whether conducted by in-house or outside personnel) should be evaluated by each attendee. A form similar to the one in Figure 7.23 can be used to determine a numerical ranking by assigning the following point values:

4 points — excellent
3 points — very good
2 points — good
1 point — satisfactory
0 points — unsatisfactory

If the overall evaluation of a program is less than 3.0, improvement is needed before that program is presented to other employees. Each course should be continually improved until the overall evaluation averages at least 3.5. The root cause of low overall ratings can be identified by computing the average rankings for Questions 2 through 5 and by

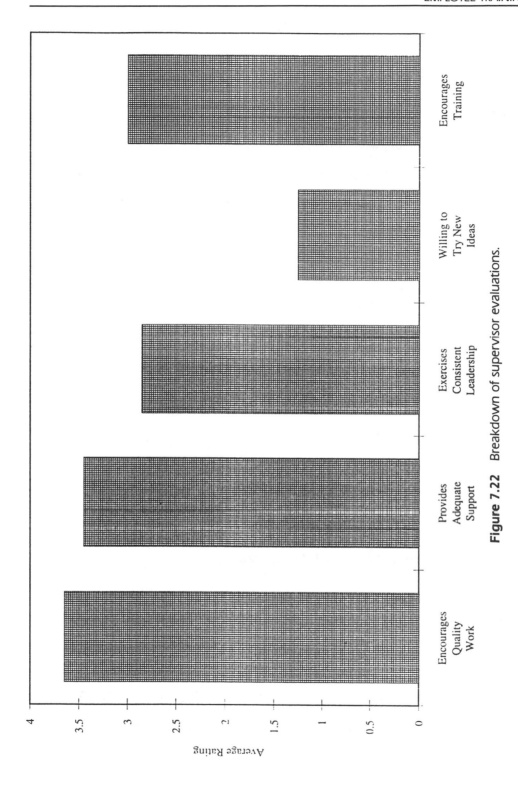

Figure 7.22 Breakdown of supervisor evaluations.

Name of Program _____*Project Management*_____ Date ___*4/10/91*___

1. What is your overall evaluation of the program?

    ( ) Excellent   *(x)* Very Good   ( ) Good   ( ) Satisfactory   ( ) Unsatisfactory

2. What is your evaluation of the program content?

    ( ) Excellent   *(x)* Very Good   ( ) Good   ( ) Satisfactory   ( ) Unsatisfactory

3. What is your evaluation of the program format?

    ( ) Excellent   *(x)* Very Good   ( ) Good   ( ) Satisfactory   ( ) Unsatisfactory

4. What is your evaluation of the handouts?

    ( ) Excellent   ( ) Very Good   ( ) Good   *(x)* Satisfactory   ( ) Unsatisfactory

5. What is your evaluation of the speaker?

    (x) Excellent   ( ) Very Good   ( ) Good   ( ) Satisfactory   ( ) Unsatisfactory

6. What did you most like about the program?   *The speaker was very knowledgeable.*

    _____

    _____

    _____

7. What would you most like to see changed for future programs?   _____*More examples of*_____
    actual projects. _____

    _____

    _____

    _____

8. Your comments: ___*Workbook needs to be easier to follow.*___

    _____

    _____

    _____

Figure 7.23   An example of program review form.

reading the narrative comments responding to Questions 6, 7, and 8.

The overall quality of firm's training programs can be measured using a bar chart similar to Figure 7.24.

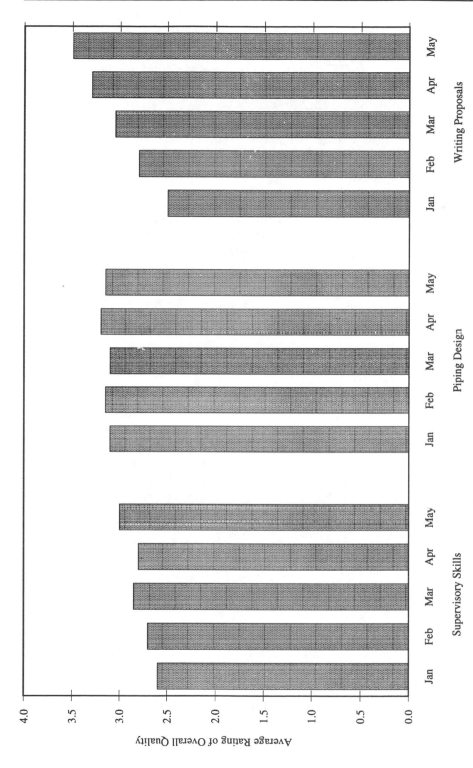

Figure 7.24 Quality improvement measurement chart for in-house training programs.

KEEPING JOBS UNDER BUDGET

Chapters 4, 5, and 6 describe ways of tracking the budget status of various kinds of projects. All of these methods yield a dollar value that describes this budget status at any point in time. For example, a project manager may determine that, as of July 1, his $120,000 project is running $8,000 over budget—an overrun of 6.7%. These results can be aggregated for a department, office, or the entire firm as shown below:

Job Number	Budget	Status*	Overruns
4216	$120,000	+ $8,000	+ $8,000
4219	68,400	+ 2,400	+ 2,400
4223	18,200	− 600	—
4224	221,000	− 2,000	—
4239	62,600	− 6,200	—
Totals	$490,200	+ $1,600	+ $10,400

*Overruns are represented by a + sign; underruns by a − sign.

Note that two totals are shown. The first represents the arithmetic sum of the budget status of all jobs; those which are under budget offset most of the overruns on the others. This value represents a picture of the quality of budget control within the group. The total of overruns (last column) represents the *potential* for further improvement. Both these values can be computed monthly and graphed using a run chart similar to Figure 7.25. The trends in these charts will tell management if the department, office, or firm is improving its budget performance.

REALIZING THE PROFIT POTENTIAL OF ALL PROJECTS

Most design firms employ job cost accounting systems that are at odds with the financial objectives of the firm as a whole. The most widely used accounting systems define "job cost" to include the following elements:

- Direct labor (salaries and wages paid to employees).
- Other salary costs (employee benefits and statutory payroll costs).

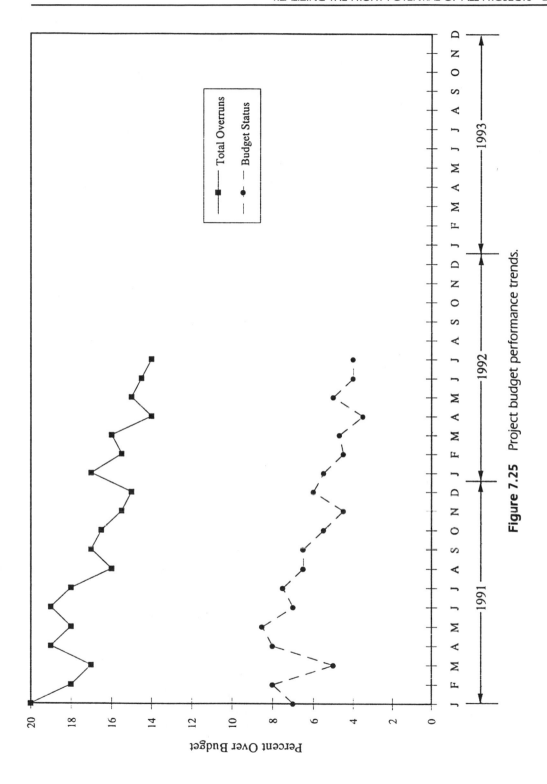

Figure 7.25 Project budget performance trends.

- Overhead (usually expressed as a percentage of direct labor or direct labor plus other salary costs).
- Other direct costs (travel, printing, CADD, etc.).

The difference between the total job costs and the contract value is the "net profit" on the project.

The problem is that these systems treat overhead as a "variable" cost, that is, a function only of the labor charged to a particular project. However, most major overhead costs are "fixed," that is, they are independent of how much labor is charged to a particular project. The need to set a fixed overhead rate means that the "net profit" generated by a project may not accurately measure that projects' real contribution to the financial well-being of the firm.

A better approach is to separate overhead into two categories: variable and fixed. Variable overhead includes costs that vary in proportion to direct labor, such as payroll taxes and employee insurance benefits. For most design firms, variable overhead equals about 50% of direct labor. Fixed overhead includes costs such as office rent, marketing costs, and vehicle leases, which are independent of the direct labor charged to a given project. Typical values are about 100% of direct labor.

Once this division of overhead is made, it is possible to compute the "gross profit" as follows:

Gross profit = Contract value − Direct labor −
              Variable OH − Other direct costs

The gross profit from a given project is the amount of money that can be used to pay for the firm's fixed overhead; once the fixed overhead has been paid, any money left over is net profit.

The use of gross profit rather than net profit job cost accounting has some interesting ramifications. To illustrate, take a hypothetical firm that has a total overhead rate of 150% of direct labor—50% for fixed overhead and 100% for variable overhead. On a net profit basis, any work done at a direct labor multiplier of less than 2.50 will result in a net loss on the project. However, a gross profit loss will occur only if the multiplier is less than 1.50. On a net profit basis, it would be better for the firm to subcontract work at a 2.25 multiplier rather than to do it in-house. On a gross profit basis, it is better to do the work in-house, even though the 2.25 multiplier is less than the firm's theoretical break-even point. Even at this low multiplier, the firm is still contributing toward paying some of its fixed overhead. (Of course, if the firm takes on *all* its work below its break-even multiplier, it will soon be out of business.)

It can be seen that both gross profit and net profit must be considered to ascertain a project's true contribution to the firm's financial well-being. It is very useful to compute both these parameters at the time each project is completed, as shown in Figure 7.26. It can be seen that some projects can reveal a very different financial result when considering gross profit as well as net profit.

KEEPING THE CASH FLOWING

Cash flow is the life blood of most design firms. Good cash flow allows the firm to grow and prosper while maintaining good credit and reasonable interest costs. Poor cash flow practices can strangle an otherwise successful firm, regardless of how good the firm's work may be. TQPM techniques can be highly effective in speeding cash flow.

The first step is to define the requirements in ways that project managers and other nonaccounting types can easily understand. Let's define the following terms:

Work in Process (WIP). Costs that have been incurred but that have not yet been billed.

Days in WIP. The average time it takes from the time a cost is incurred until it is billed.

Accounts Receivable (AR). Costs that have been billed but for which payment has not yet been received.

Days in AR. The average time it takes from the time a cost is billed until payment is received.

Working Capital. The total costs that the firm has incurred that have not been paid by its clients.

Capital Turnaround Days. Days in WIP + days in AR.

Using these simple definitions, management can set targets and the accounting department can chart the actual results against these targets as shown in Figure 7.27. This information should be shown to all project managers and others who

Job. No.	Completion Date	Net Profit			Gross Profit		
		Planned	Actual	Variance	Planned	Actual	Variance
1496	3/2/91	$14,600	$12,900	−$1,700 (−12%)	$43,900	$32,100	−$11,800 (−27%)
1627	3/18/91	6,200	7,000	+800 (+13%)	23,600	26,800	+3,200 (+14%)
1527	4/2/91	8,300	8,200	−100 (−1%)	21,600	23,200	+1,600 (+7%)
1618	4/17/91	21,800	16,700	−5,100 (−23%)	62,300	64,900	+2,600 (+4%)
1627	5/4/91	15,700	15,600	−100 (−1%)	32,700	24,200	−8,500 (−26%)
1478	5/19/91	29,800	2,600	−27,200 (−91%)	71,400	68,300	−3,100 (−4%)
1625	6/2/91	14,900	15,200	+300 (+2%)	42,100	36,100	−6,000 (−14%)
1607	6/12/91	2,300	2,300	0 (0%)	7,100	4,700	−2,400 (−33%)
Totals		$113,600	$80,500	−$33,100 (−29%)	$304,700	$280,300	−$24,400 (−8%)

Figure 7.26 Financial performance of complete projects.

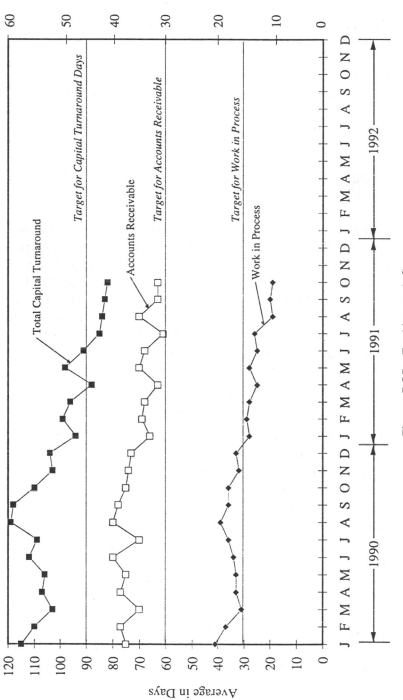

Figure 7.27 Tracking cash flow.

are involved in invoicing and collections. (Note that the right-hand axis of Figure 7.27 also shows the interest costs to the firm based on total revenues and prevailing interest rates. This helps emphasize the importance of cash flow).

It is also important to explain to nonaccounting personnel the process required to achieve good cash flow. This can be done by preparing a work flow diagram similar to Figure 7.28 and carefully reviewing it with all those who might help expedite the process.

USING TQPM TO IMPROVE MARKETING AND SALES

Unfortunately, building a better mousetrap will not necessarily cause the world to beat a path to your door. Consider the case of the Wallace Company, an oil drilling supply firm that won the prestigious Malcolm Baldrige National Quality Award in 1990: a year later, it filed for Chapter 11 bankruptcy protection. There must be an ongoing marketing effort that complements the firm's production quality initiatives. Fortunately, TQPM techniques can be used effectively to increase a design firm's client base.

Identifying Potential Projects

One way to identify potential projects is to get your firm on a lot of mailing lists and wait for requests for proposals to show up in the mail. While this approach will keep initial marketing costs down, it will also result in a miserable return on the dollars spent writing proposals. A much better way is a person-to-person approach in which an employee of the design firm establishes and maintains contact with a representative of a potential client. (Of course, the best *potential* clients are those who are happy with the firm's performance on a current or recent project.)

The first step in such an approach is to prepare a database of client representatives and assign each to an employee of the design firm (see the example in Figure 7.29). For those client representatives that are scheduled to be contracted on a regular basis, a routine updating system (such as that shown in Figure 7.30) can assure that the frequency of contacts is monitored regularly. This information, plotted on a bar chart similar to Figure 7.31, can provide management with up-to-

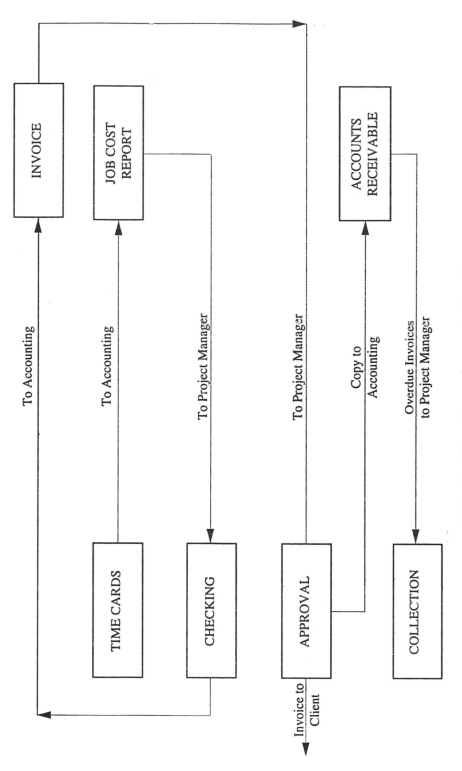

Figure 7.28 Work flow diagram for a typical invoicing process.

Client Name
Address/Phone

Paul Burton   Office: *Atlanta*
IBM Corporation   Contact: *Koon*
100 Main Street   Client Type: *I*
Dallas, TX 75301   Xmas card: *N*
214/555-5788   Newsletter: *N*
                                   Personal contact: *N*

Thomas Warren   Offfice: *Atlanta*
Martin-Marietta Company   Contact: *Alley*
P.O. Box 2000   Client type: *I*
Oak Ridge, TN 37831   Xmas card: *N*
615/555-2000   Newsletter: *Y*
                                   Personal contact: *N*

Tony Ziegler   Office: *Atlanta*
PPG Industries, Inc.   Contact: *Cox*
P.O. Box 31   Client type: *I*
Smallville, OH 44203   Xmas card: *N*
216/555-0831   Newsletter: *Y*
                                   Personal contact: *N*

Terry Haroldson   Office: *Atlanta*
City of Macon   Contact: *Spiers*
3000 Weaver Road   Client type: *M*
Macon, GA 31297   Xmas card: *Y*
912/555-2639   Newsletter: *N*
                                   Personal contact: *N*

Client types
  I—Industrial
  M—Municipal

Figure 7.29 Client database.

---

date statistical information as to how consistently the firm's lead-finding system is being followed.

Improving Proposal "Hit Rates"

Proposal preparation costs represent the single largest discretionary overhead expense for most design firms, and it is the money spent on *losing* proposals that is the costliest of all these expenditures. Deciding which proposal opportunities should be pursued is, at best, an inexact science. But a pure "gut feel" approach to making these decisions will invariably result in too many bad decisions. A more statistical approach will yield better results.

Office: *Atlanta*
Contact: *David Jones*
Date: *March 30, 1992*

| Client Name | Last | Contact This Month | | | Next |
Address/Phone	Contact	Visit	Phone	Letter	Contact
Paul Burton	3/17/92	x			5/1/92
IBM Corporation	Phone				
100 Main Street					
Dallas, TX 75301					
214/555-5788					
Thomas Warren	5/1/91		x		8/1/92
Martin-Marietta Company	Visit				
P.O. Box 2000					
Oak Ridge, TN 37831					
615/555-2000					
Tony Ziegler	10/15/91				5/1/92
PPG Industries, Inc.	Phone				
P.O. Box 31					
Smallville, OH 44203					
216/555-0831					
Terry Haroldson	10/15/91				5/1/92
City of Macon	Letter				
3000 Weaver Road					
Macon, GA 31297					
912/555-2639					

Figure 7.30 Monthly contact report.

Think of the proposal process as a poker game. The first step is to decide whether to "ante up" (that is, expend a modest amount of sales costs for the opportunity of receiving a request for proposals). Before making this decision in the poker game, you must identify some basic factors such as the potential rewards for the winner, the total cost required to play, and how tough it will be to beat the other players.

The next decision point comes when you are dealt the cards (receive a request for proposals). You must assess the cards you have been dealt and decide whether you will play the hand or fold and try your luck on the next deal. Of course, some poker players will pay virtually every hand, hoping that they will draw better cards or that they can out-bluff their opponents. Such players invariably lose lots of money. Success-

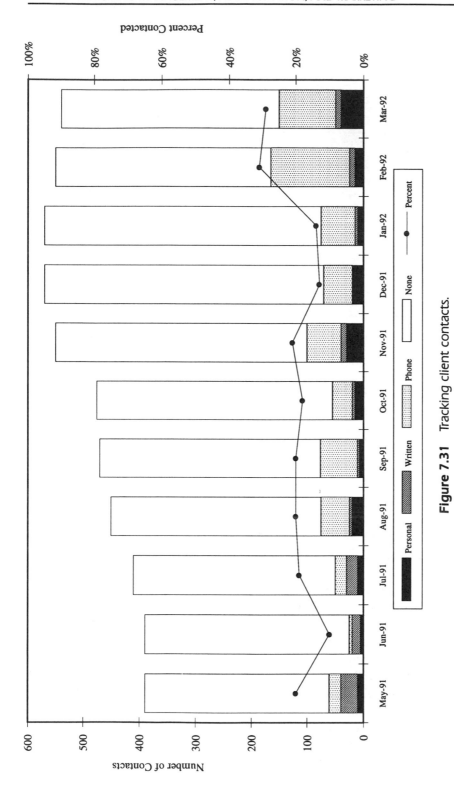

Figure 7.31 Tracking client contacts.

ful players are able to accurately assess their odds of winning and quickly fold their hand if the odds are too long.

In poker, the odds of winning are determined by: (1) the hierarchy of winning hands (three-of-a-kind beats two pair, a straight beats three-of-a-kind, a flush beats a straight, and so on), and (2) the difficulty of making a given hand (it is easier to complete a flush than to fill an inside straight). When determining the odds of winning a proposal, you must know the client's selection criteria.

For a given market, it is possible to identify generic selection factors that can be used to predict the odds of winning a particular proposal. This can be done by surveying typical clients within that market or by analyzing the results of previous proposals for that market. The result can be expressed in the form of a rating sheet similar to the one shown in Figure 7.32 (taken from a large transportation engineering firm). The higher the score, the better the chances are of being selected.

In addition to *predicting* the probably outcome of a proposal effort, the *actual results* should be tracked to determine the cost-effectiveness of the firm's proposal efforts. Most firms do this by computing proposal costs as a percentage of total sales or revenues. This approach is fundamentally flawed because it overlooks the fact that most sales come not from major proposal efforts, but as additions to existing projects or noncompetitive work from current and recent clients. In fact, one of the major objectives of TQPM is to steadily increase the amount of sales from these relatively noncompetitive sources.

A more accurate way of measuring the cost-effectiveness of proposal expenditures is to compare the costs of preparing a group of proposals with the sales results from that same group of proposals. This can be done by keeping a log of all significant proposal efforts using a format similar to Figure 7.33. The total expenditures is the sum of all variable costs (labor, variable overhead, and other direct costs) for proposals that have been decided. (Proposals that are still under consideration are not counted.) Total gross sales is the amount of sales booked from winning proposals. Gross profit is equal to gross sales minus direct labor, variable overhead, and other direct costs. The cost-effectiveness of these proposals can be expressed as gross sales per dollar of proposal costs (14.6 in the example) or gross profit per dollar of proposal costs (4.7 in the example).

Proposal cost-effectiveness is a function of: (1) how well

SCORE

I. INTELLIGENCE AND MARKET RESEARCH (40 POINTS)

A. Relationship to Sales Plan (0–5) _____

B. Our relationship to client (0–10) _____

C. Was job defined and known prior to receipt of RFP? (0–10) _____

D. Do we know selection process and who makes the selection? (0–5) _____

E. How well do we know the competition? (0–10) _____

II. COMPARISON WITH THE COMPETITION (30 POINTS)

A. Has the competition worked for the client? (10–0) _____

B. Has the competition satisfactorily done work related to this project? (10–0) _____

C. Is the competition considered local? (5–0) _____

D. Are the competition's associates better than ours? (5–0) _____

III. CORPORATE COMMITMENT (30 POINTS)

A. Project managers and staff available (0–10) _____

B. Teaming (0–10) _____

C. Local office (0–5) _____

D. Opportunity for future work (0–5) _____

Total Possible Points = 100   Total Points _____

Other Comments: _____

_____

_____

_____

Figure 7.32 Go/no go evaluation criteria.

the firm selects proposal opportunities, (2) how well the firm meets the needs of the markets it seeks to serve, and (3) the relative competitiveness of those markets. Long-term trends in these factors can be determined by updating the proposal cost-effectiveness calculation once each quarter using the most recent 12 months' results. (This is known as a 12-month moving average, updated quarterly.) These values can be plotted on a chart such as that shown on Figure 7.34.

Proposal Number	Expenditures	Results Won	Lost	Gross Sales	Gross Profit
5406	$ 1,986	√		$187,200	$ 74,200
5407	2,692		√		
5408	8,624		√		
5409	726	√		16,830	5,629
5410	284		√		
5411	1,213		√		
5412	926	√		47,920	21,320
5413	16,266		√		
5414	1,824		√		
5415	In progress	No decision			
5416	3,207		√		
5417	In progress	No decision			
5418	4,006	√		387,690	106,200
5419	In progress	No decision			
5420	2,107		√		
5421	In progress	No decision			
Totals	**$43,861**			**$639,640**	**$207,349**

Cost-effectiveness = $639,640 ÷ $43,861 = 14.6 (in terms of gross sales)

= $207,349 ÷ $43,861 = 4.7 (in terms of gross profit)

Figure 7.33 Log of major proposals.

Using Quality As A Marketing Tool

During the 1980s Total Quality Project Management became an integral part of the management of most large manufacturing firms in the United States. During the latter part of the decade, many large service firms also got onto the "quality bandwagon." More recently, local, state, and federal government agencies have also begun adopting TQPM. These diverse public and private entities represent a very large segment of clients served by architectural, engineering, and other professional service firms.

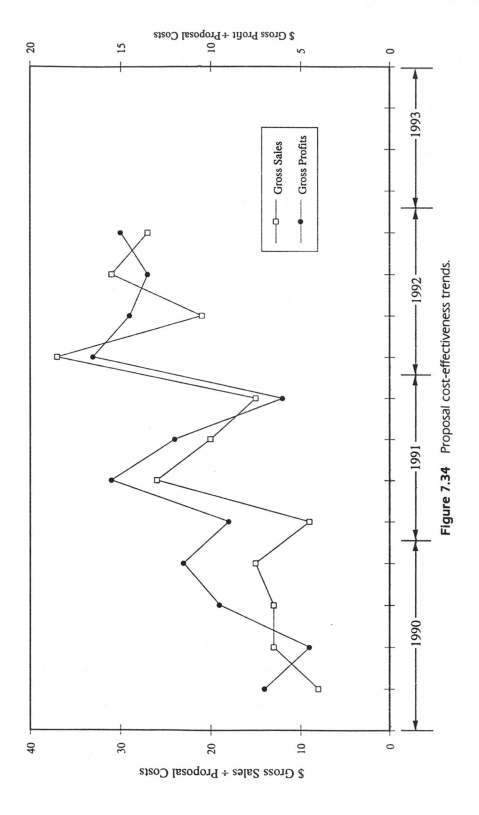

Figure 7.34 Proposal cost-effectiveness trends.

As clients develop their own TQPM systems to eliminate their quality problems, they soon discover that many of these problems are caused by their suppliers (including design professionals). This realization has resulted in many clients giving preference to suppliers (including design professionals) who have adopted their own TQPM program. Some clients are going so far as to require this as a condition of doing work.

Adopting a formal TQPM program can therefore be a powerful marketing tool for design firms. It is like CADD in the early 1980's—the few firms that had it used this capability as a powerful marketing tool. However, like CADD, as TQPM becomes more widespread in design firms, merely having it will no longer be a marketing advantage. It will become a prerequisite for working for certain clients. The marketing advantage will go to those design firms that can actually *demonstrate* how TQPM has improved quality and lowered costs. Following the methods described in this book will greatly assist in this effort.

Maintaining Diversification

Why do some design firms experience a pattern of rapid growth followed by deep cuts, repeating this cycle over and over? How are other firms able to maintain a steady record of growth and a stable workforce? The difference often lies in the firms' basic approach to marketing.

Marketing at "boom and bust" firms is often done by chasing the work that can be most easily sold. Such firms ride the crest of each new marketing wave only to crash when that wave ends. This strategy is known as "opportunity marketing." A more accurate definition might be "long-term planning by reading the *Wall Street Journal*."

More stable firms recognize that this year's hot market will, sooner or later, mature and become oversaturated. Also, markets that are relatively inactive now may well become very active in the future. The marketing strategy of these stable firms is based on a long-term view (10 to 20 years) of the markets they now serve or could gear up to serve. This long-term strategy relies on a *diversified* marketing program, which allows the firm to maintain its capabilities in markets that are down today but will probably improve in the future.

How can the principles of TQPM be used to help a firm maintain a diversified marketing effort? One way is by using

Office Location	Medical Facilities		Municipal Buildings		Office Buildings	
	Sales Costs	New Sales	Sales Costs	New Sales	Sales Costs	New Sales
St. Louis	35	320	16	260	24	180
Chicago	20	720	32	120	4	60
Detroit	82	1,020	18	180	60	220
Milwaukee	61	680	26	500	12	42
Springfield	41	50	12	120	24	360
Totals	212	2,790	104	1,180	124	862

Figure 7.35 Annual sales targets for the ABC Company (all values in thousands of dollars).

TQPM measurement techniques as a way to assure the proper blend of "opportunity marketing" (pursuing the "easiest" sales targets) and "diversified marketing" (pursuing more difficult targets that will aid in diversification). To illustrate, let's take the ABC Company, an A/E firm that provides multidisciplinary services to clients in the midwest. The managers of ABC can prepare annual budgets and targets based on their perception of the best long-term goals (see Figure 7.35). At the end of the year, the actual results can be compared to the targets (as shown in the example in Figure 7.36) and used as input to help develop targets for the following year.

If such measurements are made every year, long-term market trends can be determined using analyses such as that shown in Figure 7.37. In this example, it can be seen that the market for office buildings is steadily deteriorating, medical facilities have improved, and government buildings have remained fairly stable. It is clear that a relatively high sales expenditure will be required for the ABC Company to maintain its capabilities in designing office buildings. On the other hand, sales results will be more easily obtained for design of medical facilities. This type of information can help ABC's managers make informed decisions as to the allocation of sales budgets among its various markets.

MINIMIZING BUREAUCRACY

By this time you are probably thinking, "All this TQPM stuff is nice, but it will turn out company into a huge bureaucracy." In fact, used properly, TQPM will do just the opposite—it

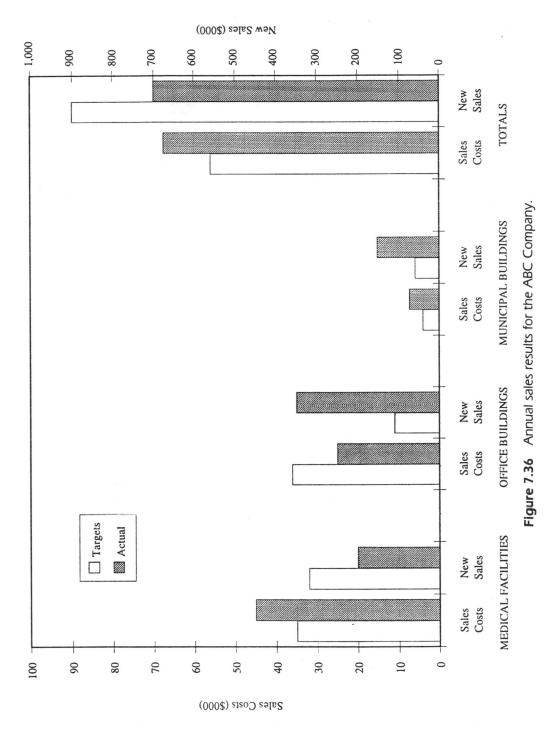

Figure 7.36 Annual sales results for the ABC Company.

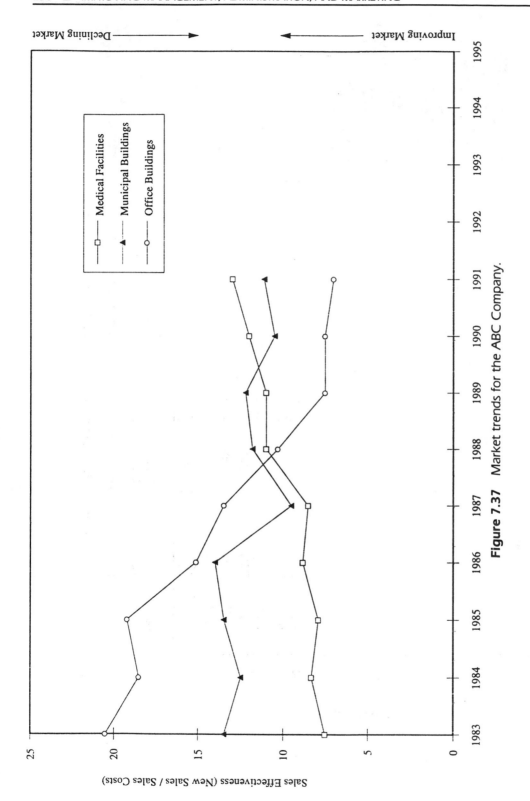

Figure 7.37 Market trends for the ABC Company.

will streamline your procedures and eliminate unproductive paperwork.

The term "bureaucracy" has a highly negative connotation, while the term "procedures" has a generally positive connotation. Yet in implementation they are almost the same. The difference is that procedures have a net benefit to the firm; bureaucracy is an unnecessary burden on the company's well-being.

To fight creeping bureaucracy, one must first understand how it develops. Most procedures are established by management for one of the following reasons:

- To avoid repeating mistakes the firm has made in the past.
- To improve efficiency of repetitive tasks.
- To make the bosses feel they are in control.

Procedures intended to avoid repeating mistakes are usually issued by management in response to a particular problem that has occurred. Suppose, for example, that in reviewing a design, the chief architect of a particular firm has a hard time following the calculations performed by one of the structural engineers. Out of frustration, he issues a new procedure specifying the precise format to be used for all calculations—with orders to follow this format or else! In his zeal to prevent this problem from recurring, the chief architect has neglected the following facts:

1. Although the structural calculations were hard to follow, they were basically sound.

2. Although it took more effort than he would have liked, the chief architect was able to convince himself that the structural design really was OK.

3. The firm has never in its 20-year existence experienced any significant liability or client relations problem associated with design calculations.

4. The chief architect's new calculations format is not well suited for certain calculations.

5. The architects in the various design disciplines had no input in developing the new format, now have they been given any training in how to use it.

6. There is no tracking procedure to determine how effec-

tively the new format is being used, or how much it is adding to the cost of performing designs.

It appears that the chief architect has overreacted to what he perceived as a problem that needed correction.

Let's continue this scenario by looking at this same firm three years after the new calculation format was issued. The chief architect again reviews a set of design calculations, finds them just as hard to follow as the ones he reviewed three years earlier, gets totally irate (narrowly averting a severe coronary attack), and sets out to find the guilty party. In this search, he finds the following:

1. The individual who prepared the calculations is one of the firm's best architects.
2. This architect had used the new calculation procedures soon after they were issued, but had found them difficult to understand, hard to use, and costly to implement. The experience of other architects has been similar.
3. As a result, during the past year, not a single project has been done using the chief architect's mandated calculation procedure.
4. The architects have been afraid to tell their bosses that they haven't been using the new procedure because they feared retribution from the chief architect.
5. Many architects have lost a good deal of respect for the chief architect. After all, if he knew what he was doing he wouldn't have come up with such impractical procedures!

During the three years since the new calculation procedure was issued, how much time has been wasted as a result? How many unnecessary delays have occurred? How much frustration has been experienced by the architects who tried to use the procedure? How much confidence have they lost in their firm's management? This is clearly a case of unproductive bureaucracy.

Had the chief architect employed the principles of TQPM to solve the initial problem, the outcome would likely have been much different. The first step would have been to define the problem and to quantitatively determine its magnitude. The problem could have been defined as follows:

Excessive time is spent in reviewing calculations that are hard to follow.

The magnitude of this problem could have been measured by first tracking the number of hours that it takes to check calculations and then dividing them by the number of drawings to establish a database on how many hours per drawing it takes to check calculations. Projects exceeding the normal range probably suffered from hard-to-follow calculations. These data could also have been collected retroactively for previously completed projects by interviewing the reviewers and checking their time cards. Once the problem was quantified, the chief architect could have decided on the most appropriate of these approaches:

- Take no action.
- Continue measuring new projects to determine whether the problem is getting better or worse.
- Take action to solve what is apparently a serious problem.

If the chief architect had decided to take action, he could have used the TQPM techniques described in Chapter 9. Handled properly, the problem could probably have been solved with a minimum of bureaucracy.

The mistakes made by the chief architect are typical of the causes of "creeping bureaucracy." He: (1) assumed that the problem was serious (even though there was no data to support this conclusion), (2) imposed a solution with little input from those closest to the problem or those who would be affected by the solution, (3) established no tracking mechanism to see if the solution was being implemented or if it was really solving the problem, and (4) assumed that the procedure could be enforced by coercion and the threat of punishment.

SUMMARY

This chapter has described how TQPM can streamline a design firm's internal systems for management, administration, marketing, and sales. The next chapter describes how to satisfy the most important customers in any professional service firm—the clients.

8 KEEPING YOUR CLIENTS HAPPY

Many TQPM programs fail because they are too internally focused. You can fine-tune every aspect of your production processes but it will do no good if you aren't meeting your clients' needs and expectations. Think about the fishing village parable in Chapter 2; the village became successful by learning what was needed to keep the fish happy and gearing its activities toward this goal. This chapter presents some specific ideas on keeping professional service clients happy.

CLIENTS DEFINE QUALITY

Never forget that the ultimate judges of quality are our clients. They judge not only the quality of our designs and reports but also the quality of our services. In fact, service quality is often more important than product quality. The objective must be to keep all your clients so happy that they will want to work *only with you* on future projects. A sole-source selection from an enthusiastic client is the ultimate win-win relationship between a technical professional and the client. The technical professional wins by minimizing marketing costs and avoiding "corner cutting" caused by undue competitive pressures. The client wins by knowing that all the project's objectives will be met or exceeded. Obviously, some clients are prevented from making sole-source selections. But they can usually manage to somehow select the firm they wanted in the first place!

Consider the method that Japanese watchmakers have used to corner the wristwatch market in Arab countries. Of course, they manufacture watches that are high in quality and reasonably priced. But other watchmakers produce similarly high quality, reasonably priced watches. The difference is the extra effort that the Japanese took to research the desires and needs of their Arab customers. The result of this research was a watch design that not only alerts the wearer five times a day when it is prayer time, but also shows the direction of Mecca so the worshippers know which way to kneel.* That is truly a case of "exceeding client expectations."

ORGANIZING FOR CLIENT SERVICE

Much has been said and written about how a design firm should be organized. The relative advantages of matrix organizations, functional organizations, and their countless derivatives have been extolled *ad nauseam*. Those discussing such organizational structures invariably neglect a key point—design firms are in business to serve their clients, who never even appear on the organization chart!

If a design firm is to be truly client-driven, its organization chart should show how it serves its clients. An excellent example of such a chart is the one developed by Schmidt Associates (see Figure 8.1). This illustrates how clients should be served—by the firm's project managers—with everyone else in the firm (including principals) serving in a supporting role. It also illustrates the fact that even clients have "customers"—the community that requires their goods and services.

ESTABLISHING REALISTIC EXPECTATIONS

As mentioned previously, the client determines whether your work meets the expected standard of quality. However, there is much that you, the design professional, can do to establish the proper expectations in the client's mind. The earlier this is begun, the better.

Establishing realistic expectations means exposing the fact that *the project will not be perfect*. Such discussions tend to be rather negative and should generally be avoided during the marketing effort. The best time to begin discussing these issues is immediately after the selection process. At that time, your credibility with the client is very high—after all, you were selected as the best choice to execute the project—and the risk of alienating the client is relatively low.

*Source: "Cars and Competition," *Journal of the American Management Association*, New York, February 1991.

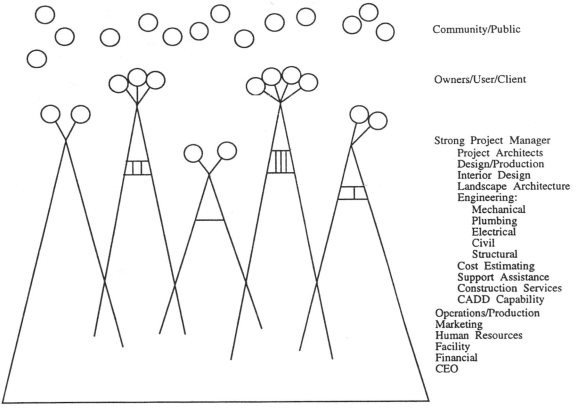

Community/Public

Owners/User/Client

Strong Project Manager
    Project Architects
    Design/Production
    Interior Design
    Landscape Architecture
    Engineering:
        Mechanical
        Plumbing
        Electrical
        Civil
        Structural
    Cost Estimating
    Support Assistance
    Construction Services
    CADD Capability
Operations/Production
Marketing
Human Resources
Facility
Financial
CEO

Figure 8.1 Schmidt Associates Architects organizational chart.

The first step is to meet with the client and mutually agree on two lists. The first list should contain all the elements that would define a successful project. The second list should identify the elements of a unsuccessful project. The following example is for a permit application for a hazardous waste storage facility:

Successful Project	Unsuccessful Project
1. Submittal of first draft to EPA by June 1	1. Permit delays beyond October 1
2. EPA approval by August 1	2. Permitting costs > \$300,000
3. EPA approval to store wastes in current manner	3. Major changes required for storage of hazardous wastes
4. Total permitting costs < \$150,000	

The "successful project" list contains the desirable goals that will be set and tracked throughout the project; however, the client should recognize that the project *may* fall short of one or more of these goals. The "unsuccessful project" list contains only *critical* objectives. If any of these objectives are not met, the project will not be considered a success.

It is important that these lists of expectations be prepared in a quantitative, not qualitative manner. Consider the difference between the following lists:

Qualitative Objective	Quantitative Objective
Attractive building design	Approved by design review committee
Highly automated	Able to be operated by six people
Reasonable construction cost	Construction cost < $100 per square foot
Minimal construction changes	Construction change orders < $200,000
Adequate parking	Parking for 240 cars

The above technique has two objectives: (1) to understand *precisely* what the client wants and needs, and (2) to assure that the client's expectations are reasonable.

ESTABLISHING TOLERANCES

It is important that clients understand the concept of "tolerances." If you order a steel rod 1 inch in diameter and 4 inches long, you wouldn't measure the dimensions to the nearest micron and reject it if it were 2 microns too short. The rod would probably be suitable for your intended use if the length and diameter were within $\frac{1}{8}$ inch of the specified size. Thus, we can say that the allowable tolerance of the steel rod is $\pm \frac{1}{8}$ inch. To make a steel rod accurate to within 1 micron would not only be unnecessary, but also prohibitively expensive.

The same concept should be applied to architectural, engineering, and other technical projects. Is it necessary for a report to have zero typographical errors? If so, the budget must include adequate time for several thorough reviews to find and eliminate "typos." If the requirements of the report do not justify this effort, an acceptable tolerance should be defined with respect to typos.

Is it necessary for a set of plans and specifications to have zero conflicts? If so, the budget for checking and corrections must be very high. If this expenditure of time and money is not acceptable to the client, a suitable tolerance level for design conflicts should be established. The following are examples of well defined tolerances for commonly required deliverables:

Deliverable	Example of Well Defined Tolerances
Report	No more than one typographical error per page (on average). No typographical or grammatical errors that alter the intent of the text.
Plans and specifications	Allowance of 2% of construction budget for change orders to correct conflicts and other common design errors and omissions.
Cost estimate	Accurate within ±10% compared to actual construction cost.
Monthly progress report	Issues within five working days of the end of the month. Reported budget and schedule status accurate to within ±5% of actual.
Meeting minutes	Issued within three working days of the meeting.
Laboratory analyses	No more than 10% of samples rejected (for any reason).

MEETING SUBMITTAL DATES

An all-too-common complaint from clients is that project managers promise to deliver something (proposal, report, drawings, etc.) by an agreed-upon date, then let that date pass by without either submitting the document or calling the client to request an extension to a later date. These instances greatly damage a design firm's credibility and reduce its chances of securing future work with that client.

Before this problem can be solved, it must be measured. This can be done by the secretaries who are responsible for sending these documents to the clients. Once a week or once a month, each project manager should identify all documents scheduled to be delivered to clients during that week or month. Each secretary can keep a list of these deliverables using a form similar to Figure 8.2. Once a month, these logs can be tallied and the results presented graphically in a format similar to Figure 8.3. This chart should be updated regularly and displayed in a conspicuous location so that everyone will be reminded of the importance of maintaining clients' confidence by meeting commitments.

PLANNING FOR CONTRACT MODIFICATIONS

Even the best defined scope of services inevitably spawns changes that affect the schedule or budget. Because such contract modifications are often necessary, it is helpful to establish a procedure for handling them. At the outset of the project (perhaps at the "kick-off" meeting), the client's project manager and the design firm's project manager should mutually agree on how to handle such changes should they arise. This procedure should be documented and should answer the following questions:

- What kind of notification is required?
- What is the basis for estimating extra costs?
- Whose approval is required?
- How long should the approval process take?
- What should be done while awaiting approval?

It is also helpful to agree on a standard format (such as the example in Figure 8.4) that can be used by the design firm to request contract modifications.

Holding such procedural discussions *before* the need arises has two major client relations benefits. First, it establishes in the client's mind the possibility that changes *may* become necessary; when they do, it isn't a total surprise. Sec-

Document Tracking Number	Job Number	Description of Deliverable	Original Due Date	Revised Due Date	Departure Date (late or on time)	Overtime Required
1	26054	Draft work plan to EPA	8/15/91		8/15/91 on time	
2	26054	Monthly report to EPA	8/15/91		8/15/91 on time	
3	26054	Site 1 final proposed plan	8/19/91		8/17/91 early	
4	26295	Monitoring plan—Rev. 1 to Client	8/9/91		8/13/91 late	Support—1 hr.
5	26295	Monitoring plan—Rev. 1 to EPA	8/27/91		8/27/91 on time	Support—3 hr.
6	26328	30% design drawings to client	8/31/91	9/5/91	9/5/91 revised	
7	26054	Analytical bid document	9/9/91		9/9/91 on time	Support—1 hr.
8	26295	Monthly report to EPA	9/9/91		9/9/91 on time	Support—1 hr.
9	26328	Geotech bid documents	9/11/91	9/14/92	9/14/91 revised	
10	36328	30% design drawings to bldg. dept.	9/9/91		9/11/91 late	

Figure 8.2 Client deliverable log.

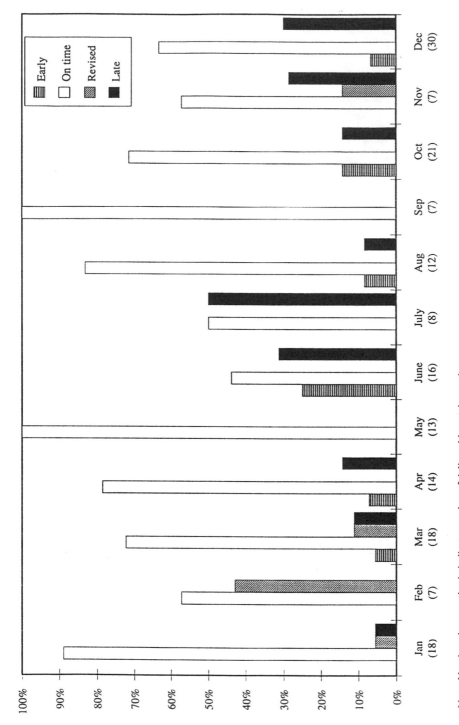

Note: Numbers in parenthesis indicate number of deliverables each month.

Figure 8.3 Deliverables tracking charts.

CONTRACT NO.	CLIENT CONTACT		CLIENT NAME		CHANGE ORDER NO	REVISION
PROJECT NUMBER	PROJECT MANAGER		PROJECT TITLE		DATE PREPARED	
CHANGE REQUESTED BY	DATE REQUESTED	CHANGE REQUESTED ☐ BY LETTER (ATTACHED)	☐ BY TELEX/TELECOPY (ATTACHED)		☐ VERBALLY	

DESCRIPTION OF CHANGE TO CONTRACT SCOPE:

IMPACT OF CHANGE ON COST AND/OR SCHEDULE BASELINE (IF APPLICABLE, DESCRIBE CONSTRUCTION IMPACT):

MANAGEMENT AND ENGINEERING COST ESTIMATE

LABOR COST				OTHER DIRECT COSTS	
TASK/DISCIPLINE	MANHOURS	BILLING RATE	LABOR$	DESCRIPTION OF ODC/SUBCONTRACT	ODC$
TOTAL MANHOURS		TOTAL LABOR $		TOTAL OTHER DIRECT COSTS	
TOTAL COST FOR THIS CHANGE $				PROJECT MANAGER APPROVAL	DATE

NEW COST BASELINE		NEW SCHEDULE BASELINE
PREVIOUS CONTRACT VALUE $_____ ADDITION (REDUCTION) THIS CHANGE $_____ NEW CONTRACT VALUE $_____ FOR CPFF, THE NEW FIXED FEE $_____		

APPROVAL SIGNATURES

A/E OFFICER (PRINT OR TYPE NAME)	DATE	AUTHORIZED CLIENT (PRINT OR TYPE NAME)	DATE
SIGNATURE OF A/E OFFICER		AUTHORIZED CLIENT SIGNATURE	

Figure 8.4 An example of a change order form.

ond, it avoids procedural problems from disrupting discussions related to the *merit* of a particular request for a contract charge.

PREPARING FOR CLIENT MEETINGS

Good preparation is the key to good client meetings. Plan the meeting objectives by considering the following questions:

- Do we want a decision?
- Do we need advice?
- Do we want to update the client on the project status?
- Must we warn the client about impending problems?

Be sure the objectives of the meeting are clearly communicated to the client and understood by both parties before the meeting begins.

The next step is to develop and formulate an *agenda* that will accomplish the objectives. A good agenda should serve as an outline to identify work to be done before the meeting. For example, the following agenda identifies specific "homework assignments" that are required for a meaningful discussion of each item:

Topic	Lead Presenter	Required Preparation
A. Update on budget/ schedule status	M. Robinson	• Update CPM schedule • Update costs to date • Update forecast costs
B. Rezoning possibilities	L. Narilan	• Contact zoning board • Call Commissioner Morrison
C. Construction problems	H. Lewis	• Update status of piling work • Determine quantities of rock encountered
D. Surveying contract	M. Robinson	• Negotiate fee with surveyor

Just as important as planning is *follow-up* after the meeting. Get "action" minutes out quickly, and follow up to be sure that everyone is doing what was promised during that meeting. Once a commitment is made, make sure that it is carried out, whether the person making the commitment is a member of the design firm's project team, a consultant, or the client.

DEVELOPING AN IMAGE AS A COMPETENT MANAGER

Today it is not enough to be recognized as a competent design professional. Clients also expect the managers of their projects to know the status of key activities at all times. Projecting an image as a competent manager requires style as well as substance. The following is a list of suggestions that will enhance your image with your clients:

1. Keep project files in order so that when a client calls asking for information about a document you will have it readily available.
2. Always arrive at meetings a few minutes early—and well prepared.
3. Respond to client requests at once. Don't wait for a convenient time even when requests appear to be trivial.
4. Be prepared to discuss the project status (technical, budget, and schedule) at any time.
5. Learn to articulate ideas clearly, both verbally and in writing.
6. Keep the client informed by routinely sending copies of correspondence, telephone notes, and other important project documentation.
7. Schedule weekly update meetings, either in person or by telephone. They should be held on the same day of the week and at the same time of day.
8. Issue formal progress reports at least once a month, whether or not the contract requires it.
9. Review all invoices before they go out and be prepared to answer any questions the client may have about them.

10. Be sure your office is neat whenever a client comes to visit (even if it reverts to its normal condition after the visit).

THE CLIENT SPONSOR

An all-too-common problem in client relations occurs when a design firm's project manager is unable to cope with a client who is becoming dissatisfied with the firm's work. This can result from the project manager failing to recognize subtle signs of client dissatisfaction. Or it may be that the project manager knows there is a problem but, for whatever reason, fails to request help from the firm's senior managers.

A solution to this problem is the assignment of a "client sponsor" for each project. The client sponsor should be a senior manager who:

- Keeps in touch with the client from time to time, assuring that the client remains well satisfied with the firm's services.
- Acts as an in-house advocate for the client, assuring that the project receives the appropriate priority within the office.
- Serves as a point of contact when the client has a problem that he or she does not wish to discuss with the firm's project manager.
- Obtains both informal and formal performance evaluations upon completion of the project.
- Keeps in touch with the client periodically as a way of identifying potential future projects.

A recommended procedure for implementing a client sponsor program is described below:

1. A client sponsor is selected for each client.
2. The client sponsor keeps in touch with the client periodically to assure his or her total satisfaction. During project execution, the client sponsor takes whatever measures are necessary to correct any client relations problems.
3. Upon completion of the project, the client sponsor calls or visits the client to obtain an informal debriefing on

the firm's performance and asks the client to fill out an evaluation form (see example in Figure 8.5). If the client was satisfied, the client sponsor should also inquire about future projects in which the firm may be involved.

4. The client evaluation forms are given a numeral value based on the following:

4 points—exceeded expectations
3 points—met expectations
2 points—needs improvement
1 point—serious problem

A point can be plotted for each project based on the completion date and overall assessment ranking of each project (see Figure 8.6). These data will provide a quantitative measure of client satisfaction.

5. After collecting data for a year, bar charts can be developed showing the overall ranking of the firm's performance (Figure 8.7), as well as the average ranking for each evaluation category (Figure 8.8). These data can be used to prioritize areas that need the most improvement.

In implementing a client sponsor program, it is imperative that the firm's client sponsor and project manager work as a *team*. This requires open communications in which all contacts with the client are discussed frankly and objectively. If the project manager feels that he or she is being subverted, rather than assisted, by the client sponsor, the client will quickly observe this friction and the program will be counterproductive. Both the client sponsor and project manager must focus on a single common objective—total client satisfaction—and all personal goals must be subordinated when they deviate from this objective.

PROACTIVE CLIENT COMMUNICATIONS

Virtually all communications between the client and design firm are initiated because one of the parties needs something from the other. Such communications are always reactive and often negative. The best that can be hoped for is that each person is reasonably responsive to the needs of the other. Of-

ELEMENT	EVALUATIVE CRITERIA	Exceeded Expectations	Met Expectations	Needs Improvement	Serious Problem
Technical Quality	Completeness; accuracy; relevance	☐	☒	☐	☐
Timeliness	On-time delivery; process cycle time	☒	☐	☐	☐
Cost-Effectiveness	Actual cost of service (direct or indirect)	☐	☐	☒	☐
Dependability	Consistency; promises kept; credibility, trustworthiness	☐	☒	☐	☐
Cooperativeness	Responsiveness; flexibility; approachability; courtesy	☐	☒	☐	☐
Communication	Listening; feed forward information on progress/problems	☐	☐	☒	☐
Overall assessment of performance		☐	☒	☐	☐

Would you hire us again? _Yes, for certain types of projects._

Other comments _Project manager should have considered more options to reduce costs and communicate their impacts to me._

The following information is optional:

Evaluator's Name _S.F. Randolf_

Project _City Hall Expansion_

Figure 8.5 A form for client evaluation of service quality.

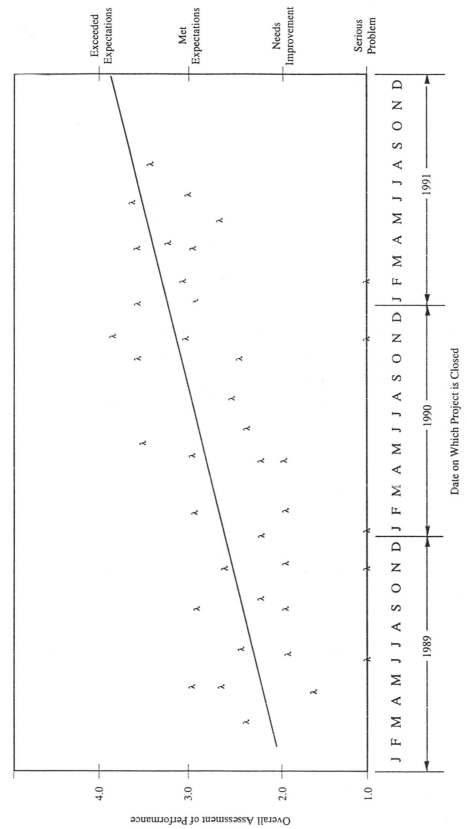

Figure 8.6 Overall assessment of design firm performance.

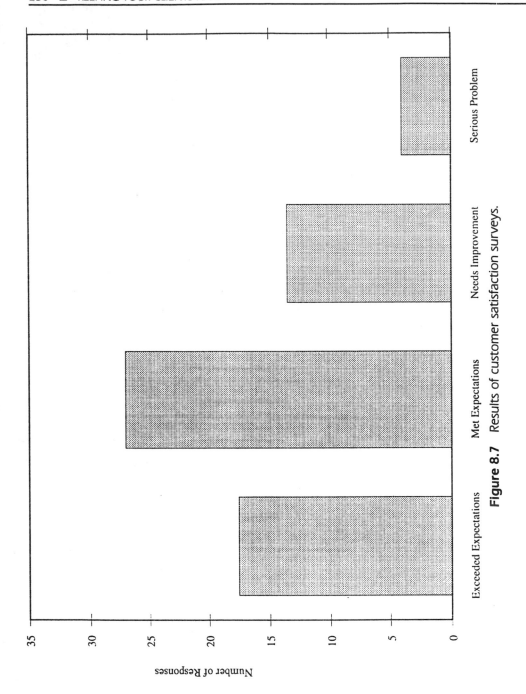

Figure 8.7 Results of customer satisfaction surveys.

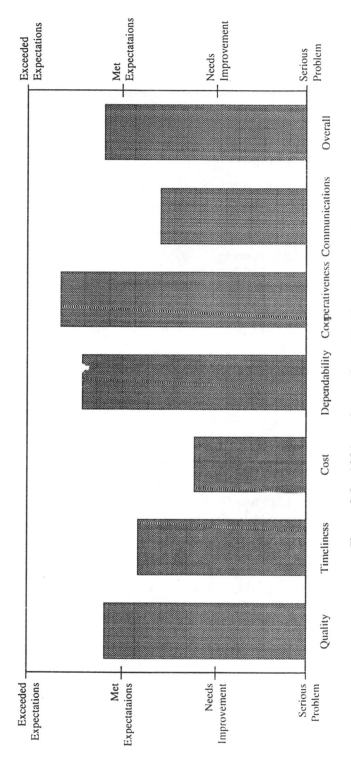

Figure 8.8 1991 service quality evaluations by category.

ten, the price for being responsive is interrupting other previously planned activities.

Client communications can be improved significantly by being *proactive,* rather than reactive. Each project should have an agreed upon communications plan that includes written progress reports, meetings, and phone calls.

Written Progress Report

Whether required by contract or not, the design firm should submit progress reports to the client on a regularly scheduled basis (such as "every Monday" or "by the 5th of every month"). The contents should also be agreed upon with the client, including such items as:

- Summary of work done last period.
- Forecast of activities during next period.
- Changes in scope made last period.
- Budget status.
- Schedule status.
- Input required from client.
- Other problems.

Meetings

In addition to written updates, it is often useful for the client and design firm to plan regular meetings to discuss the status of the project and resolve problems that have arisen. It is important that such meetings be held on the same day, at the same time, and in the same place. For example, the agreement may be for a meeting to be held every Friday at 10:30 A.M. at the design firm's office. The agenda of such regularly scheduled meetings can be similar to the items described above for written progress reports.

Phone Calls

When regular meetings are considered impractical or where there are long time intervals between such meetings, regularly scheduled phone calls can effectively fill in the gaps. Again, it is essential that these calls always be scheduled for the same time and day (such as every Tuesday at 9:00 A.M.). It is also necessary to identify who will initiate the calls (usually the design firm's project manager).

Measuring Conformance

Developing a client communications plan, then failing to follow it, is worse than having no plan at all. Such failure to follow through with a commitment can seriously damage the design firm's credibility with the client. Nonconformances must therefore be measured to assure that appropriate actions are taken to eliminate them before they become a problem. One way to accomplish this measurement is for the project secretary to receive copies of written reports, meeting minutes, and notes of telephone conversations. Once a month, these can be tallied and compared to the requirements for all the projects for which that secretary is responsible (see Figures 8.9 and 8.10).

SACRIFICING SHORT-TERM GAINS

A prevalent fear among clients is that design firms tend to increase a project's size and complexity in order to increase their fees. Unfortunately, there have been many cases where such fears were well founded and, as a result, most sophisticated clients will enter into professional service contracts with one hand firmly on their wallet. This lack of trust causes stress between the design professional and the client whenever the scope of work is altered during the course of the project, and produces an unhappy ending to many projects that at first appeared very promising.

Managers in professional service firms must be sensitive to this built-in distrust among clients and should go out of their way to allay these concerns. The client's interests must be placed above the short-term interests of the design firm—and the client must know that the design firm has the client's interests as its first priority.

A real-life example will illustrate the point. An environmental engineering company had a contract with an industrial client to design a $5 million treatment facility to remove nitrogen from the wastewater. During the study phase of the project, the design firm's project manager discovered that another industry in the same town was purchasing nitrogen. It was technically feasible and very economical to transport the

Department: _Medical Care Facilities_ Month: _August 1991_

Secretary: _J.P. Franklin_

Job Number	Written Progress Report			Meetings			Phone Calls		
	Required	Actual	Nonconformances	Required	Actual	Nonconformance	Required	Actual	Nonconformances
2794	1	1	0	2	1	1	4	4	0
2946	1	0	1	4	4	0	0	2	0
2967	2	2	0	2	2	0	8	7	1
3126	1	1	0	1	1	0	4	3	1
Totals	5	4	1	9	8	1	16	16	2

Figure 8.9 Client communications log.

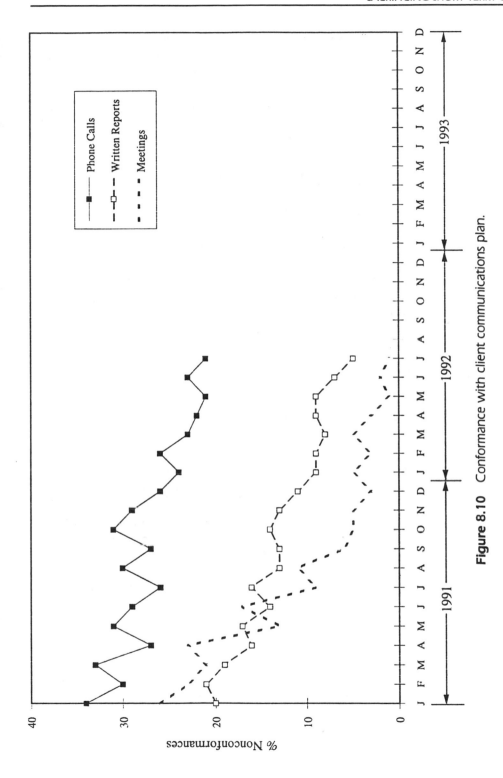

Figure 8.10 Conformance with client communications plan.

excess nitrogen from one plant to satisfy the needs of the other. Such a solution would not only save both firms a great deal of money, but would also eliminate the need for the planned $5 million treatment plant. An internal discussion was held within the design firm to determine whether the client should be informed of this option, thereby risking cancellation of a substantial design project. Despite the potential loss of business to the design firm, the decision was made to: (1) advise the client of this option, and (2) work with him to try to make this option feasible.

It turned out that the option of sending excess nitrogen to the other plant was politically impractical and the $5 million project proceeded as planned. However, the client was very impressed with the high level of professionalism on the part of its design firm. In fact, the client expanded the scope of work to include full construction management and long-term operations and maintenance of the waste treatment facility.

Have you ever found your firm in a similar situation? How did you handle it? What will you do the next time this happens?

GIVING MONEY BACK TO THE CLIENT

Most professional services contracts are based on some type of cost-plus-fee arrangement with a budgetary not-to-exceed amount. Such contracts have traditionally been managed like the old television game of "The Price is Right." The design firm tries to spend up to the not-to-exceed amount without going over. This approach has been so commonplace that clients expect to spend the full not-to-exceed amount on every project. In evaluating competitive proposals, clients often use proposed not-to-exceed budgets as a way of judging which design firm will provide its services at the lowest cost.

Design firms can dramatically improve client relations by planning to spend *less* than the not-to-exceed amounts of their contracts. By returning 2–5% of the authorized expenditure value to the client, the firm presents an image of being efficient and concerned about the client's money. The fact that very few design firms employ this practice will make it even more impressive to the client. Doing it on a regular basis will also reduce the client's tendency to compare the firm's not-to-exceed estimates with those of competing firms.

How do you handle projects whose scope and level of effort increase during the course of doing the job? Most design firms try to handle these extra efforts *within the original authorization* if at all possible. Their intent is to give the client "a little extra" in the name of good client relations. Unfortunately, the design firm usually discovers in time that this extra service cannot be accommodated within the original authorization, then has to ask for an increase as the project is nearing completion and running out of money.

A much better approach is for the design firm to request an increase in authorization *as soon as the scope change or extra level of effort is identified.* The client does not necessarily have to formally amend the contract, but should agree that such an amendment will be made if required prior to reaching the existing authorization. At the end of the project, the design firm can total all the extra work activities and show the client that the actual costs are less than the authorized amount.

SELECTING QUALITY CLIENTS

In our fishing village parable (Chapter 2), the village leaders learned that long-term success was based more on the *quality* of the fish they caught than on the initial *size* of the fish. When treated well, high quality species grew larger and tasted better than poor quality species. The objective was to seek only high quality species of fish, even if the individual fish were small when caught.

This philosophy can also be applied to the way design firms pursue their marketing objectives. Most firms focus on individual projects. They base proposal decisions on how large and profitable they expect each project to be. But, as the fishing village leaders learned, these are the *wrong* criteria. Instead, the long-term success of a design firm lies in the *quality* of the clients it serves.

Most design firm managers instinctively respond to virtually any opportunity to add new clients. But a true commitment to quality requires that certain clients be avoided. Let's look at some characteristics of such clients.

Poor Credit Ratings

Many design firms will eagerly pursue projects for clients without bothering to check their credit worthiness. Constant collection battles, disputes over invoices, threats to stop work, and other symptoms of slow paying clients will eventually sour the relationship between the design firm and the client. A high level of energy is always needed to prevent payment problems from exploding into major confrontations. Such an atmosphere is not conducive to a long-term relationship based on quality service and mutual respect.

Litigiousness

Some clients have a record of suing their engineers, architects, and other technical professionals whenever they perceive any problems on the project. Working for one of these clients is almost always detrimental to the long-term interests of the firm who is contracted.

Attend meetings of your fellow professionals (American Institute of Architects, National Society of Professional Engineers, Professional Services Management Association, etc.). Talk with your fellow professionals. Inquire about previous problems with the potential client. If someone has had legal problems with that client, he or she will generally be quite willing (even eager) to discuss these problems. A pattern of such incidents paints a clear picture.

Excessive Cost Sensitivity

There is another type of client to avoid—the one who selects technical service firms based *solely* on the lowest price for the client's defined scope of work. This selection process is in direct conflict with the basic definition of quality— conformance with *agreed-upon* requirements. The requirements of a project cannot be *agreed upon* if the scope of work is defined unilaterally by the client. As described in previous chapters, a project's requirements must be defined through a series of meetings and phone calls between the client and the design firm. And this agreement of requirements must be continuously revisited as the project develops. Bids based solely on a client's scope of work usually lead to claims by the design firm for scope changes and unanticipated conditions. The client invariably responds by trying to limit these changes. The end result is a combative relationship between client and design professional, not the "partnering" relationship that is successful in the long-term as well as the short-term.

Long-Term Workoad

The payoff for providing quality service is the development of a long-term relationship. If a client has little prospect for future work, such a relationship cannot develop. Marketing expenditures are better spent with clients who will have a long-term workload that the design firm can help satisfy.

DEVELOPING A "PARTNERING RELATIONSHIP"

The widespread use of TQPM in Japan has resulted in *keiretsu*, a system of long-term partnerships among customers and suppliers. These partnerships benefit the suppliers by providing them with a steady source of sales made with minimal marketing expenditures. The customers benefit by: (1) reduction of "learning curve" costs by the suppliers, (2) improved customer-supplier communication, and (3) a long-term commitment by suppliers to meeting their customer's needs. (Repeated failures to meet a customer's needs results in elimination of the supplier from the *keiretsu*.) In Japan, the *keiretsu* system also includes sharing of financial interests, such as stock ownership or loan swaps. Its overall intent is to strengthen all firms within the *keiretsu* through teamwork and synergy of efforts.

While legal barriers prevent the use of Japanese-style *keiretsu* in the United States, some elements of this approach are being adopted successfully by U.S. industry, government agencies, and institutional organizations. Known as "partnering," the objective is to establish customer-supplier relationships that extend beyond an individual project. In a 1989 report, The Partnering Task Force of The Construction Industry Institute (an association of owners, architect/engineer firms, and construction companies,) defined "partnering" as follows*:

> Partnering is a long-term commitment between two or more organizations for the purpose of achieving specific business objectives by maximizing the effectiveness of each participant's resources. The relationship is based upon trust, dedica-

*Source: "Partnering: Meeting Challenges of the Future," Task Force Interim Report, 1989 Annual Construction Industry Institute Meeting, San Diego, Calif.

tion to common goals, and an understanding of each other's individual expectations and values. Expected benefits include improved efficiency and cost effectiveness, increased opportunity for innovation, and the continuous improvement of quality products and services.

The Construction Industry Institute task force contacted seven owners who were known to be involved in formal partnering agreements. Among the findings were:

- 86% believed project schedules were more dependable.
- 100% believed there would be fewer design errors and omissions.
- 71% believed constructability would improve.
- 100% believed resource planning would improve.
- 100% believed innovation would improve project performance.

The task force also interviewed 11 design and construction firms involved in partnering and drew the following general observations:

- The planned duration of the relationship should be at least four years, with provisions for extension.
- The scope of services performed should encompass a broad spectrum of services from conceptual development and planning to detailed design, procurement, expediting, construction, and commissioning.
- The employees involved in the partnering activities should be predominantly located in one area or building. In many respects, the partnering arrangement resembles a task force or even a separate business division.
- The employees involved in the partnering relationship should be predominantly employees of the design firm or contractor. A core group of employees consisting of one to a few owner representatives and five to ten design firm or contractor representatives should be established to lead the group and should remain employed even if the workload reaches a very low level.
- A quality improvement process should be a common theme that leads to higher quality services and products, and hence lower costs. Partnering is thought to be an effective vehicle to accomplish these improvements.

At the 1990 Construction Industry Institute Annual Conference in Nashville, Tennessee, a breakout session was held on "partnering for success." Representatives from Union Carbide Corporation and the Bechtel Corporation evaluated their successful partnering relationship and listed the following "lessons learned":

- Procedures should be merged before taking on large volumes of work.
- Staff should be trained in new procedures and in TQPM.
- Contractor employees must act like owners by placing the highest importance on the owner's needs.
- Some owner staff should perform tasks, not just oversee the work.
- Contractor personnel should perform new aspects of work.
- The owner has to establish some methods and procedures.
- The contractor needs to learn to say "no" to the owner.
- The owner needs to be concerned about the partner.
- The contractor works beside the owner, not always for him.

Can partnering work with clients in the public sector where procurement practices do not permit the kind of relationships described above? The views of Lt. General Henry J. Hatch, Chief of U.S. Army Engineers, provide an insight*.

> We describe partnering as the creation of a relationship between Owner and Contractor that promotes the achievement of mutually beneficial goals. We're talking about applying that basic philosophy to the public sector, which, because of our requirements to enter into competitive processes for each project, cannot have [an] enduring relationship. We're talking about an attitude and an adjustment of that attitude within our particular structure. Under partnering, the contractor and the government representatives focus as a team on the project's mission, its goals and objectives, finances and schedule. The idea is to win.

*Source: Speech at The Construction Industry Presidents Forum, Washington, D.C., April 24, 1991.

A good example is a $34-million contract, one part of the overall $320-million Bonnevelle Navigation Lock Project, administered by our [Corps of Engineers] Portland District. To begin their new relationship, the Corps resident engineer and the contractor's project manager attended a one-week leadership development program that allowed them to establish the beginning of a trusting environment.

Once the significant players in the Bonneville project became well acquainted, they began to develop a win-win charter, as they call it, both sides winning. The charter—not a contract, but a charter laid out on paper—became the basis for goals for their efforts. It was a noncontractual, written statement of principles, which defined mutual expectations.

The project was completed last year, on schedule, within budget. In addition, it had a two-thirds reduction in the letters and case-building paper work that we normally accumulate for the purpose of entering into litigation. Two-thirds reduction. Probably sold off some filing cabinets. With value-engineered savings of nearly $2-million included, cost growth was only 3.3%, which compares to about a 10% average that we normally experience for major construction projects. And there were no lost-time injuries.

[Corps of Engineers] projects where partnering principles have been used have resulted in better cost control through the life of the project. At our Portland District, construction projects show an 80% reduction in cost growth. More importantly, none of the Portland District projects using partnering have today any outstanding claims or any litigation. Additionally, there have been no late deliveries, no fatal accidents. And a reduction in lost-time accidents rates. Also, a reduction of the amount of rework.

Now we admit very openly, this is not a panacea. No one believes a new type of teamwork is going to eliminate all the problems. Undoubtedly, some will continue to arise. But by promoting trust, cooperation and up-front information-sharing, both parties can focus, not on building a successful case against the other, rather on how to effectively solve problems.

Even if formal partnering agreements are not used—and for most projects they are not—fostering this kind of client relationship should be the goal of every member of every design firm.

SUMMARY

This chapter has discussed effective ways that design firms can invest in long-term client relations. The payoffs for this investment are: (1) more repeat business, (2) reduced marketing expenses required to replace lost clients, and (3) fewer lawsuits. The next chapter presents some specific techniques that can be used to solve a wide range of quality problems typically encountered in design and other technical service firms.

9

ELIMINATING QUALITY PROBLEMS— PERMANENTLY

The previous chapters have discussed how to identify and measure recurring quality problems that are common in design firms. This chapter describes some techniques to resolve them—and assure that they won't return. The prevention of future problems is the payoff for the investment made in TQPM.

THE REAL COST OF QUALITY

The "1—10—100 rule" describes the following ratios:

Cost to prevent quality problems	$1
Cost to correct quality problems discovered during in-house review	$10
Cost of quality problems discovered by contractors or clients	$100

Figure 9.1 presents a list of cost elements associated with quality problems that arise on design projects. Can these costs be quantified? Let's look at some examples.

Lack of Coordination Between Civil and Structural

During construction of a new county hospital, the contractor observed several major discrepancies between the civil and structural drawings. He filed a claim for $75,000 of additional construction costs, which the county paid and deducted from the design firm's fees. Upon learning of this problem, the

Costs of Preventing Problems	Costs of Correcting Problems Discovered During In-House Reviews	Costs of Dealing with Problems Discovered by Contractors or Clients
• Leadership training	• Time spent checking	• Resolving claims and change orders.
• System improvement	• Time spent making corrections	• Redoing documents
• Defining client requirements	• Time spent backchecking	• Reduced employee morale
• Learning problem-solving skills	• Additional supervision	• Dissatisfied clients
• Maintaining measurement charts	• Making multiple changes resulting from "ripple effect of errors"	• Lost future business
• Internal team-building	• Missed deadlines	• Damage to reputation
• Determining causes and remedies	• Overtime	• Lawsuits
	• Employee frustration, reduced morale	
	• Productivity decline	
	• Client dissatisfaction due to extra costs, missed deadlines	

Figure 9.1 Costs of quality for design projects.

design firm's principal-in-charge conducted a search for the guilty. Carol Smith, the project structural engineer, perceived that she was being blamed for a problem not of her making and quit, taking a job with the county's engineering department. Because of her departure, the redesign team was unable to identify all the structural conflicts; more discrepancies were eventually discovered by the construction contractor, resulting in $43,000 of additional change order claims, which were also charged to the design firm. Ms. Smith also spread the word to her colleagues at the county engineering department about the poor quality of work produced by her former employer. As a result, the firm stopped getting new projects from the county—a loss of over $600,000 per year in fees.

Improperly Approved Shop Drawings

During construction of a chemical plant expansion, it was discovered that 42 anchor bolt locations shown on the shop drawings were incorrect. Unfortunately, these errors had not been caught during the design firm's review of shop drawings and were not discovered until the anchor bolts had already been set. The required corrections cost $8,000 in redesign and $14,000 in additional construction costs. The client refused to pay for the additional $22,000 for rework, telling the design firm and the contractor to work it out between themselves. After considerable debate and threats of legal action, the design firm agreed to "absorb" all the additional engineering costs and pay half of the additional construction costs. Unfortunately, two of the 42 replaced anchor bolts were improperly installed and didn't provide adequate anchorage for a large air compressor. During start-up, these bolts came loose and the compressor owner suffered major damage. The owner sued both the design firm and the contractor for the costs of repairing the compressor and the revenue lost because the facility was three weeks late in starting up. A negotiated settlement was finally reached in which the design firm paid the owner a total of $187,000.

Missed Holding Times for Waste Samples

A field team leader working on a hazardous waste site was responsible for collecting samples from a series of wells and sending them to a laboratory for analysis. Due to a mix-up, the samples were not analyzed until after their allowable holding times had elapsed, thus invalidating the results. The direct costs to reperform the work included $76,000 for the driller to remobilize and reinstall the wells, $16,000 for time and expenses associated with resampling, and $37,000 to redo the analyses, for a total direct cost of $129,000.

But there were other indirect costs as well. By the time the resampling and reanalyses had been completed, the report was delayed by two months, causing the client to miss a regulatory deadline. The client not only terminated the consultant, preventing the firm from performing the remaining phases of the project, but also sued to recover the cost of the fines. The consultant then sued the analytical laboratory to recover the extra costs it incurred for resampling as well as the costs of the client's fine. The laboratory countersued the consultant to recover the unpaid analytical costs on the grounds that the consultant's field team leader had improperly prepared the manifest form for the original waste samples. Total costs to all parties, including legal fees, were in excess of $800,000.

Errors in Computing Proposal Costs

In preparing a cost proposal for a major project, a design firm had improperly set up a computer spreadsheet. The result was that the costs for one of the tasks was counted twice in the total. Because everyone was working until the last minute, no one caught the error, which resulted in a $19,000 overestimate. As a result of this error, the firm lost a $100,000 project.

During the time this proposal was being prepared, the firm had several projects nearing completion and had counted on securing the proposed project in order to keep its staff busy. Upon losing this opportunity, management concluded that four employees had to be laid off. One of these employees filed a complaint with the Equal Employment Opportunity Commission, claiming that he was discriminated against because of his age. The firm had to answer formal charges and, after a two-year administrative and legal battle, was found to be innocent of the discrimination charge. Total legal costs were $32,000 plus a total of over 200 man-hours of unbillable time spent by the firm's managers in successfully defending against these charges.

CAN THE COSTS OF QUALITY BE MEASURED?

There is considerable disagreement between TQPM experts as to the measurement of cost of quality. Philip Crosby believes it is essential to convert quality problems to dollars in order to: (1) attract management's attention to the problem, and (2) help prioritize among various problems. W. Edward Deming disagrees, saying that indirect costs (especially lost customers) are so great and so hard to measure that the whole exercise is a waste of time. Regardless of which philosophy is believed, quality problems must be *measured* using some parameter that represents their *total* cost (direct and indirect). The measurement system must answer the following questions:

1. What process is to be measured?
2. Which part of the process will be measured? Which requirement(s)?
3. Why was this part/requirement chosen?
4. How will data be collected?
5. Who will be responsible for collecting the data?
6. What kind of chart will be used and how will it be labled?
7. Who will be responsible for recording information?
8. Who routinely needs to be aware of the data?
9. How will the information be communicated to those identified above?
10. Who should be responsible for taking action based on the information?

To avoid misunderstandings, a blank form should be prepared that can be used to chart the actual measurements. For example, measurement of the lack of coordination between civil and structural drawings can be defined as follows:

Parameter. Number of conflicts found during checking of civil and structural drawings divided by total number of civil and structural drawings.

Frequency. Each time the 90% complete civil and structural drawings are given an internal review.

Procedure. Drawing checkers tally each conflict found during the checking process. The total is then divided by the number of civil and structural drawings to determine the average number of conflicts per drawing.

Responsibility. Checkers will provide data to the chief engineer, who will tally the results.

Blank Form. A blank tracking chart similar to Figure 9.2 can be used to plot a data point for each 90% design review.

It is essential that measurement begin as soon as a quality problem is identified. This measurement activity can continue as the causes and remedies are being developed so that a substantial amount of baseline data have been collected prior to implementing any corrective actions. These baseline data can then be compared to the measurements

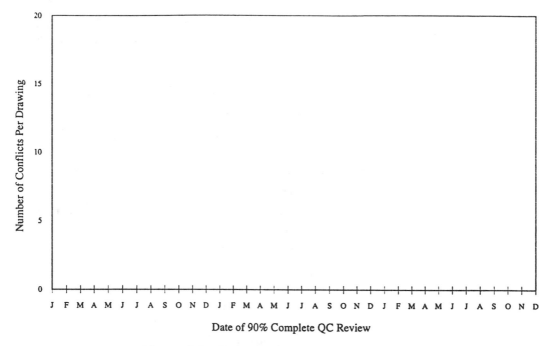

Figure 9.2 Example of a blank tracking chart.

made *after* corrective action is implemented to determine if the proposed remedy is *really* producing the desired effect.

Quantitative measurement of problems is often the first major hurdle faced when a design firm begins to implement TQPM. Chapters 4–8 presented many examples showing how common quality problems can be measured. The techniques presented generally fall into two categories: objective data and surveys.

The most accurate measurement technique is the collection of hard data regarding a specific quality problem. Counting the actual number of errors caught during the drawing checking process is an example of measurement using objective data.

If direct measurement of objective data is not feasible, surveys can be used to quantify a problem. Client satisfaction surveys are a common example. To be effective, surveys must be brief (one page if possible), have easy-to-follow instructions, be worded to avoid biasing the responses, and be formatted to facilitate quantifying the results. If possible, the individuals who are asked to fill out surveys should receive feedback regarding the results of the survey and how these results will be used.

A SYSTEM FOR ELIMINATING QUALITY PROBLEMS

Dr. J. M. Juran has developed what he refers to as the "journey from symptom to cause to remedy" (see Figure 9.3). The "steering arm" consists of one or more individuals representing the firm's management. Its role is to provide guidance and make policy decisions based on management's view of the firm's goals. The "diagnostic arm" consists of employees assigned to solve a specific quality problem. When the diagnostic arm is a group, Philip Crosby refers to this group as a "corrective action team" (CAT). Such teams should consist of four to eight individuals who are intimately familiar with the problem—but from differing viewpoints. Each step in Juran's approach is described below in the context of a typical design firm.

Step 1—Assign Priority to Projects

Most design firms can list many areas in which quality could be substantially improved. Chapters 4–8 of this book describe some common ones and how they can be measured quantitatively. No firm has the resources needed to tackle all these areas at once, so management must decide which problems should have the highest priority. This decision should consider two factors:

1. The firm's most serious problems should be identified so that the first steps toward solutions can be made. It must be recognized that measurable progress on these difficult problems may take months or years to achieve. Examples of such problems might include chronic project budget problems or inadequate coordination among design disciplines.

2. The firm should also select some relatively simple problems that can be solved quickly so that the staff can see the benefits of TQPM. An excellent example is the number of errors made in filling out time cards. This problem plagues virtually every design firm, and it is easy to measure using the techniques described in

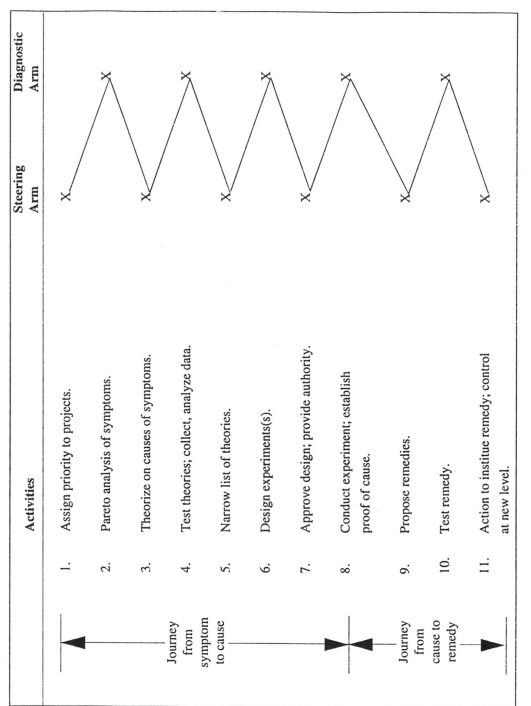

Figure 9.3   Journey from symptom to cause to remedy. Source: Juran, J. M., Quality Control Handbook.

Chapter 7. Because each employee fills out a time card, everyone can personally relate to the problem and appreciate the improvement that will occur as a result of TQPM.

Once the quality improvement projects have been prioritized, management should select the "diagnostic arm" for each one. For simple problems, the diagnostic arm may consist of one person whose job it is to measure nonconformances and advise those who caused them. For complex, deeply rooted problems, a corrective action team is usually required to adequately address all aspects of the problem.

Step 2—Pareto Analysis of Symptoms

The diagnostic arm's first activity is to prioritize the symptoms of the identified problem. For example, a design firm may have collected data on time card errors and determined that they average 120 nonconformances per week. These time card errors may have the following symptoms:

- Not submitted on time.
- Invalid job numbers.
- Omitted task numbers.
- No approval signature.
- Job number does not match project name.

The Pareto principle states that 80% of the results come from 20 percent of the causes. The purpose of a Pareto analysis, therefore, is to find which symptoms account for most of the problem. In the case of time card errors, this can be done by the keypunch operator tallying the number of each type of error during a representative period of time. Attention can then be directed to the most common sources of errors. (Pareto analyses for more complex problems are discussed later in this chapter.)

Step 3—Theorize on Causes of Symptoms

Once the symptoms have been identified and prioritized, the steering arm should work with the diagnostic arm to postulate possible causes. This can best be done using brainstorming techniques, which are described later in this chapter. In the case of time card errors, the possible causes might include:

- Delays in obtaining job numbers for new projects.
- Carelessness by employees.
- Inadequate access to current job listing.
- Misunderstood task breakdowns.
- No system for handling time cards for out-of-town employees.
- Supervisors unavailable for approval signatures.
- Keypunch errors.
- No knowledge of when jobs are closed.

Step 4—Test Theories; Collect and Analyze Data

The diagnostic arm should collect and analyze data to determine which potential causes are *truly* causes of the identified problem. In the example of time card errors, this could be done by asking employees to fill out a simple questionnaire identifying which of the potential causes are most common (see Figure 9.4).

Step 5—Narrow List of Theories

Once the data have been compiled and analyzed, the steering arm is once again involved, this time to help narrow the list of theories down to a manageable number. For discussion purposes, let's say that the responses to the time card questionnaire were as follows:

Potential Causes	Average Ranking
Delays in obtaining job numbers for new projects	6.2
Carelessness by employees	8.3
Inadequate access to current job listing	7.9
Misunderstood task breakdowns	5.2
No system for handling time cards for out-of-town employees	2.3
Supervisors unavailable for approval signatures	3.1
Keypunch errors	1.2
No knowledge of when jobs are closed	5.2
Other	3.1

To: Employees of XYZ Consultants

From: Sally Hammer

Subject: Errors on Time Cards

As you may know, we have been plagued by an excessive number of errors on time cards. Such errors result in additional administrative costs, delays in processing the data, and frustration by almost everyone involved. Please help us solve this problem by giving us your opinion on the possible causes. Rank each cause on a scale of 0 to 10 based on how big of a problem you perceive it to be.

_____ Delays in obtaining job numbers for new projects

_____ Carelessness by employees

_____ Inadequate access to current job listing

_____ Misunderstood task breakdowns

_____ No system for handling time cards for out-of-town employees

_____ Supervisors unavailable for approval signatures

_____ Keypunch errors

_____ No knowledge of when jobs are closed

_____ Other (describe): _____

_____

_____

_____

Please return this form to my office by August 14.

Figure 9.4 Questionnaire regarding time card errors.

The list of theories can thus be narrowed to:

- Carelessness by employees.
- Inadequate access to current job listing.

This narrowing does not mean that the other theories do not contribute to the problem. It is merely a way of prioritizing those causes that have the most impact. These are referred to as "root causes."

Step 6—Design Experiments

At this point, the diagnostic arm develops one or more experiments to determine whether the identified root causes are *really* root causes. In the time card example, the following experiments could be conducted:

> *Carelessness by Employees.* A representative of the diagnostic arm selects an experimental group and advises each employee in that group every time a time card error is detected. After six weeks, the number of time card errors in the experimental group is compared with the number of errors in the control group (i.e., those whose procedure was not changed).
>
> *Inadequate Access to Current Job Listing.* A different experimental group is selected and each employee in that group is given a complete job listing every week. After six weeks, the number of time card errors in this experimental group is compared with those of the control group.

Step 7—Approve Design; Provide Authority

The steering arm reviews the design of the experiments to insure that: (1) they will yield conclusive results, and (2) they are not too disruptive to day-to-day operations. If these conditions are met, the diagnostic arm is given authority to begin the experiments.

Step 8—Conduct Experiment; Establish Proof of Cause

If the experiments confirm the suspected causes, the process can then move to the journey from cause to remedy. If not, the experiment(s) should be revised and repeated or a different experiment begun.

Step 9—Propose Remedies

Given the results of the experiment, the steering arm (with consultation from the diagnostic arm) is in a position to propose solutions that will eliminate the root causes of the problem. In the case of the time card errors, the following remedies could be proposed:

1. Have the keypunch operator send a notice to each employee who makes a time card error. The notice should

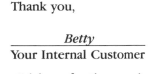

To: *R. C. Alexander*

Date: *6/1/92*

Subject: Time Sheet Errors

Your time sheet errors for week ending   *5/29*   were:

- *Job No. 5629 is closed.*
- *No task identified for Job 2794.*

If there is a problem with our system that makes it difficult for you to fill out your time card correctly, please advise Rose. Otherwise, please take care, beginning next week, to fill out your time card correctly.

Thank you,

Betty
Your Internal Customer

Figure 9.5   Nonconformance advisory for time card errors.

not threaten reprisal, nor should copies be sent to the offending employees' supervisors; it should merely describe the error that was made and ask the employee to be more careful next time (see example in Figure 9.5).

2. Each employee should be given an updated job listing every week.

Step 10—Test Remedies

Before a proposed solution is implemented on a firmwide basis, it is often useful to test it on a "pilot" group. Such a test not only will verify that the solution really works, it also provides an opportunity for "fine tuning" prior to full-scale implementation. In our time card example, the test could be conducted for a single department before time card procedures are revised on a company-wide basis.

Step 11—Action to Institute Remedy; Control at New Level

After the test has been successfully completed, the remedies can be instituted and the results compared with the previously collected data. For example, in the case of time card errors, the keypunch operator should continue measuring the number of erroneous entries and compare them with the previous data to be sure that they have been reduced significantly. This reduced error rate then becomes the norm. If the level of errors is still excessive, the steering arm should go back to the process to consider additional remedies.

THE QUICK FIX

There will be cases where quality problems are so severe that they cannot wait until all 11 steps have been accomplished (a process that often takes several months). In these cases, a "quick fix" may be needed as a stop-gap measure. This is acceptable under certain conditions. First, the magnitude of the problem should be quantified *prior* to instituting the quick fix. (This will avoid overreacting to visible symptoms and enable valuable baseline data to be collected.) Second, everyone (including management) must understand that the quick fix will be in effect only while a permanent systemic solution is being developed.

To illustrate how a quick fix can be used, let's say that a design firm has had serious problems resulting from inaccurate construction cost estimates. These problems have included loss of client confidence and even an occasional lawsuit. The first step (as always) is to *measure* the magnitude of the problem. This can be done using a scatter chart showing the difference between estimated and actual construction cost. Once these data have been compiled and plotted, it serves as the baseline against which to measure progress that results from corrective actions. However, it is apparent that such actions will probably take many months before measurable progress is achieved. The seriousness of the problem demands some sort of quick fix as an interim measure.

In this case, the quick fix might be a requirement that every construction cost estimate be reviewed by the firm's chief engineer prior to issuing it to the client. This quick fix must *not* be confused with a permanent cure. In our example, the quick fix consisted of merely adding an additional quality control step to what is apparently a flawed process for preparing cost estimates. This will no doubt improve the quality of the cost estimates, but at the price of increased cost and time required to perform the estimate (not to mention the additional burden imposed on an already overworked chief engineer). However, this stop-gap measure may be desirable to prevent major problems while the root cause of the

problem is determined and a permanent solution is identified.

USING TEAMWORK TO SOLVE PROBLEMS

Traditional quality assurance and quality control approaches
have been based on the concept that an independent group
must be used to identify quality problems. The TQPM process, on the other hand, requires that both the identification
and solution of problems involve the *same people* who are
most intimately involved with these problems. The implementation of this approach involves the use of corrective action teams (CATs) (also known as "quality circles" or "quality
action teams"), who serve as Juran's "diagnostic arm" (see
Figure 9.3). The CAT works closely with the management
representative(s) who serve as Juran's "steering arm."

Once a quality problem is identified, the responsible man-
ager(s) should assemble and "steer" the CAT. To do so, the
manager(s) must become familiar with the problem before
any time is spent on solving the problem. The manager(s)
should: (1) write a synopsis of the problem, its impact, and
the efforts to date to remove the problem; (2) prepare a charter for the CAT; and (3) select and assign the members, name
a chairperson, and hold a kickoff meeting to initiate the effort
and provide documentation.

In selecting the CAT members, the manager should consider the probable functional areas impacted; the talent, experience, availability, and authority to be given to the members; overall time schedule to solve and implement the
corrective action, and budget for the analysis/planning work.

Selection of the team leader is critical to achieving results.
A good team leader will:

- Bring in creativity and/or technical experts when
  needed.
- Not browbeat anyone into volunteering.
- Not dominate the other participants.
- Assure meetings start on time with all members present.
- Prepare a clear agenda for each meeting.
- Not force solutions on the group.
- Assure that the meetings do not drag on too long.

- Secure the full attention of team members during meetings.
- Assure that team members fulfill their assignments.
- Avoid predetermined solutions.
- Obtain the authority for the team to accomplish its goals.
- Break down territorial protection among team members.
- Assure that the team's accomplishments are recognized.

To accomplish all these objectives, the team leader must have the full support and cooperation of all team members. Specifically, the following examples of counterproductive behavior must be avoided by everyone on the team:

- Coming to a meeting with another agenda.
- Criticizing ideas of others.
- Dominating other participants.
- Holding opinions until the boss speaks.
- Irregular or late attendance.
- Bringing other things to do during the meeting.
- Failing to fulfill assignments.
- Refusing to take appropriate roles (especially leadership).
- Negative mind set.
- Failing to participate in group discussions.
- Not sharing honest opinions.
- Giving low priority to CAT activities.
- Holding sidebar conversations.
- Protecting territorial "turf".
- Falling asleep during meetings.

A CAT is typically composed of four to eight people, all of whom deal with a particular problem on a regular basis, but each of whom views the problem in a different way. The team should include suppliers and customers as well as people who actually perform the work. For example, if a corrective action team were formed to reduce recurring errors in filling out time cards, this CAT could consist of:

- The keypunch operator who enters the data into the computer.

- Someone in the accounting department who uses the data.
- Someone whose time cards often have errors.
- Someone whose time cards rarely have errors.
- Someone who regularly reviews and approves time cards.

The CAT's charter might include developing ways of measuring a particular problem or it may be formed after these measurements have already been demonstrated. Either way, the work of the CAT is not complete until the problem has been solved, as demonstrated by quantitative measurements. In the above example, let's say that the keypunch operator counted an average of 100 errors per week that required correction. The members of the CAT should establish an acceptable tolerance level, say 10 errors per week. Their job is not done until this level has been achieved *consistently.*

To be effective, CATs must be formed in accordance with the following principles:

1. The focus must be on the problem itself, *not* whose fault it is.
2. All CAT members must be given the freedom to make any statements or observations without fear of retribution.
3. There can be no "sacred cows." Members of the corrective action team must be allowed to find *all* the sources of the problem. (Policies and procedures established by senior managers are often the sources of quality problems.)
4. Members should be selected to avoid those with "hidden agendas" that would interfere with the goal of solving the problem.
5. A team leader should be selected who will schedule meetings, keep discussions on track, and document the results.

The activities of the CAT should generally follow Juran's journey from symptom to cause to remedy (Figure 9.3). In solving relatively simple problems, it may be expedient to combine some of the 11 steps, as long as there is a clear distinction between the journey from symptom to cause and the journey from cause to remedy. For example, in the following agenda, a total of five one-hour meetings were designed to solve a relatively straightforward quality problem:

Meeting No. 1. Discuss the problem statement, review the CAT process, and establish a way to measure the magnitude of the problem.

Meeting No. 2. Using brainstorming techniques, list possible causes of the problem. By consensus of the CAT, determine one or two *root causes.*

Meeting No. 3. Using brainstorming techniques, list possible solutions to the root cause(s). By consensus, select a small number of solutions to be considered for implementation.

Meeting No. 4. Evaluate the potential solutions, make a final ranking of solutions, and develop a pilot study.

Meeting No. 5. Evaluate results of the pilot study and prepare recommendations for presentation to management.

BRAINSTORMING

Brainstorming is more than a verbal free-for-all in which everyone speaks until a brilliant idea suddenly emerges. Conducted properly, it is an orderly process that leads to sound conclusions with a minimum of wasted effort. A brainstorming session held among the members of a CAT should include the following phases:

1. *Objective Definition.* The CAT leader should define the objective of the particular brainstorming session. Is it to develop a measurement technique, determine the root cause of a problem, or identify the best solution? If the objective of the brainstorming session is not clearly understood by all the participants, the discussion will meander along many blind alleys.

2. *Solicitation of Ideas.* During this phase, the CAT leader solicits ideas from all the attendees. Any ideas that relate to the objective are welcomed and written on a blackboard or easel for all to see. The leader must *not* permit any discussion of the merits of ideas expressed during this phase. He or she must also encourage everybody to present their ideas, and to build on previously

presented ideas. A good way to encourage participation is to call on each person in turn and ask for ideas. This phase ends when everyone "passes."

3. *Screening.* At this point, each idea should be discussed. Those that are duplications should be combined. Those that obviously hold no promise should be eliminated from further consideration. In most brainstorming sessions, this screening process should reduce the number of ideas by 50 to 75%.

4. *Prioritization.* The remaining ideas should be prioritized to determine which ones deserve further study. One way of doing that is by "multivoting." For the first vote, each CAT member selects the best half of the list of ideas. (For example, if there are 12 ideas on the list, each person gets 6 votes.) A natural break is identified by the CAT leader and approximately half the original list is eliminated. The next step in the multivoting process is the "ten/four vote." Each person gets a total of ten votes to cast, with no more than four votes for any single idea. The written secret ballots are given to the CAT leader, who counts them and prioritizes the ideas accordingly.

5. *Homework Assignments.* If the brainstorming session is unable to totally meet the meeting's objective within the previously agreed-upon time (which is not unusual), it may be necessary to make individual assignments to be completed by CAT members prior to the next scheduled meeting. Any remaining issues should then be resolved expeditiously at this second meeting.

6. *Documentation.* It is essential that all results of each brainstorming session be fully documented by the team leader with copies distributed to each participant and to the managers involved.

PARETO'S PRINCIPLE

As mentioned previously, the Pareto principle states that 80% of the results (either good or bad) come from 20% of the causes. This principle can be used to prioritize potential solutions for complex quality problems. For example, a design firm established 12 categories of errors that often occur on electrical drawings. On one project, quality control reviews of 20 electrical drawings revealed a substantial number of design errors. These errors were categorized and tabulated as follows:

Type of Error	Number of Errors
1. Does not conform to client's design criteria	6
2. Does not conform to code	5
3. Does not conform to calculations	0
4. Interdisciplinary coordination problem	12
5. Operability/constructability problem	9
6. Does not conform to vendor data	0
7. Dimensional error	7
8. Callouts incorrect or missing	56
9. CADD-related problem	0
10. Incorrect notes	33
11. Additional views/details needed	4
12. Does not conform to drafting standards	21

These data can be displayed in the form of a Pareto chart showing the most frequent errors on the left (see Figure 9.6). In this example, most of the effort should be devoted to correcting error types 8, 10, and 12 (assuming that the number of errors corresponds to their impact on overall quality).

In the above example, these three kinds of errors comprise 74% of the total observed errors. However, a word of caution is in order. The example was for a single group of electrical drawings on a single project. TQPM is a long-term process to seek out recurring problems and correct them. It is, therefore, essential to collect this same kind of data for a variety of projects and use Pareto's law to prioritize the long-term problems. For example, Figure 9.7 is a Pareto diagram of reasons for shop drawing rejections, based on data collected for *all projects* performed by the firm during a two-year period.

SEPARATING CAUSES FROM EFFECTS

Quality problems manifest themselves in many ways. These effects can be measured; for example, how many errors in filling out time cards, how many drawing errors, and so on. But to *eliminate* the problem, one must understand the causes as

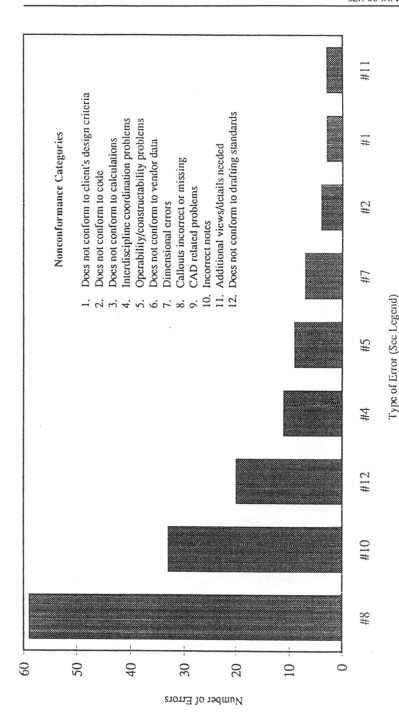

Figure 9.6 Example of a Pareto chart for errors on electrical drawings.

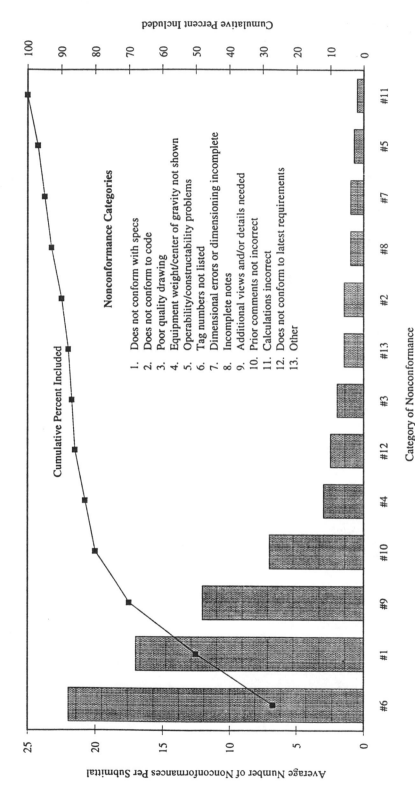

Nonconformance Categories

1. Does not conform with specs
2. Does not conform to code
3. Poor quality drawing
4. Equipment weight/center of gravity not shown
5. Operability/constructability problems
6. Tag numbers not listed
7. Dimensional errors or dimensioning incomplete
8. Incomplete notes
9. Additional views and/or details needed
10. Prior comments not incorrect
11. Calculations incorrect
12. Does not conform to latest requirements
13. Other

Figure 9.7 Pareto analysis of nonconformances on shop drawings.

well as the effects. This is not as easy as it seems. Root causes may be intentionally concealed by those who cause the problems. More often, they are unconsciously concealed in order to preserve the *status quo*. After all, we are more comfortable with what we have always done than with what we have never tried. These obfuscations often make it necessary to employ some analytical techniques to dig out the root causes of serious quality problems.

The first step is to precisely define the problem. This problem definition should identify:

- Who?
- What?
- Where?
- When?
- How?

During problem definition, no one should place blame or predetermine a cause or solution. The problem should be stated simply and unambiguously—in one sentence if possible. For example, a good problem statement might be: "Field work is often delayed due to equipment breakdowns." A contingency diagram (Figure 9.8) can be used to identify both the causes and remedies for relatively simple quality problems.

More complex problems can be tackled using the cause-and-effect or "fishbone diagram," a technique developed by Dr. Ishikawa, a well-known Japanese quality expert. The "head" of the fish is the problem statement and the "bones" are the potential causes sorted into categories. The fishbone diagram is typically developed on a blackboard or easel by the leader of a corrective action team as a way to focus a brainstorming session. Once all the potential causes are identified, they need to be evaluated to determine one or two *root causes*. This can be done by: (1) collecting hard data, (2) conducting a survey of those affected by the problem or (3) multivoting among CAT members (as described previously in this chapter). Figure 9.9 is an example of how a corrective action team from Florida Power and Light Company used a cause-and-effect diagram to analyze their problem of too many projects past due.

Another technique is the root cause "why" process, in which a series of "why" questions is asked about a problem

The Problem   **The Causes**

Field Work
is Often Delayed
Due to Equipment
Breakdowns

Equipment not checked out prior to sending in the field

Equipment abused in the field

Spare parts are not readily available to field crews

Field personnel do not know how to repair equipment

Corrective Actions

1. Develop checklists of equipment and spare parts for various types of field projects.

2. Prepare field packs with all equipment and supplies required for most types of projects.

3. Assign Marilyn Johnson to maintain spare parts inventory.

4. Train field staff in proper operation and maintenance of equipment.

5. Set up a logging system to charge equipment usage to jobs.

Figure 9.8 Contingency diagram.

---

until the root cause emerges. (This technique has been perfected by five-year olds, who use it whenever they are told that they can't have something they want.) To illustrate how this technique can be used by adults, let's take the problem of "too many orders on construction projects." The "why" process works as follows:

Problem: There are too many construction change orders.
    Why? Because field inspectors answer questions without checking with the designers.
    Why? Because the field inspectors think that it's their responsibility to answer all questions immediately.
    Why? Because no one has told the field inspectors to check with the designers first.
    Why? Because there are no written procedures for field inspectors.
    Why? Because no one has been assigned the job of writing field inspection procedures.

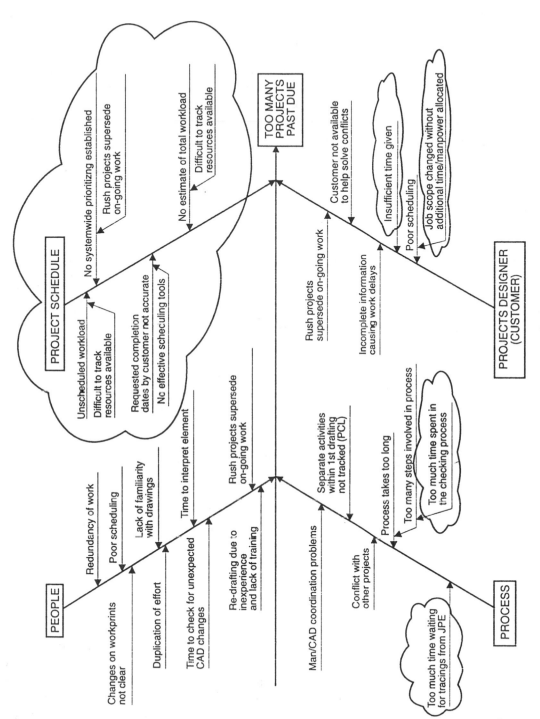

Figure 9.9 Cause-and-effect diagram.

Week _10/10/89_

Employee	Start Date	Home Office/ Field	Recruiter/ Checker	Error	
				Pre-Check-In	Received by Records
Fred Smith	8/30	Pasadena	P. Carlson	Source code incorrect on ESR because data collection forms incorrect (2 forms).	
Bill London	9/5	Pasadena	B. Famile	Was only a position status change from full-time temporary to full-time regular but was treated as a new hire - whole package was completed.	
Sally Jones	9/11	Pasadena	M. Chen		Both letters of employee verification are not valid. Need to have employee redo.
Li Wong	10/10	Saugus	W. Tiscount		Need alien registration number and date of entry. Need country of citizenship; employee is not a U.S. citizen.

Figure 9.10 Case history: HRD hiring package—collecting nonconformance data.

It is now clear what the root cause is and what actions are necessary to solve the problem.

INCREASING VISIBILITY

Some kinds of quality problems can be solved very simply by merely increasing their visibility. For example, a large West Coast engineering company observed problems in the accuracy and timeliness of the paperwork associated with hiring new personnel. The company's human resources department decided to apply TQPM to eliminate this recurring problem.

Their first step was to collect data on the kinds of nonconformances that were causing the problem (see Figure 9.10).

The same group then reviewed the data and made a commitment to become more exact in their work process. They decided to track their progress in the form of a line graph and post it on the bulletin board to provide constant feedback regarding the success of their efforts. Their success was remarkable (see Figure 9.11).

PROVIDING FEEDBACK

Many errors are made by well-intentioned employees who simply do not know that they are doing anything wrong. A simple feedback mechanism can work remarkably well to prevent these problems. In 1990, the Atlanta office of Engineering-Science, Inc. discovered that it was averaging over 100 time sheet errors per week, resulting in the following costs:

Required Corrective Actions	Man-Hours per Week	Other Direct Costs
Rekey corrections	3.0	
Fix invoices	3.5	
Express late time cards to headquarters	1.0	$20
Additional data line charges		$25
Follow up corrections	3.0	$20
	10.5	$65

Total weekly costs = 10.5 hr @ $50 + $65 = $590
Total annual costs = 52 weeks @ $590 = $30,680

A simple feedback system was employed in which the keypunch operator sent a handwritten note to each employee who had a time sheet error. Writing the notes initially *increased* the amount of time it took to handle errors. However, as shown on Figure 9.12, the error rate soon dropped dramatically and reached a consistent level of less than ten errors per week.

THE WORK PROCESS MODEL

Some quality problems are too large or too complex to be solved simply. It is often helpful to divide these into their el-

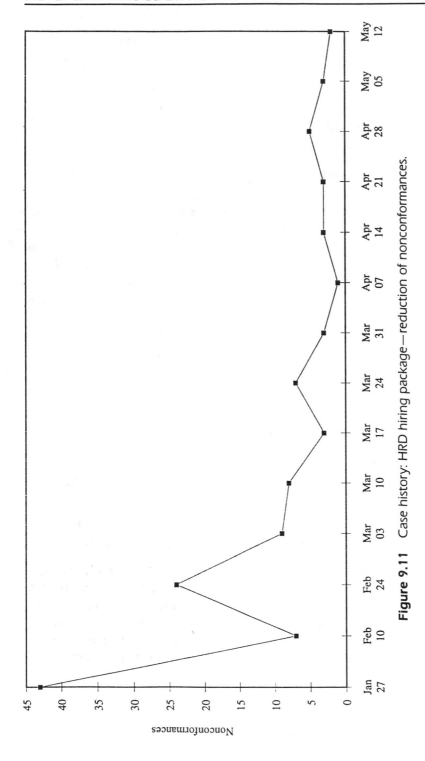

Figure 9.11 Case history: HRD hiring package—reduction of nonconformances.

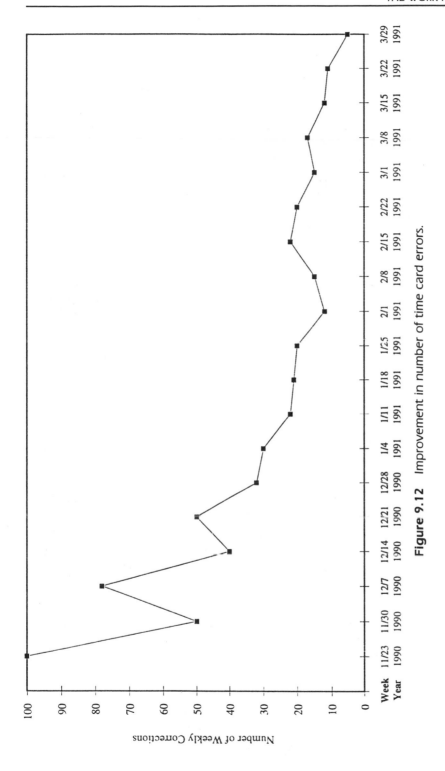

Figure 9.12 Improvement in number of time card errors.

emental components in order to identify potential break-downs in the system. This can be done using a work process model in which each step is shown in a flow chart that also includes possible nonconformances that lead to quality problems.

For example, a planner in a large architectural firm observed that most of his reports were going out to the clients late, in spite of his attempts to prepare the handwritten drafts in plenty of time for typing and graphics. To help identify the source of the problem, he prepared a work process model (Figure 9.13) beginning with "Give handwritten draft to secretary" and ending with "Ready for reproduction." Careful evaluation of his model revealed the following:

1. The secretary was directly involved in the work process at least six different times, all on the critical path. Any delay in any of these steps would delay the final completion time.

2. There were at least four steps where delays could occur due to word processing or graphics personnel not understanding the author's requirements. Because there was no built-in direct communications between the author and these departments, there was no opportunity to clear up any confusion until the next round of corrections.

3. There were at least five steps in which the report production could be delayed due to equipment breakdown or work overload by someone other than the author. Because the author was not in direct communication with the individuals handling the report at those steps, he had no way of knowing about these delays or of taking action to remedy them.

These observations led the planner to revise the work process model, as shown on Figure 9.14. This new model accomplished the following:

1. The secretary's involvement was eliminated, greatly reducing the possibilities of delays due to her being out of the office or busy on other work.

2. In steps 1, 2, 5, and 6, the author gave the work directly to the word processor and graphic artist who were assigned to work on his report. He spent a few minutes

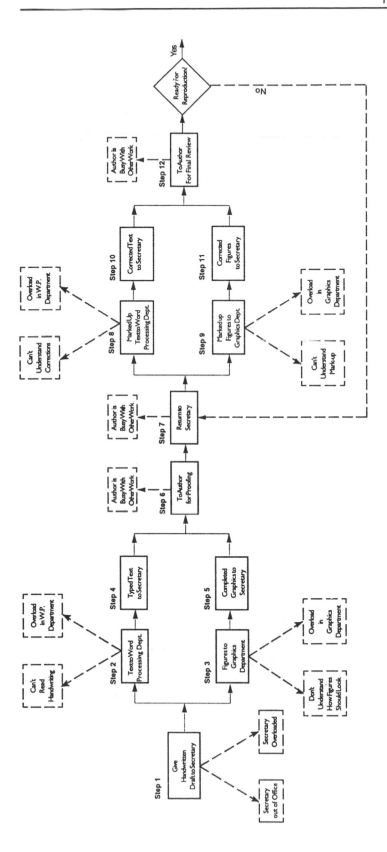

Figure 9.13 Work process model for report production: Approach #1.

LEGEND

—— Correct Path

– – – Potential Delays

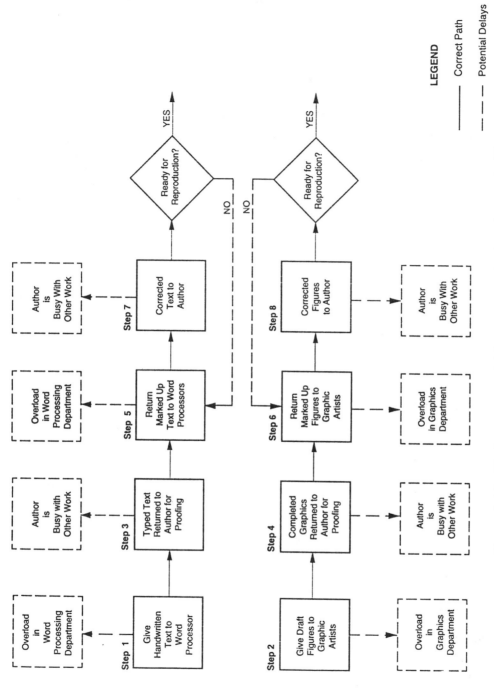

Figure 9.14 Work process model for report production: Approach #2.

with each person to be sure there were no questions or misunderstandings that could delay production. He also verified that these individuals understood their deadlines and could meet them. The word processor and graphic artist agreed to notify the author immediately if any unanticipated events threatened the deadline.

Implementing this revised work process model reduced the opportunities for potential delays from 12 to 8 and improved on-time performance. But the planner was still not satisfied. After brainstorming the problem with other planners in the office, a third approach emerged (see Figure 9.15). In this work process model, the author prepared the initial draft of both the text and graphics on a personal computer using the firm's standard software. All the word processing and graphics departments had to do was: (1) assure that the document was in the proper format, (2) make any final corrections needed, and (3) file it in the system for future retrieval. Total steps were reduced to six, and total opportunities for delays were reduced to four.

Using the revised work process model, the author will have to spend *more* of his time during the report preparation process. But in return for the extra time invested, the planner will receive the following benefits:

- Less time charged by the secretary.
- Less time charged by word processing and graphics personnel.
- Greater control of the process by the author.
- Reports delivered to the client more quickly.
- Reduced frustration level for all parties.
- Happier clients and greatly improved prospects for future work.

Another type of work process model is shown on Figure 9.16 for the preparation of electrical single-line diagrams. In this example, Jane, the head of the electrical department, has been besieged by complaints about the high number of errors on single line diagrams. She starts with a precise definition of the process output—electrical single-line diagrams. She then identifies the customers (the electrical designers) and the requirements (short-circuit current calculation and

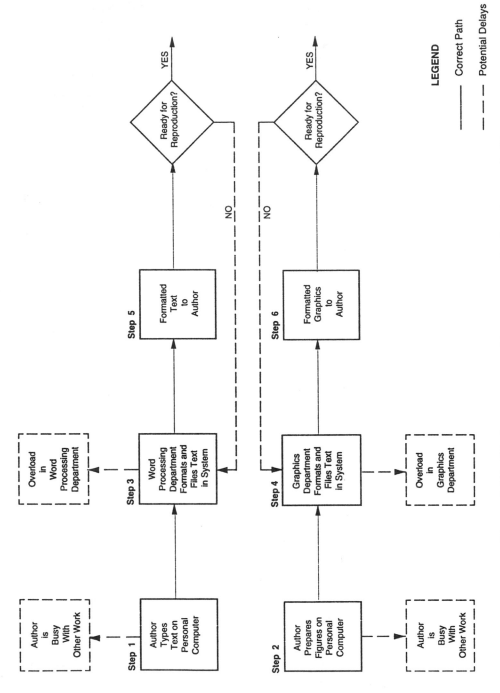

Figure 9.15 Work process model for report production: Approach #3.

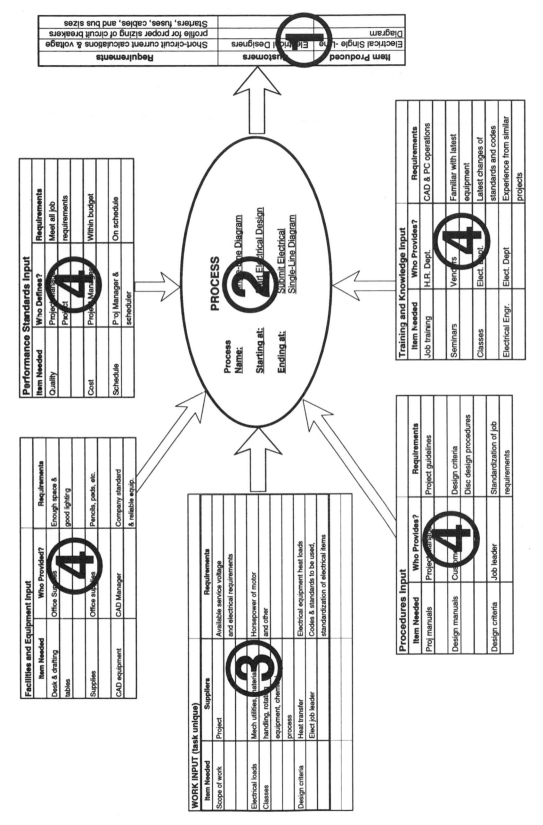

Figure 9.16 Example of a work process model.

voltage profile, starters, fuses, cables and bus sizes). This information is entered in the "process output" block.

Next, she precisely defines the starting point for the work process as "start electrical design" and the end point as "submit electrical single-line diagram." This information is entered in the "process" block.

Finally, she identifies all the required work inputs including facilities and equipment, performance standards, procedures, training and knowledge, and any task-unique inputs. These inputs, along with their suppliers and requirements, are entered into the respective input blocks.

When it has been completed, this work process model provides a systematic way of identifying all the possible causes of the problems experienced in producing electrical single-line diagrams.

BENCHMARKING

A relatively quick and inexpensive way to solve quality problems is to identify someone who has already solved the same problem and copy the solution. This technique, known as "benchmarking," can be used within the same firm, within the same industry, or outside the industry. A "road map" for using this technique is presented below*:

1. Determine the factors critical to the long-term success of the organization and establish the parameters by which performance should be measured. Parameters might be technical (e.g., errors per sheet of drawings) or administrative (e.g., accounts receivable collection days).

2. Measure current performance in your own organization.

3. Gather information about which organizations are the best-in-class for the technique or process being benchmarked. These may be another office within the same firm, another design firm, or another professional service firm.

*Source: Bhote, Keki R., *Next Operation as Customer*, American Management Association, New York, 1991.

4. Prepare a questionnaire for use during visits to benchmark organizations.

5. Visit a few leading organizations and gather information not only from their managements but also from working levels. (Workers may have a more realistic perspective on their achievements.)

6. Record the gap between the benchmark organizations and your own for each parameter within the discipline being benchmarked; then determine the reasons for the gaps.

7. Act to close the gaps by establishing goals, timetables, and teams to achieve these goals. Adapt the techniques used by the benchmark organizations to suit your own organization.

8. Repeat the process periodically to ensure a narrowing of the gap. (The benchmark organizations are not likely to stand still.)

Let's look at how an engineering company recently used benchmarking to solve a common quality problem—slow collection of accounts receivable. The first step was internal benchmarking, that is, looking at various offices within the firm to determine which offices consistently had the fastest cash collections. The following differences were noted in the procedures used at the most successful offices:

1. Individuals who prepared the invoices were degreed accountants with over five years of experience. Less successful offices often used inexperienced clerks to perform this task.

2. Invoicing and collections were the *primary* responsibility of a single individual. In less successful offices, this responsibility was often disbursed among several people.

3. Project managers were given three working days to review invoices; if no comments were received in that time, invoices were mailed to the clients. In less successful offices, project managers were allowed to delay mailing of invoices for weeks until they were able to review them.

The next step in the benchmarking process was to identify other design firms that had excellent records of collecting accounts quickly. In this case, the data sources were several surveys conducted by *Professional Services Management Journal* as well as information obtained from management consultants who specialize in working with design firms. The following additional techniques were identified.

1. Large projects were billed weekly or biweekly rather than monthly.
2. Labor costs were billed separately from expenses so that questions about minor expenses did not delay payment of large labor invoices.
3. Sample invoices were attached to the contract and reviewed with the client prior to mailing the first invoice. This prevented delays due to format or procedural problems.

Finally, successful firms in *other* industries were studied to see if some of their techniques might be applicable in speeding payment of accounts. The following procedures were identified:

1. Up-front retainers were requested in the amount of approximately two months' charges. These retainers were then held until the end of the project. (Taken from a law firm.)
2. A late charge of $1\frac{1}{2}\%$ was automatically billed for all accounts more than 45 days past due. (From a dentist.)
3. Original invoices were sent directly to clients' accounts payable departments in addition to being sent to the clients' project managers. This permitted invoices to get into clients' payment queues while their project managers were still reviewing the invoices. (From an accounting firm.)

When all these ideas were consolidated into a unified company-wide strategy, the total capital turnaround (time spent preparing invoices and collecting accounts) was reduced from an average of over 100 days to less than 70 days.

FORCE-FIELD ANALYSIS

A common problem in TQPM is *plateauing*, that is, substantially improving a particular quality problem, but reaching a plateau before the desired level of improvement has been reached. The force-field analysis is an excellent tool for analyzing this situation and determining a course of action to revitalize the quality improvement process. In the example in Figure 9.17, a horizontal scale shows the initial error level — the degree of nonconformance prior to initiating any corrective actions. The lower horizontal line shows the plateau that has currently been achieved. Vertical arrows pointing from the initial error level to the plateau level identify the corrective actions that have already reduced nonconformances. Vertical arrows pointing up to the plateau level show the impediments to further improvement.

Like the fishbone diagram, a force field diagram provides a graphical framework that can be used to brainstorm a list of causes for continued nonconformances. It can also help to prioritize those causes.

MULTIVARIABLE ANALYSIS

After determining the root cause of a quality problem and identifying ways of solving the problem, measurements must be taken to be sure that the desired results really occur. For example, if a new procedure is instituted to solve a particular quality problem, conformance with that procedure can be correlated with the accomplishment of the desired results.

Let's take the hypothetical case of ABC Surveyors, a small surveying firm that performs mostly small projects on a fixed price basis. After a year and a half of tracking budget performance, Arlene Conklin, the president, concluded that ABC was losing a lot of potential profits as a result of budget overruns (see Figure 9.18). To solve this problem, she developed a system for weekly updating of project budget status. Arlene then issued the system to all the project managers for their use *on a voluntary basis* to help them keep their jobs under budget. Upon the close-out of each job, the project manager identified the number of weeks of project duration and the number of weekly budget updates he or she had prepared in accordance with the new system.

After a year of collecting these data, Arlene used multivariable analyses to correlate procedural compliance with actual results (see Figure 9.19). There was considerable scatter in the data, indicating that budget performance is a function of many factors. However, a curve of best fit showed a definite correlation between compliance with the new procedure

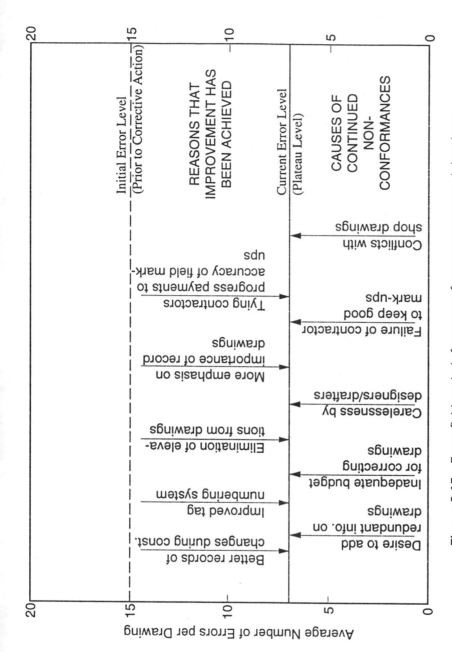

Figure 9.17 Force-field analysis for nonconformances on record drawings.

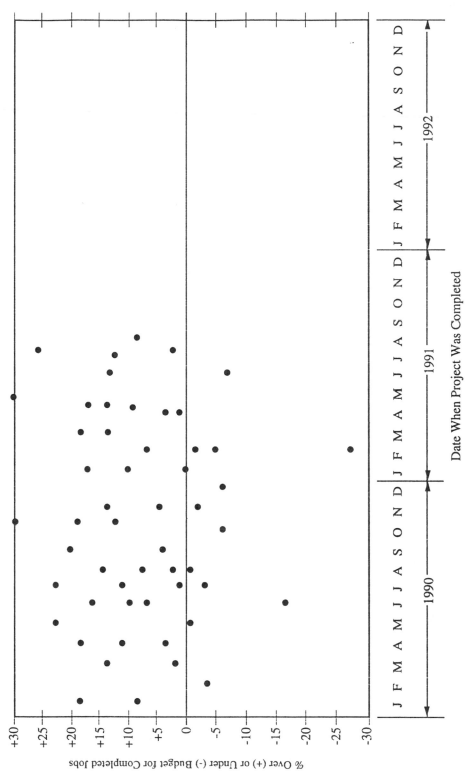

Figure 9.18 History of budget overruns at ABC Surveyors.

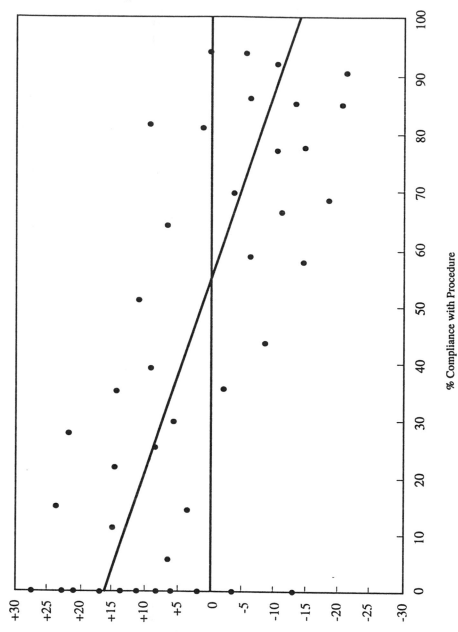

Figure 9.19 Multivariable analysis of budget performance.

and results in budget performance. It was clear that the procedure produced the desired results. Arlene therefore implemented this procedure on a firmwide basis. If no such correlation had been evident, Arlene would have known that proceeding with this approach would simply waste the valuable time of her project managers.

GUIDELINES AND PROCEDURES

Recurring quality problems can often be solved by improving guidelines and procedures. As discussed in Chapter 7, guidelines are similar to procedures but some subtle differences are critical. Procedures are *mandatory*; they must be followed unless there is an approved waiver. Guidelines are *voluntary*; they should serve as a resource to help people avoid "reinventing the wheel" and prevent repeating mistakes.

To be effective, both guidelines and procedures must be readily accessible, easy to find, easy to use, and hard to forget. In addition, procedures must include a systematic way of monitoring compliance. For example, if the firm has a requirement that all field personnel receive health and safety training, records must be kept as to which employees have actually received such training.

TRAINING

The solution for many quality problems includes training and education. Training is generally done to fulfill one of the following functions:

Motivation. Many errors are caused by simple carelessness and can be easily prevented if the employees are motivated to be more careful. The first step is to explain *why* the particular task is important and what adverse consequences result when it isn't done correctly. For example, if the drafters frequently forget to date-stamp check prints, management should explain: (1) what can happen when the wrong version of a drawing ends up on the construction site, and (2) how date-stamping can help prevent this problem.

Technique. Some errors result from employees' lack of understanding of procedures or techniques. For example, if project managers are frequently exceeding their budgets, management should train them in techniques for accurately monitoring and controlling their budgets.

Exercises. Training can also be used to allow employees to practice newly acquired skills prior to using them in the real world. For example, a group of drafters can go through a hands-on training session on the use of a new CAD program prior to actually using it on a project. Such exercises accelerate the learning process and prevent mistakes resulting from lack of familiarity with new techniques.

Vision. Training can also be used to expand employees' horizons. The objective here is to expose them to issues that their bosses normally address. The result is that the employees' vision is expanded so they strive to accomplish a *goal*, not simply perform a *task*.

MISTAKE-PROOFING

One Japanese auto manufacturer, as part of its TQPM program, identified a recurring problem—workers were installing a carburetor part upside down, resulting in premature failures in the carburetor. Had this occurred in a U.S. auto maker, management would have attacked the problem by finding out who was responsible for this error and administering appropriate punishment. But it happened in a Japanese company that did not believe in placing blame for such problems. Instead, a corrective action team was formed to study the problem and recommend a solution. They quickly arrived at a recommendation to management—stamp an "up" arrow on each part so that workers would see which way the part should be installed. The recommendation was adopted and these nonconformances immediately dropped by 75%. But, despite the dramatic improvement, a significant number of carburetor parts were still being installed upside down. After more in-depth analysis, it was decided to redesign the carburetor so that the part would fit only if it were installed right-side up. Nonconformances immediately dropped to zero. This technique is known as mistake-proofing.

Most firms have a spell-checking program as part of their word processing system. This is a form of mistake-proofing.

Some firms have taken the additional step of installing spell-checking on their CADD program, thus preventing "typos" and spelling errors from entering their drawings as well as their reports and specifications.

Another example of mistake-proofing is the REDICHECK system (described in Chapter 4) for preparing and checking drawings. By drawing all plans at the same scale, regardless of discipline, the checker can overlay the various discipline drawings on a light table and quickly identify conflicts. Some CADD programs now include this feature.

Mistake-proofing can also be used to sole serious quality problems that often occur when a complex computer program contains a minor error. Error traps can be installed in the program to check the computed results against independent rule-of-thumb values. Inconsistencies can be quickly identified and programming errors corrected.

THE DECISION MATRIX

After using several of the techniques described previously in this chapter, a corrective action team may be left with a small number of alternative solutions that cannot be further screened or reduced without resorting to arbitrary selections. At this point, a mechanism is needed to establish potential solutions and how they should be implemented. The decision matrix is a very useful tool for this purpose.

The first step is to establish the criteria that will be used to evaluate the final list of alternatives. These might include the following:

- Potential benefits (high, medium, low).
- Costs (high, medium, low).
- Difficulty of implementation (high, medium, low).
- Client receptiveness to solution (yes or no).
- Other problems.

The next step is to determine what possible decisions may be made for each alternative. These might include:

1. Bad idea—forget it.
2. Good idea, but not now—postpone it.
3. Has potential—pilot it using an experimental group.

4. Looks like a winner—set up a full-scale test for a limited period of time.
5. Can't miss—proceed with full-scale implementation immediately.

The matrix can then be set up as shown in Figure 9.20 and the blanks filled in based on discussions among the corrective action team.

TESTING A TENTATIVE SOLUTION

Managers of design firms tend to be action-oriented and decisive. Having identified a problem, its cause, and a remedy, they instinctively order immediate firmwide implementation of that remedy. This works well for simple problems that lend themselves to easy solutions. But for more complex problems, such an across-the-board approach can be disastrous—even if the potential remedy is a good one. One problem is the *Law of Unanticipated Consequences*, which states that any action taken to remedy one problem may create others. Also, when implementing a new system, policy, or procedure, it is often wise to test it to: (1) verify that it will indeed achieve the desired results, and (2) debug the new system. Testing can be performed using pilot studies or full-scale tests.

The Pilot Study

Pilot studies are conducted using an experimental group that is representative of the entire firm. The results of the experimental group can then be compared with the rest of the firm (or some other control group) to determine the efficacy of the proposed remedy, as well as to identify any unanticipated consequences. The following questions should be answered prior to beginning any pilot test:

1. What proposed corrective action(s) will be tested?
2. Who will comprise the experimental group?
3. How long will the test be run?
4. What resources will be required for the tests?
5. Who will monitor the test?
6. Whose approval is needed to run the test?

Problem: _How can we speed up collection of accounts receivable_

Potential Solutions	Potential Benefits (H-M-L)	Costs (H-M-L)	Difficulty (H-M-L)	Clients Receptive? (Yes - No)	Other Problems (H-M-L)	Decision*
1. Hire full-time billing clerk	L	H	L	Yes		3
2. Give discounts for early payment	M	H	L	Yes		1
3. Eliminate PM Review of invoices	L	L	M	No	Could cause client relations problems	1
4. Send 45-day collection letters	M	L	L	No	Need to set up system to generate letters	4
5. Stop sending back-up with invoices	M	L	L	No	Could delay payments	1
6.						
7.						
8.						
9.						
10.						

L - Low _M - Medium_ _H - High_

*Possible Decisions
 1. Bad idea - Forget it!
 2. Good idea, but not now - Postpone it
 3. Has potential - Pilot it on an experimental group
 4. Looks like a winner - Set up full-scale test
 5. Can't miss - Immediate full-scale implementation

Figure 9.20 Decision matrix.

7. What is the test procedure?

8. How will the results be analyzed?

To illustrate how a pilot test can be used, let's take a multi-office firm that has identified a quality problem common to all its operations—too many drawing errors are being identified during final design reviews. The high number of design errors results in schedule slippages, design budget overruns, excessive change orders during construction, and unhappy clients. The firm's management assigns a corrective action team that measures the problem, identifies its causes, and proposes a remedy—put all design engineers, architects, and CADD operators through a 40-hour CADD training course.

When this recommendation is presented to the firm's management, it is met with less than total enthusiasm. Some principals think it is a great idea that should be implemented immediately. Others are dead set against spending a great deal of money on such a training program. To break the deadlock, a pilot program is set up by the corrective action team using one of the firm's smaller offices as the experimental group. An office is selected that has about an average record for making design errors. The proposed training program is implemented and data are kept for the following six months.

After completion of the six-month test period, the office has achieved a 50% reduction in design errors. The corrective action team then looks for unanticipated consequences. The only one observed is positive—a significant reduction in the turnover rate of the firm's CADD operators—presumably because of improved morale resulting from the training. The corrective action team then looks for ways to fine-tune the remedy. After interviewing each member of the experimental group, it is decided that each CADD operator should be given the full 40-hour course, while experienced architects and engineers can be given an abbreviated 16-hour version. After the results of the pilot program are presented to management, there is unanimous approval.

In the above example, the test program not only resolved a debate about whether a new program should be implemented, but also significantly improved the program. Had the pilot test not been performed, the firm would have spent more than was necessary for CADD training of experienced architects and engineers.

The Full-Scale Test

Another testing technique is the full-scale test, in which the experiment is conducted for the entire organization, but for a limited time. For example, let's say that a geotechnical firm has had recurring problems in collecting its accounts receivables due to excessive billing errors. After considerable study, a corrective action team recommends the purchase of a new billing program. The program is thoroughly evaluated, including reference checks with other professional services firms that have purchased it.

To test the program, it can be used for all the firm's billings during a three-month period. During the test period, the firm's project managers are advised to carefully review the invoices and report any problems to the firm's accounting manager. At the end of the test period, the firm may elect to: (1) discontinue use of the new program, (2) adopt it permanently, or (3) make certain modifications, then test it again.

ASSURING THAT PROBLEMS DON'T COME BACK

With traditional management approaches, most quality problems are "solved" by devoting management attention to establishing and enforcing procedures. These apparent solutions last only as long as management keeps a watchful eye on the situation. As soon as management feels that the problem has been solved, its attention is directed to other areas and the original problem gradually returns. This approach is like cutting weeds with a string trimmer; it may be fast, but the weeds soon grow back. By contrast, the intent of TQPM is to *remove the roots* so the weeds *never* come back.

For example, let's say that a firm has a problem with client communications—too many project managers fail to submit their monthly progress reports to their clients on time, resulting in slowdowns in invoice payment and unhappy clients. The traditional "solution" would be for a senior manager to call a meeting or issue a nasty memo complaining about the problem and threatening offenders with some sort of punishment. If the threat is taken seriously, dramatic improvement occurs almost instantly. The manager congratulates himself or herself on being "tough but fair" and moves on to solve other pressing problems.

Soon after the memo is issued, the project managers turn

their thoughts to other matters and the threat from management begins to recede into their subconscious minds. The timeliness of monthly progress reports slowly deteriorates and eventually reaches the same poor condition it was in before management took action. The perceptive manager discovers that the problem has returned and the cycle repeats itself, this time with more serious threats from management.

Eventually, the manager either gives up in exasperation or embarks on a witch hunt to find and punish the offenders. During this "search and destroy" mission, the manager discovers that some of the worse offenders are also some of the firm's best performers. This finding presents a major dilemma: to punish (and alienate) some of the firm's best performers over what they view as a minor issue or to "look the other way" and lose respect because of a failure to carry out the previous threats.

TQPM offers a better approach. First, the manager should meet with the project managers to discuss the problem and its ramifications. They should then *agree* on a specific requirement for monthly reports that will satisfy these concerns, not be overly burdensome to implement and, most important, be measurable. Let's say that a firmwide standard is adopted as follows:

> *Every active project will have a written progress report submitted to the client at least monthly, submitted by the 5th of the following month. Each report will include at least the following information:*
> - *Summary of work done this period.*
> - *Budget status.*
> - *Schedule status.*
> - *Problems requiring client assistance.*
> *Copies of all progress reports will be sent to Sally Jones.*

On the 6th of each month, Sally can review the list of active projects and the copies of all progress reports to identify which project managers failed to conform to this requirement. Any project managers who fail to conform receive a nonconformance notice from Sally. (As mentioned previously, such notices must be nonthreatening in tone, should not express or imply retribution, and most important, copies should *not* be sent to the person's boss.) Once the project managers get in the habit of doing their progress reports on time, very few nonconformance notices will be required. However, this tracking and advisory system must become a permanent part of the firm's procedures in order to assure that the problem doesn't recur.

Instead of trying to control the actions of each project manager, senior management can monitor the effectiveness of the overall system by reviewing a tracking chart (similar to Figure 9.21) which is updated each month by Sally Jones. The firm's senior managers need to take action only if the system is not producing the overall results that are desired.

SUMMARY

This chapter has presented a variety of techniques that can improve quality and increase productivity. The next (and final) chapter describes a systematic approach that can be used to introduce and ultimately institutionalize TQPM within a design firm.

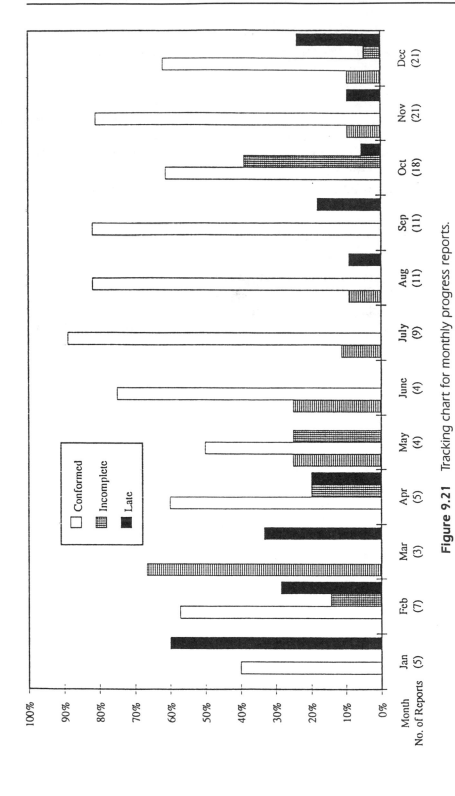

Figure 9.21 Tracking chart for monthly progress reports.

10 IMPLEMENTING TQPM IN YOUR ORGANIZATION

This chapter pulls together the concepts presented thus far into a cohesive method for implementing TQPM in a technical service organization. It also describes how to continually improve the TQPM process so that it is not merely a one-shot program but an ongoing process that will gradually transform the organization into one that embodies the concepts of customer service, responsiveness, production efficiency, and improved competitiveness in the marketplace.

A STANDARD FOR MEASURING TOTAL QUALITY

This book has defined "quality" in very broad terms. Unlike traditional quality control and quality assurance, we have dealt not only with the quality of work produced by a design firm, but also with the quality of *the firm itself*. We have presented many methods for measuring the quality of various elements of the firm. We now combine all these elements into an overall concept of how well the firm is managed.

A number of systems have been developed to measure the overall quality of an entire organization. Perhaps the oldest is the Deming Award, named after Dr. W. Edward Deming and widely used for many years by Japanese companies as a way to measure the success of their quality programs. (As of 1990, only one U.S. Company—Florida Power and Light—had won this award.)

In the mid-1980s, the U.S. Department of Commerce developed a list of evaluation criteria that could be used as a uniform standard by which an organization's quality could be measured. Responsibility for this effort was assigned to the

National Institute of Standards and Technology, the same agency responsible for developing standards for weights and measures, scientific measurement techniques, and test methods. The result of this effort was the Malcolm Baldrige National Quality Award—an annual award presented to organizations exhibiting outstanding achievements in quality management. Up to two awards may be made each year in each of the following categories:

- Manufacturing companies.
- Service companies.
- Small businesses.

The award examination varies slightly from year to year, but is generally based on the following key concepts:

1. Quality is defined by the customer.
2. The senior leadership of businesses needs to create clear quality values and build these values into the way the company operates.
3. Quality excellence derives from well-designed and well-executed systems and processes.
4. Continuous improvement must be part of the management of all systems and processes.
5. Companies need to develop goals, as well as strategic and operational plans, to achieve quality leadership.
6. Shortening the response time of all operations and processes of the company needs to be part of the quality improvement effort.
7. Operations and decisions of the company need to be based upon facts and data.
8. All employees must be suitably trained and developed and involved in quality activities.
9. Design quality and defect and error prevention should be major elements of the quality system.
10. Companies need to communicate quality requirements to suppliers and work to elevate supplier quality performance.

The 1993 award examination categories and point weighting system are presented in Figure 10.1. The scoring system is

1993 Examination Categories/Items	**Point Values**
1.0 Leadership	95
1.1 Senior Executive Leadership 45	
1.2 Management for Quality 25	
1.3 Public Responsibility and Corporate Citizenship 25	
2.0 Information and Analysis	75
2.1 Scope and Management of Quality and Performance Data and Information . . .15	
2.2 Competitive Comparisons and Benchmarking 20	
2.3 Analysis and Uses of Company-Level Data 40	
3.0 Strategic Quality Planning	60
3.1 Strategic Quality and Company Performance Planning Process 35	
3.2 Quality and Performance Plans 25	
4.0 Human Resource Development and Management	150
4.1 Human Resource Planning and Management 20	
4.2 Employee Involvement 40	
4.3 Employee Education and Training 40	
4.4 Employee Performance and Recognition 25	
4.5 Employee Well-Being and Satisfaction 25	
5.0 Management of Process Quality	140
5.1 Design and Introduction of Quality Products and Services 40	
5.2 Process Management: Product and Service Production and Delivery Processes 35	
5.3 Process Management: Business Processes and Support Services 30	
5.4 Supplier Quality 20	
5.5 Quality Assessment 15	
6.0 Quality and Operational Results	180
6.1 Product and Service Quality Results 70	
6.2 Company Operational Results 50	
6.3 Business Process and Support Service Results 25	
6.4 Supplier Quality Results 35	
7.0 Customer Focus and Satisfaction	300
7.1 Customer Expectations: Current and Future 35	
7.2 Customer Relationship Management 65	
7.3 Commitment to Customers 30	
7.5 Customer Satisfaction Results 85	
7.6 Customer Satisfaction Comparison 70	
TOTAL POINTS	1000

Figure 10.1 Malcolm Baldrige National Quality Award 1993 examination categories and items.

based on the following evaluation dimensions for each category and examination team.

> *Approach.* The method the company uses to achieve the purpose addressed in the examination item.
>
> *Deployment.* The extent to which the approaches are applied to all relevant activities in the examination item.
>
> *Results.* Outcomes and effects in achieving the purposes of the examination item.

A summary of how points are awarded for each examination item is presented in Figure 10.2. Additional details regarding the scoring system are presented in Appendix F.

Applying for the Baldrige Award is very costly, time consuming, and may divert management's attention from day-to-day operations. Furthermore, winning the award is no guarantee of financial success (see Figure 10.3). When management adopts the goal of winning the award rather than that of improving quality, the rigid adherence to the process takes precedence over common sense. The results are often the opposite of what was intended.

Instead of viewing the award itself as a goal, management should look upon it as a score card that can be used *internally* to measure progress in the quest for real quality improvement. Only when the organization has demonstrated major accomplishments in all aspects of its operations should management even consider applying for the award.

COMMITMENT FROM THE TOP

Total Quality Project Management is not a grass roots or bottom-up approach; it's a top-down system. The firm's principals *must* take the lead in becoming committed to quality improvement. They must establish the philosophy of zero defects as the only standard of quality. They must establish the attitude that no one will knowingly submit to the client any deliverable that does not conform to requirements, no matter what the pressure for maintaining schedule or budget. (This is very painful the first few times it is implemented, but becomes easier once people are convinced that management is absolutely serious and uncompromising.)

The principals must make time for implementing TQPM

Score	Approach	Deployment	Results
0%	• anecdotal, no system evident	• anecdotal	• anecdotal
10-40%	• beginnings of systematic prevention basis	• some to many major areas of business	• some positive trends in the areas deployed
50%	• sound, systematic prevention basis that includes evaluation/improvement cycles • some evidence of integration	• most major areas of business • some support areas	• positive trends in most major areas • some evidence that results are caused by approach
60-90%	• sound, systematic prevention basis with evidence of refinement through evaluation/improvement cycles • good integration	• major areas of business • from some to many support areas	• good to excellent in major areas • positive trends – from some to many support areas • evidence that results are caused by approach
100%	• sound, systematic prevention basis refined through evaluation/improvement cycles • excellent integration	• major areas and support areas • all operations	• excellent (world-class) results in major areas • good to excellent in support areas sustained results clearly caused by approach

Figure 10.2 Scoring guidelines for the Baldrige award.

Award Year	Company/Location	1990 Sales	Performance Since WG
1988	Globe Metallurgical; Cleveland Privately held; produces metal alloys	$100 million (est.)	In a depressed market, Globe has increased market share, operates at 90% of capacity. Big companies more eager to buy from Globe.
	Motorola; Schaumburg, Illinois Produces radio equipment, cellular phones, microprocessors, and other electronic gear	$11 billion	Earnings per share dropped for the first time in five years in 1990; design glitches led to delay in delivery of critical chips.
	Commercial Nuclear Fuel Division, Westinghouse; Pittsburgh Provides fuel rods for nuclear power plants	$350 million (est. for division)	Two other divisions were runners-up for the Baldrige in 1989 and 1990. But corporate earnings are down.
1989	Milliken; Spartanburg, South Carolina Privately held; makes auto and apparel fabrics and carpeting	$2 billion (est.)	The textile industry has been in a slump, but Milliken kept its sales even, thanks to its grip on niche markets.
	Business Products and Systems Group, Xerox; Rochester, New York Produces copiers, printers, workstations, and software	$14 billion (for group)	Improved quality has raised its share of the copier market from 8.6% in early 1980s to 16% today. But profits are down and stock remains below 1987 highs.
1990	Cadillac Motor Car, General Motors; Detroit Makes luxury cars	$8 billion (est. for division)	GM is losing money in a terrible car market, but Cadillac is holding its market share in competition with new Japanese luxury models.
	S/400 Unit, IBM; Rochester, Minnesota Makes intermediate computers	$14 billion (est. for unit)	Rochester unit stands out, increasing its market share, while IBM as a whole flounders.
	Federal Express; Memphis Ships parcels around the world	$7 billion	Has lost money in new international operations. Profits are down and shares are worth half their 1987 and 1988 highs.
	Wallace; Houston Privately held; distributes pipes, valves, and fittings for oil and chemical companies	$90 million	No windfalls, but has lined up more potential customers than past 40 years; gets respect from CEOs and presidents, instead of having to kowtow to purchasing agents. [Despite these benefits, Wallace filed for Chapter 11 backruptcy protection in 1992.]

Source: Main, Jeremy, "Is the Baldrige Overblown," *Fortune*, July 1, 1992.

Figure 10.3 How Baldrige Award winners did in 1991.

and must give this time top priority. *This job cannot be delegated.* Realistically, successful implementation will take a minimum of 20% of senior managers' time. They must do enough homework to always come to quality meetings prepared. Principals must:

- Take action to assure that the other managers are devoting adequate time and priorities to TQPM.
- Take time to recognize contributions to TQPM.
- Communicate regularly to technical staff regarding quality issues.
- Assure that corrective actions are being properly implemented and that there is follow-up to assess the effectiveness of corrective actions.
- Most importantly, listen to what clients and technical and administrative personnel say about what is important to them in implementing TQPM.

Principals must install a sense of *ownership* of TQPM within the firm's personnel, not just a sense of participation. This can be facilitated by assuring that everyone is actively participating in quality improvement. Some of the more timid people may have to be encouraged individually, perhaps by creating special assignments for them. Everyone needs to be encouraged to speak out and volunteer both their opinions and their time.

The firm's principals must not only manage, but lead in the implementation of TQPM. This means they must *actively* participate to the same or greater extent that they are asking others to participate, including:

- Taking part in the corrective action system.
- Hanging quality posters, awards, and so on in their offices.
- Having at least one area for posting of personnel measurement charts in their offices.
- Making quality management a part of their regular staff meetings, perhaps the first agenda item.

Principals must take the lead in creating a nonintimidating environment for problem solving. They must always assume (until proven otherwise) that personnel are doing their best to produce a quality product. Principals need to take the initiative through their own examples of depersonalizing problem solving; they must shift people away from finger pointing toward searching out root causes. They must not become defensive about their systems and management approach but instead recognize that they may often be *part of the problem* without realizing it.

Implementation of TQPM initially will take more of everyone's time. There is no way to shortcut this. Every employee must realized that TQPM is not another separate duty assigned, but a different way of performing everyone's present duties. Implementation of TQPM will initially be a liability to the organization; it will cost before it can save, and will probably cause some friction. Because everyone is already busy on priority efforts, the firm's principals must, when necessary, rearrange some priorities and workloads for key personnel involved. Successful implementation means that people must spend *priority time* on this effort.

Most important of all, principals must "walk what they talk." Each principal should evaluate his or her real commitment to quality improvement by estimating how many hours in the average week are spent on the following activities:

1. Personally servicing clients.
2. Controlling overhead.
3. Visiting projects in the field.
4. Talking to other managers.
5. Finding out what clients, ex-clients, and potential clients want.
6. Talking to principals and stockholders.
7. Learning what clients think of your service.
8. Writing proposals.
9. Recognizing employees who provide excellent service.
10. Planning and scheduling.

The odd-numbered activities above are directly associated with implementation of TQPM. Principals who spend most of their time on these are sending a loud message to their subordinates that they are truly committed to quality. Those who spend most of their time on the even-numbered activities are unintentially transmitting the opposite message.

An excellent example of commitment to the principles of TQPM is the story of the Michael Baker Corporation, a large A/E firm named after its founder, Michael Baker, Jr. When Baker died in 1977, his son, Michael III, took over the company. By 1983, employee morale had deteriorated badly, company losses topped $1 milion, and Michael III was looking to sell his father's company.

Upon taking over as CEO, Richard Shaw developed a recovery strategy based on two principles. First, he made every effort to open lines of communication. Senior management communicated with employees both in writing and in person. Regular "brown-bag" sessions were begun with Shaw at headquarters in Beaver, Pennsylvania. And employees were encouraged to submit questions to management. "We've tried to be open, honest and aboveboard with employees. We try to tell them the good things and the bad things," Shaw said.

Shaw went even further. In 1988, more than 900 employees filled out a 26-page survey. The result? Over 200 recommendations were submitted to the human resources department and then distributed to appropriate managers and business units. All recommendations (both positive and negative) were responded to, each with a thorough answer. Results were published in an employee bulletin in November 1989. The survey proved to be very enlightening to senior management. Shaw commented, "The survey told us a lot of things—some of which we didn't want to know."

Open communication, however, was not the sole solution to Baker's woes. The company needed to grow and diversify. The company had to start from scratch, proving itself to old customers and trying to attract new ones. And it had to improve its performance reputation. "We didn't do anything on time, we didn't meet the schedules, we didn't meet the budgets, and our performance was lousy," Shaw admitted.

In 1984, Baker nearly lost one of its faithful customers for good. The Secretary of Transportation of the Pennsylvania Department of Transportation (PennDOT) vowed that he would never give the Michael Baker Corporation another job. It took a lot of hard work on the company's part to finally change PennDOT's mind.

Things are looking up now for the Michael Baker Corporation. It's been a long hard road back from near bankruptcy and a challenge to introduce a new management style. As a result, the corporate environment has experienced a significant change. "We have a much more open and participative management style," Shaw says. "We have a lot of folks around here who ask a lot of hard questions and they are not a bit backwards about criticizing what I do or asking questions about what I do," Shaw admits. "That is valuable—to me and to the company*."

PEER REVIEWS

To begin the implementation of a TQPM program, management must determine the underlying quality problems that currently exist. This can be a difficult task because the *real* quality problems are often hidden or disguised by those who fear retribution. Therefore, in most organizations, management's view of the firm's quality problems is badly distorted.

One way to overcome this problem is through a process known as "peer review." The generic definition of a peer review is "a documented, fully traceable review performed by qualified specialists who are independent of the original work, but have the expertise to perform the work." An organizational peer review is a review of the practices and procedures of the entire firm.

One of the best developed, most effective, and least costly peer review programs is sponsored by the American Consulting Engineers Council (ACEC). Its program has received endorsements from such groups as:

- American Institute of Architects.
- American Society of Civil Engineers.
- Association of Consulting Engineers of Canada.
- Coalition of American Structural Engineers.
- Design & Construction Quality Institute.
- DPIC Companies.
- Fédération Internationale des Ingénieurs Conseils.
- Hazardous Waste Action Coalition.
- Professional Engineers in Private Practice, a division of the National Society of Professional Engineers.

*Source: Mason, Julie Cohen, "On the Road to Recovery," *Management Review*, April 1991.

- Shand, Morahan & Company, Inc.
- South African Association of Consulting Engineers.
- The California Council of Civil Engineers and Land Surveyors.
- Victor O. Schinnerer & Company, Inc.

In 1990, the cost for a one-person, one-day review ranged from $600 to $1,100. For large firms, the cost could range from $1,600 to over $8,000, depending on the number of reviewers and the number of days spent at the office. These costs include the review team's travel, lodging, and honoraria as well as an administrative fee to cover the ACEC peer review program's costs. Some liability insurance carriers offset these costs by reimbursing policyholders for peer review costs; others offer an annual premium credit on their liability insurance.

The heads of the firms that have been reviewed under the ACEC program have unsolicited testimonials as well as an overall rating of results of 95 on a scale of 100.

The goals of the ACEC peer review are to identify the firm's objectives, policies, and procedures and then examine how these policies and procedures are implemented. The peer review covers the following areas:

- General management.
- Professional development.
- Project management.
- Human resources management.
- Financial management.
- Business development.

The firm's managers decide if the review team should emphasize any of these areas over the others.

The peer review is confidential. Members of the review team sign statements of nondisclosure before they arrive at the firm's office. All material provided them and all discussions are covered by this statement of nondisclosure, and all material provided to the reviewers is returned or destroyed after the review. The review team also maintains confidentiality with respect to the sources within the firm of various information that the review team reports to management. After the review, the team's notes are destroyed. Any information that is sensitive from the firm's standpoint or that of its clients can be withheld.

The review team's report to the senior manager(s) of the firm during the exit conference at the end of the site visit is oral, not written. This enhances the confidentiality of the review. The firm may, if the reviewers agree, make an audio or audiovisual tape of the exit conference.

The peer review focuses on practices and procedures. The review team looks for a sense of logic and orderliness in the designer's approach to a project—*not* for the correctness of calculations, and so on. Similarly, the review team examines deliverable documents only from the standpoint of apparent conformance with the firm's policies on work planning, production, and quality control/quality assurance.

The review team does not evaluate the firm against national or regional standards. If the review team makes reference to other firms, other policies, or results of surveys, such references are only for general information.

For more information on the ACEC peer review program, contact:

Organizational Peer Review Administrator

American Consulting Engineers Council

1015 15th Street, NW

Suite 802

Washington, DC 20005

Phone: (202) 347-7474

ORGANIZING FOR TQPM

A sound organizational structure must be established for TQPM to function in a well-coordinated manner. This structure must consider the size and organization of the firm itself. For very large, centralized firms, the organization might look like Figure 10.4. For smaller firms, the TQPM organization might be superimposed over the firm's existing organization. Some of the key TQPM functions in a "typical" multidepartmental design firm are described below.

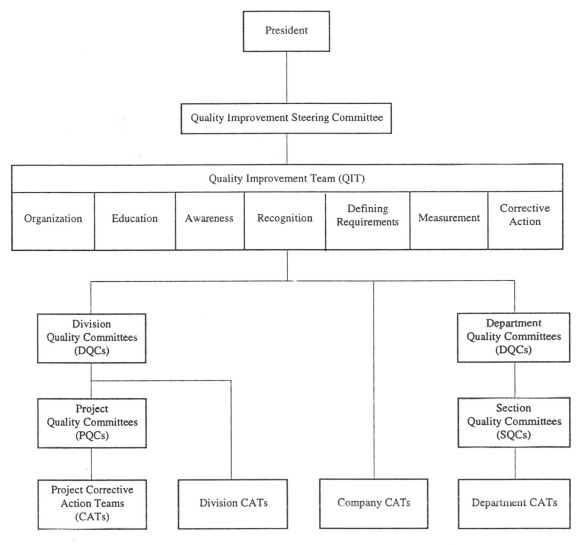

Figure 10.4 Typical TQPM organization for a large design firm.

Clients

The final judges of the success of TQPM are the firm's clients. They will ultimately decide if the work meets their requirements for schedule, costs, and technical quality. The firm's principals, project managers, and others who interface with clients must: (1) understand their clients' requirements, and (2) do whatever is necessary to meet them. The firm's organization must include a way of obtaining direct client input to the quality process.

Senior Management

Someone must provide ongoing impetus to keep the TQPM process moving on track. This can be a single principal (TQPM manager), a "steering committee" consisting of a small group of principals, or a "quality improvement team" consisting of representatives of the organization's middle and upper management. Philip Crosby has defined the strategic functions of this person or group to include the following:

Management Commitment. Demonstrating to everyone in the organization that all levels of management are dedicated to TQPM.

Quality Education. Teaching everyone the tools needed to implement TQPM.

Quality Measurement. Developing systems that can be used to quantitatively measure the various elements that define "quality" in the organization.

Cost of Quality. Quantifying the cost of doing things wrong and the costs required to do them right.

Goal Setting. Setting specific objectives for improving quality over a 12- to 18-month period.

Corrective Action. Identifying, studying, and correcting recurring quality problems.

Error Cause Removal. Establishing a quick, simple process to identify and eliminate the causes of quality problems.

Quality Councils. Establishing teams to continually improve the organization's production processes.

Recognition. Assuring that those who demonstrate active participation and/or accomplishment in TQPM are provided with positive reinforcement.

A TQPM administrator should also be assigned to handle the paperwork and other logistics associated with implementing TQPM. For organizations of over 100 employees, this will probably be a full-time position.

Middle Managers

Once the overall objectives and strategies have been defined, each line manager must: (1) determine how his or her group can contribute to the process, and (2) direct a program that will accomplish the agreed-upon goals. Because most employees report to middle managers (branch office managers, department heads, etc.), the active participation of these managers in TQPM is *crucial* to the success of the total effort.

In most technical service organizations, the department and branch office managers are in the best position to observe and understand quality problems that tend to recur from project to project. This knowledge must be translated into specific actions by implementing the following elements within each manager's area of responsibility:

1. Organize the department TQPM program according to the guidelines established by the TQPM manager, steering committee, or quality improvement team.
2. Support the TQPM programs for training, awareness, recognition, and so on.
3. Develop department procedures that specifically define the requirements to be met for key work activities.
4. Measure key work activities and analyze the results.
5. Take corrective actions including, if necessary, the assignment of department CATs to analyze internal functions needing improvement.

Each department manager should be supported by a department secretary or other administrative assistant who serves as the TQPM administrator for that department.

Project Managers

Each project manager is responsible for overseeing and supporting the implementation of the TQPM program on his or her own projects. On major multiyear projects, the project manager may form a project quality committee (PQC) made up of representatives from each functional group assigned to the project (the various design disciplines, CADD, permitting, surveying, etc.).

Whether or not a PQC is created, each project manager is responsible for holding regular project quality meetings with key staff members and for placing the following quality-related items high on his or her agenda:

1. How well has the project's scope of work been defined and communicated at every level on the project? Is the scope of work being accomplished in accordance with these requirements?

2. Is full and effective use being made of standard company guidelines and procedures?

3. Does everyone understand the attitude required for a successful customer/supplier relationship? If not, what is being done to improve this understanding?

4. What quality parameters are being measured, and what are the results of these measurements?

5. How is the corrective action process being implemented on the project to resolve known problems?

6. Are the approaches of the company and department TQPM programs supporting the needs of the project?

All project quality meetings must be conducted in a positive team-building way. Discussions regarding existing problems should focus on finding ways of improving methods for producing work that conforms to requirements—*not on assigning blame.* Suggestions for preventing problems from happening should be encouraged. The performance of error-free work should be promoted, and each member of the team should be trained to recognize his or her role in achieving this.

TRAINING EVERY EMPLOYEE

Employee training in the principles of TQPM must begin with senior management and must eventually include everyone in the firm. The education process should begin with the firm's top management learning about TQPM from someone who already has an in-depth understanding. One source for such information is a consultant who specializes in TQPM training for a wide variety of clients (e.g., manufacturers, service organizations, government agencies, etc.). The following is a partial listing of known TQPM consultants:

- Philip Crosby & Associates, Winter Park, FL
- Development Dimensions Pittsburgh, PA
- Gunneson Group Landing, NJ
- United Research Morristown, NJ
- ODI Burlington, MA
- Ernst & Young New York, NY
- Walker Customer Satisfaction Indianapolis, IN
- Qualtec Palm Beach, FL
- General Systems Pittsfield, MA
- Juran Institute Wilton, CT

Another source of quality training is consultants who specialize in management training for design firms. Some of these firms are now offering TQPM training. They include:

- The Coxe Group
  Seattle, WA
- William M. Hayden, Jr., Consultants, Inc.
  Jacksonville, FL
- Management Design
  San Francisco, CA
- Martin-Simonds Associates, Inc.
  Seattle, WA

A third source of information and training is professional societies that are dedicated to the implementation of TQPM. They include*:

- American Society for Quality Control
  Milwaukee, WI
  Founded 1946
  85,000 members, mainly quality control specialists
  Sponsors array of seminars and conferences
- Association for Quality & Participation
  Cincinnati, OH
  Founded 1977
  8,000 members
  Emphasis on employee involvement, self-directed work team in the quality movement
- Quality & Productivity Management Association
  Schaumburg, IL
  Founded 1979
  1,000 members, most senior and middle managers
  Emphasis on networking quality professionals
- American Productivity & Quality Center
  Houston, TX
  Founded 1977
  450 corporate members
  Sponsors workshops, is assembling a clearinghouse on benchmarking

*Source: "Quality 1991," *Business Week*, January 15, 1992.

	Object		Employee	Course Name	Hours	Instructor
Compulsory Training	Directors		All	Executive course (within company)	11	External Instructor
	Department and section managers		All	Department and section management course	38	Specialized Instructor
			Senior Managers	Refresher course	19	
	Staff	Technical	All	QC (staff) course	32	Instructor in each plant, division, and office
		Clerical	All	QC (staff) course	24	
	Line	Supervisors	All	Supervisor course	24	
		Group leaders and circle leaders	All	Group leader course	24	
		Workers	All	QC worker course	8	
	New Employees		All	New Employee course	8	
	Part-time Employees		All	Part-time employee course	8	
Specialized Training	Staff		Selected Staffs	1. Basic course (A)	192	Specialized Instructor
				2. Basic course (B)	114	
				3. Reliability	39	
				4. Design of experiment	36	
				5. Multivariable analysis	36	
				6. Others	As req'd	

Figure 10.5 Master quality training schedule for a Japanese manufacturer. Source: Labovitz, George H. and Chang, Yu Sang, "Learning from the Best," *Quality Progress*, May 1990.

The type and level of employee training is a subject of considerable debate. Figure 10.5 shows the training program of a Japanese manufacturer that has won the prestigious Deming Award for Quality. This level of training is probably overkill for a design firm that is just beginning to implement the quality improvement process. A more appropriate level of training was developed by The Ralph M. Parsons Company, which provides an eight-hour training course for all its employees. Known as "Quality Improvement Fundamentals," it includes the following topics:

- Managing quality.
- Improving customer/supplier relationships.
- Developing teamwork.
- Identifying requirements.
- Using prevention.
- Understanding zero defects.
- Cost of quality.
- Measuring to improve.
- Analyzing problems.
- Eliminating a problem's cause.

This level of training is generally adequate for the purpose of introducing the basic concepts to all employees. However, it cannot adequately address the problem-solving techniques that are critical to the success of TQPM. Another four to eight hours of training should be provided to all supervisors and managers. This follow-up training should teach the techniques described in Chapter 9 of this book and should include extensive use of group exercises to utilize these techniques on real-world problems.

It is also desirable to provide a two-hour refresher course to each employee one year after receiving the initial eight-hour course. This will rejuvenate enthusiasm and provide the perspective of having worked with the system for the past year. Additional refresher courses should then be given every year or two.

Like all procedures, compliance with training requirements should be tracked. In a small firm, this can be done by identifying which individuals have received training and keeping this list updated periodically. Figure 10.6 illustrates a simple way to monitor the progress of the training program in a large, multidisciplinary organization.

EMPOWERING EVERY EMPLOYEE

TQPM cannot succeed without the dedication and involvement of the firm's employees. The more employees are in-

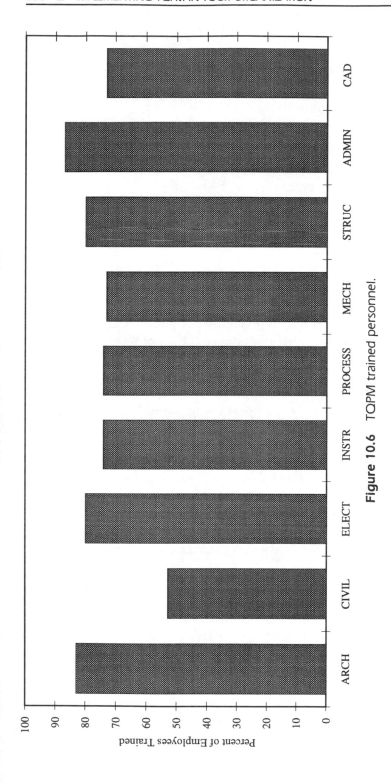

Figure 10.6 TQPM trained personnel.

volved, the more rapid will be the improvement. Managers must empower the employees in two different ways.

First, employees must be encouraged to bring quality problems and suggested improvements to management's attention. This *cannot* be done effectively by the traditional "suggestion box" approach because the employee rarely receives feedback as to what happened to the suggestion after it went into the box. To be effective, managers and employees must make the following pact:

1. Employees have an *obligation* to advise management of any problems that affect the quality of the company.
2. Employees who raise quality problems must be willing to help management solve these problems.
3. Management must not permit retribution *in any form* against those employees who raise quality problems.
4. Management must respond honestly and openly to all quality issues raised by employees; verbal comments may be answered verbally, written comments *must* be answered in writing.

The most effective employee involvement programs are those based upon written comments from employees. Making this a formal process reduces intimidation, prevents misunderstandings, and provides a mechanism for follow-up. Figure 10.7 is a corrective action request form used by Engineering-Science, Inc. Note that copies are sent to the TQPM administrator as well as to the employee's supervisor. The TQPM administrator assures that the request is handled properly.

In addition to identifying quality problems, employees must be empowered to help resolve them. This is accomplished by using the team-oriented problem solving techniques described in Chapter 9. One of the best examples of how effective empowerment can work is the Toyota Automobile Company, winner of the Deming Award for Quality. Since beginning this process in 1951, Toyota has achieved the following remarkable successes:

- Increase from 0.1 to 47.7 suggestions per employee per year.
- Increase in employee participation from 8% to 95%.
- Increase in the implementation of suggestions from 23% to 96%.

QIP Log _____

Project Log _____

✓ which

☐ CORRECTIVE ACTION REQUEST
☐ "I COULD DO MY JOB BETTER IF..."

Call TQPM administrator if assistance is needed with this procedure.

PART A - By Originator (statement of problem and impact):

Suggested Solution (optional):

Originator_____cc_____Date_____Ext_____Loc_____

Your supervisor's name_____Ext_____Loc_____

Send a copy to TQPM Administrator and a copy to your supervisor.

PART B - By Supervisor of Originator (describe your solution to originator's problem):

Or: The solution to this problem is outside the area of my responsibility, and I am forwarding this CAR to

_____for further action.

Supervisor_____Date_____

Figure 10.7 Corrective action request form.

As shown in Figure 10.8, this achievement was accomplished over many years of constant management attention. How did Toyota do it? Some of their techniques are listed below:

- All submitted suggestions receive a response *within 24 hours* from the employee's direct supervisor.
- Good suggestions are rewarded in a variety of ways. (Rewards are discussed later in this chapter.)
- After a while, employees begin to think like managers, making suggestions that really make sense from a business point of view.

DEMONSTRATING SUCCESS QUICKLY

Management's initiatives to implement TQPM will be greeted by considerable skepticism by the firm's middle managers and employees. It will be viewed as another management fad that, like those before it, will die of its own weight within a few months. This normal reaction will become increasingly negative as it becomes apparent that implementing TQPM will be much more time-consuming than the firm's traditional command-and-control approach. Resentment will be particularly strong among the firm's branch office managers, department heads, and project managers, who will view it as an increasing imposition on their time with little or no tangible benefits to them.

Everyone must be prepared to take a long-term view. It will take *at least* a year before the investment in TQPM will begin to pay off in ways that are visible to middle managers and employees. This period can be minimized by selecting some relatively simple quality problems that can be solved quickly. It is also helpful if such problems can be understood by a broad cross section of the firm's employees. An ideal place to start is with the problem of time card errors. Virtually every design firm uses time cards and almost all of them have problems with employees filling them out incorrectly. Because every employee fills out a time card, it is easy to explain the problem to them. (These are the same reasons that we have used time card errors as a way to explain TQPM concepts in this book.)

As we have discussed in previous chapters, the first step in attacking the time card error problem is to measure it. This

Year	Total of Suggestions Submitted	Suggestions per Employee per Year	% of Employees Participating	% of Suggestions Implemented
1951	789	0.1	8	23
1952	627	0.1	6	23
1953	639	0.1	5	31
1954	927	0.2	6	53
1955	1,087	0.2	10	43
1956	1,798	0.4	13	44
1957	1,356	0.2	12	35
1958	2,682	0.5	18	36
1959	2,727	0.4	19	33
1960	5,001	0.6	20	36
1961	6,660	0.6	26	31
1962	7,145	0.6	20	30
1963	6,815	0.5	21	34
1964	8,689	0.5	18	29
1965	15,968	0.7	30	39
1966	17,811	0.7	38	46
1967	20,006	0.7	46	50
1968	29,753	0.9	43	59
1969	40,313	1.1	49	68
1970	49,414	1.3	54	72
1971	88,607	2.2	67	74
1972	168,458	4.1	69	75
1973	284,717	6.8	75	77
1974	398,091	9.1	78	78
1975	381,438	8.7	81	83
1976	463,442	10.6	83	83
1977	454,552	10.6	86	86
1978	527,718	12.2	89	88
1979	575,861	13.3	91	92
1980	859,039	19.2	92	93
1981	1,412,565	31.2	93	93
1982	1,905,642	38.8	94	95
1983	1,655,868	31.5	94	95
1984	2,149,744	40.2	95	96
1985	2,453,105	45.6	95	96
1986	2,648,710	47.7	95	96

Figure 10.8 Employee suggestion system used by Toyota. Source: Labovitz, George H. and Chang, Yu Sang, "Learning from the Best," Quality Progress, May 1990.

can be done easily by the person who ultimately handles all the time cards and inputs the data into the firm's computer (or logs them onto a manual tracking system). He or she should count all incorrect charges each time the data are entered. At the same time, a nonthreatening note (similar to Figure 9.5) is issued from the data entry person to all employees who had errors on their time cards. (To avoid creating a threat, copies of these notices must *not* be sent to supervisors, nor should they be filed for future punishment of offenders.) If you follow this simple approach, you should experience results similar to that obtained from an actual case history shown in Figure 9.12.

RECOGNIZING SUCCESS

Nonconformance charts, emphasis on zero defects, corrective action teams, nonconformance notices, and other tools presented in this book can cast TQPM in a negative light in the eyes of the employees. The constant focus on things that are wrong can degenerate into an attitude that, "This company is really screwed up!" To counterbalance this overly negative view, there must be equal emphasis by management on what the firm and its employees are doing well. Recognition must be given for *all* significant accomplishments by individuals and teams, and should include specific events as well as achievement of long-term goals. Recognition should include those successes achieved through the TQPM process as well as those that resulted from other means.

Customer-Based Recognition

The most important recognition of performance must come from the firm's clients. It is they who judge the quality of service provided, regardless of what the firm's managers believe it to be. This fact should be the foundation of any design firm's recognition program.

An excellent source of such recognition is commendation letters written by clients to compliment the firm and its employees on a job that was particularly well done. A copy of each commendation letter should be sent to the home of each employee who contributed to the effort, along with a handwritten note from one of the firm's senior managers thanking the employee for his or her contribution. Copies of the letters should also be framed and hung on the wall in a prominent location for all to see.

Internal "customers" can also serve as sources of recognition for employees who do not routinely come in contact with clients. Some firms have a bulletin board on which people are encouraged to place handwritten notes thanking other employees for their contributions when they were deemed to be of outstanding quality.

Peer Recognition

Peer recognition is another powerful recognition tool. Some firms have formalized this by establishing annual awards for those individuals whose performance was consistently outstanding during the year regardless of the employee's position description. Each year, a selection committee is appointed that represents a vertical cross section of the firm (or each office for multioffice firms). One representative is selected for each major category of personnel, for example, clerical, drafters, technicians, engineers, project managers, and so on. The selection committee publishes selection criteria and solicits nominations from everyone in the firm (see example form in Figure 10.9). All nominations are reviewed by all members of the committee; *unanimous* approval is required for a nominee to be selected. Those selected are then presented with an award, usually a work-related item of high quality but modest cost such as an engraved desk set, or leather briefcase. The presentation of the awards should be made by a senior manager at an office-wide ceremony, attended by spouses if possible, to emphasize the importance of these achievements.

Publicizing Accomplishments

Annual awards are nice, but they do little to offset the day-to-day negative emphasis that TQPM efforts often generate. An effective counterbalance must include frequent publicity about real accomplishments.

Some firms have instituted an employee-of-the-month system of recognizing quality accomplishments over a short-term. Such awards are often accompanied by reserved parking spaces, free coffee, or use of a company car for the month. Some firms find them very effective. However, there can be drawbacks to such systems. By limiting the award to only one employee each month, an artificial scarcity of quality employees is implied. This can create unhealthy competition for the

I wish to nominate: _____

Describe how the nominee has consistently exceeded expectations. Be as specific as possible citing particular accomplishments in quantitative terms.

_____

_____

_____

_____

_____

_____

_____

_____

_____

_____

_____

_____

_____

_____

_____

_____

_____

Nominated by: _____ Date: _____

Figure 10.9 Excellence award nomination form.

award (especially if it has substantial monetary value), which can detract from team building efforts. This problem is sometimes dealt with by limiting each employee to one award per year; however, such limitations can actually *demotivate* the best employees by making them ineligible once they have won an award. It is far better to establish award systems that are noncompetitive but, rather, reward everyone who meets preestablished criteria.

In addition to regularly scheduled formal awards, it is also necessary to give on-the-spot recognition of specific accomplishments. One such approach is "Doughnut Day" in which a manager buys doughnuts for everyone in the office (or a department) in recognition of a particular accomplishment. The firm pays for the doughnuts, and each box contains a note identifying the person(s) and event being recognized.

In all these forms of recognition, both individual and team accomplishments should be recognized. Also, the accomplishments must be significant so that the awards do not become trivialized. It is also important that recognition procedures be formalized and monitored in order to assure that they are being performed as planned.

Monetary Rewards

When discussing the issue of recognition, the question of money always arises. Advocates of substantial monetary incentives argue that money is the most effective way of motivating employees toward desired behaviors. Opponents argue that such approaches can pit one employee against another, thereby destroying attempts at team building. Both views have merit. Substantial monetary rewards can successfully motivate door-to-door encyclopedia salespersons, who operate almost totally independently. But TQPM relies on strong teams working together to achieve continual improvement. Attempts have been made to structure monetary incentive programs based upon group performance; however, it is impossible to recognize each individual's contribution in a truly objective way. Therefore, in the case of either individual or group programs, the jealousy and bickering that generally accompanies large financial rewards are incompatible with the environment needed for effective teamwork. If financial awards are given, they should not be of such magnitude that they jeopardize team building efforts.

MONITORING PROGRESS OF THE TQPM PROGRAM

The beginning of this chapter described how standards of quality can be established for technical service organizations. Following are some approaches to measure how a design firm can measure its progress in achieving these standards.

Commitment to Quality

A successful TQPM program will result in major cultural changes within the firm. One of these is an increase in the importance of customer service. Remember, the term "customer" doesn't just refer to a firm's clients—it also includes internal customers such as the word processor who is given a handwritten draft of a report to type.

Prior to beginning a formal program in Total Quality Project Management, it is important to obtain "baseline" data regarding the commitment of the firm to customer service. This can be done by asking each employee to anonymously fill out a survey such as the one in Figure 10.10. Reperforming the survey once or twice a year will then provide a quantitative measure of how much improvement has been achieved since the last survey. The firm's management will also be able to identify those areas that are rated lowest and plan their efforts to improve them.

Client Evaluations

The ultimate judges of quality are the clients. Chapter 8 described how to obtain quantitative feedback regarding client satisfaction. To determine how well the TQPM program is working, it is necessary to look at long-term trends in client ratings. This can be done by aggregating all the ratings obtained during each year and plotting them on a run chart such as Figure 10.11.

Long-Term Cost-Effectiveness

Design firms traditionally have relied on in-depth checking and auditing to achieve quality in their studies, designs, and construction projects. These QA/QC approaches have forced a correlation between cost and quality—higher quality has been achieved by increased spending on reviews and corrections. But this linkage is really artificial. Most design organizations spend 25–40% of project budgets on rework, but only 2–5% on reviews. By implementing TQPM, a design organization can improve quality by eliminating errors rather than by catching and correcting them. Error elimination not only improves quality, it also reduces costs. Thus, with TQPM, costs go down as quality goes up.

To illustrate how this can work, let's take a hypothetical design firm that is embarking on a TQPM program. The firm's progress is illustrated in Figure 10.12 and described below:

Baseline Conditions (Year Zero)

- 30% of project costs are spent on rework.
- Quality of work is about average for the industry.
- No one has heard about TQPM.

To evaluate your organization's culture on the key factors in customer driven service, rate the statements below on the following scale:

1 = Never   2 = Rarely   3 = Sometimes   4 = Usually   5 = Always

Note: "Internal customers" include anyone who relies on input from someone else in the firm in order to do a job.

Customer Orientation	Circle Your Rating
1. We "listen" carefully to our clients' needs through a formal feedback system and act on this information.	1 2 3 4 5
2. When we lose a client we know why. Or we find out.	1 2 3 4 5
3. Our repeat business exceeds the industry average.	1 2 3 4 5
4. Our day-to-day activities are in harmony with our values and goals about client satisfaction.	1 2 3 4 5
5. Our clients have advocates in our organization.	1 2 3 4 5
6. We see ourselves as customers and suppliers in our work relationships with each other.	1 2 3 4 5
7. My manager's concerns and activities have convinced me that care of internal customers is important.	1 2 3 4 5
8. We have a formal process in place to determine our internal customers' wants, needs, and expectations, now and for the future.	1 2 3 4 5
9. We have clear measures and tracking systems to tell us how we are meeting our customer's requirements—in every department.	1 2 3 4 5

Management Climate

1. Our managers "walk what they talk."	1 2 3 4 5
2. The predominant attitude around here is seeking opportunities rather than acting defensively.	1 2 3 4 5
3. Managers give workers the responsibility and authority to take care of clients and internal customers.	1 2 3 4 5
4. People think "competition" means other companies, not the person down the hall.	1 2 3 4 5

Cooperation/Integration

1. People at all levels can participate in decision making.	1 2 3 4 5
2. Supervisors and managers in different departments work well together.	1 2 3 4 5
3. Very few things fall through the cracks because the left hand doesn't know what the right hand is doing.	1 2 3 4 5
4. Our systems make clear who has responsibility for various activities.	1 2 3 4 5
5. The organization's goals are set at the top, based on our mission, and are clear and achievable.	1 2 3 4 5
6. Results and goal achievement are rewarded both formally and informally.	1 2 3 4 5

Attitude, Skills, and Results

1. What happens in the organization really matters to all our people—executives and workers alike.	1 2 3 4 5
2. People feel responsible, needed, and empowered to do what needs to be done to take care of our customers and keep them satisfied.	1 2 3 4 5
3. Our senior managers know how to identify and solve customer service-related problems.	1 2 3 4 5
4. Problem-solving skills are used in every department and are standard operating procedure.	1 2 3 4 5
5. Our managers and supervisors have the skills to influence others, communicate effectively, and motivate and lead subordinates, particularly through periods of economic challenge and change.	1 2 3 4 5
6. Our focus is on preventing problems rather than fixing them after the fact.	1 2 3 4 5
7. We concentrate on exceptional care of clients, rather than cost-cutting, to increase our profits and earnings.	1 2 3 4 5

Figure 10.10 Customer commitment survey. Source: Cannie, Joan Koob and Caplin, Donald, *Keeping Customers for Life,* **American Management Association,** New York, 1991.

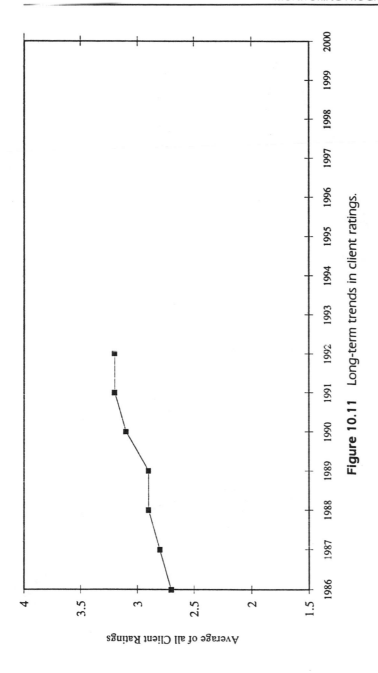

Figure 10.11 Long-term trends in client ratings.

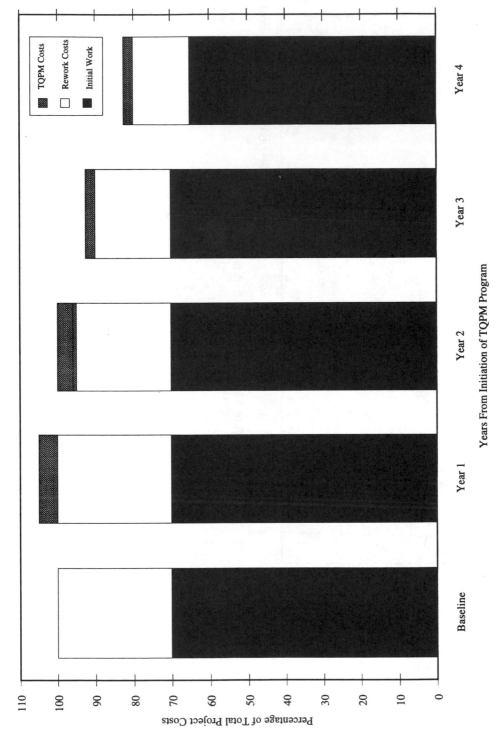

Figure 10.12 How TQPM can reduce project costs.

One Year Later

- TQPM has increased costs by 5%.
- Rework remains at 30% of total costs.
- Total cost of production is now 5% more than when TQPM was begun.
- Quality has improved only slightly.
- There is much grumbling about TQPM.

Two Years Later

- TQPM costs remain at 5% of total production costs.
- Rework is reduced to 25% as a result of TQPM efforts.
- Total cost of production is now the same as baseline.
- Quality improves significantly.
- Grumbling about TQPM decreases but is still considerable.

Three Years Later

- TQPM costs decrease to 2.5% of total production costs.
- Rework is reduced to 20% as a result of TQPM efforts.
- Total cost of production is now 7.5% less than baseline.
- Quality is now on a par with the best firms.
- Existing clients begin to recognize improvements in quality.
- A few die-hards are still grumbling about TQPM.

Four Years Later

- TQPM costs remain at 2.5% of total production costs.
- Rework is reduced to 15% as a result of TQPM efforts.
- Firm is acknowledged by its clients to have the best quality in the industry, resulting in more repeat business.
- Decrease in required sales and marketing costs reduce overhead rate by 5%.
- Total cost of production is now 17.5% less than baseline.
- Critics of TQPM have been converted or have left the firm.

Every firm embarking on a TQPM program must maintain a cost-effectiveness chart (or charts) showing long-term trends. For example, Figure 10.13 is such a chart in which

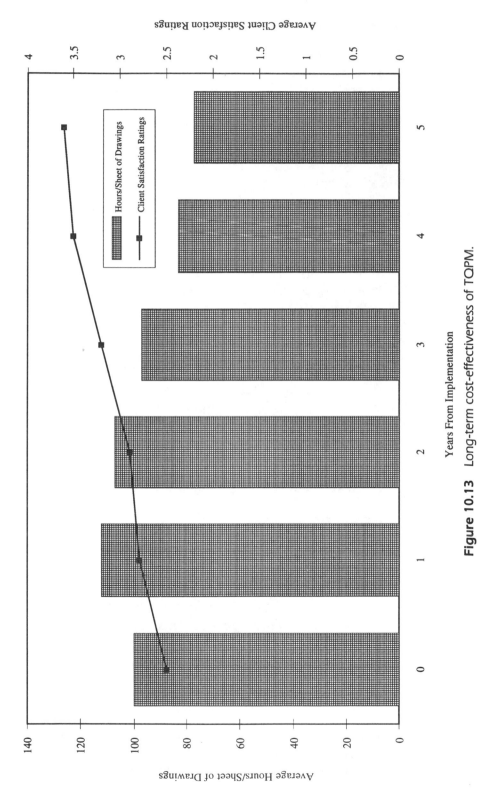

Figure 10.13 Long-term cost-effectiveness of TQPM.

quality is measured by client satisfaction ratings and efficiency is measured by the average man-hours per drawing required for design projects.

CONTINUOUSLY REVISING YOUR STANDARDS

It is important to think of quality as a journey, not a destination. While "zero defects" is an appropriate performance standard, it is not an achievable goal. It is better to think of quality improvement targets as a logarithmic scale. If the current quality level for a given parameter is one nonconformance in 10, the next step should be to reduce the nonconformance rate to one in 100, then one in 1,000, and so on. (Of course, the benefits of each successive step in quality improvement must be greater than the costs to achieve that improvement.)

Some firms have simplified this concept by measuring nonconformances in parts per million. For example, let's say a construction cost estimate has a total of 25 line items and each line item includes an estimate of unit price, quantity, and extension. In this example, there are a total of 75 opportunities for error (76 if one counts the addition of the 25 line items). The next step would be to define the acceptable tolerance levels, say ±20% for unit prices, ±5% for take-offs, and ±$100 for calculations of extensions. If, after final prices are received, it turns out that three unit prices and two take-offs fell outside the predetermined tolerance levels, then that process would have a nonconformance rate of approximately 6.5% percent (5 ÷ 76) or 65,000 defects per million opportunities.

At this point a word of caution is in order. The use of sigmas or parts per million to measure nonconformances is not an *absolute* way of measuring quality. It is meaningful only when taken in the context of the definition of nonconformances in a given process. For example, consider a common nonconformance in technical reports—typographical errors. If a report has an average of one page in three with typos, its conformance can be said to be 333,000 defects per million opportunities, or about one sigma. The same typographical errors can be said to occur an average of 6 times every 1,000 words or 6,000 defects per million opportunities. The same report can be said to have 10 nonconformances in every 10,000 characters, or 1,000 defects per million opportunities. We can see that this statistical approach is valid only when dealing with a precisely defined nonconformance.

These statistical measurement tools are most useful when dealing with nonconformances that occur infrequently but whose consequences can be very serious. Let's take the case of structural calculation errors. Such errors, if not caught, can cause serious structural damage and even loss of life. Because no quality control system will catch 100% of these errors, it is essential that their frequency be reduced to as low a level as possible. Expressing these calculation errors as parts per million or sigma values will place them in proper perspective and provide a useful way to measure improvements in a process that is already 99+ % correct. For example, Motorola, a Baldrige Award winner, has targeted a standard of two defects per million as its goal for manufacturing quality.

A similar approach has been used successfully for many years in measuring worker injuries. When a large American manufacturing firm first began measuring worker injuries in 1924, they found an incident rate of almost 6 per 100 full-time workers. The cost of these injuries was high, both in human terms and in dollar costs to the company. As soon as the importance of this problem became apparent to management, steps were taken that cut this rate in half within three years. Since then, many programs have been initiated to further reduce worker injuries. Some worked well; some didn't. But through the years, the firm has continued to reduce worker injuries so they are now less than one-tenth the originally measured rate (see Figure 10.14). Despite these impressive long-term results, the firm is still working hard to reduce injury rates even further. Their goal continues to be "zero defects."

SUMMARY

In the late 1980s, TQPM began as an *avant garde* movement in the design profession. Much like CADD in the late 1970s, it was first tried at large engineering and architectural firms. By 1995, most design firms will have embarked on some type of TQPM program. By the end of the decade, TQPM will be like CADD is today—a requirement for survival in an increasingly competitive marketplace. Those firms who begin early and implement TQPM intelligently will prosper during the 1990s and beyond. Those that fail to do so will likely be relegated to the dustbin of history. Which course will your firm take?

Figure 10.14 Safety history for a large manufacturing firm.

A GLOSSARY OF TERMS COMMONLY USED IN TOTAL QUALITY PROJECT MANAGEMENT

There are many variations of the TQPM process developed by Dr. W. E. Deming in the early 1950s. Each has its own techniques and vocabulary. This glossary is a compilation of terms used by many different TQPM systems. Although many of these are not used in this book, it may be useful for the reader to have a convenient source of reference when he or she hears these terms.

Acceptance: Agreement, indicated by signature and date, that a document or item conforms to specified requirements.

Agenda: Outline of a meeting that lists the items to be discussed and the objectives or decisions to be reached, as well as the location, date, and start/finish times.

Approval: Acceptance of a document or item by a specified authority from the organization responsible for its production or use.

Audit: A type of review used to ensure that the required work processes and procedures are being followed and that the work produced is conforming to the specified requirements.

Auditor: An individual who is qualified to perform any portion of an audit.

Brainstorming: A method for generating ideas within a group about problems, their causes, and their solutions;

members take turns speaking, record suggestions without immediate comment, and defer discussion or evaluation until everyone has finished contributing.

Bubble Up: Process of forwarding (oral or written) constructive suggestions and ideas for formal consideration when their apparent scope exceeds an individual's authority to act.

Cause-and-Effect Diagram: A graphic tool used to collect and structure ideas about possible root causes of a problem. Categories of potential causes (people, equipment, procedures, process inputs, etc.) appear as "bones" branching off the spine. The fishhead is the problem or effect. (Also known as a fishbone or Ishikawa diagram.)

Centering: A process used by a team to determine whether a problem has been correctly identified and defined.

Churn: Unnecessary rework created because performance was not right the first time; also refers to frustration and inefficiency resulting from unclear requirements (see Price of Nonconformance).

Conformance: A condition in which a product, service, or work process meets the requirements of the customer.

Consensus: General agreement by team members on a specific decision or issue.

Contingency Diagram: A two-part graphic tool used to collect ideas about root causes of a problem by listing the possible negative actions that would create the problem. Then, positive solutions are found to the negative actions listed in order to identify the possible corrective actions that will prevent those root causes from recurring. Similar to the cause-and-effect diagram, but not as formal.

Corrective Action: Specific actions taken to eliminate the root cause(s) of a nonconformance so the problem is eliminated. The corrective action should be followed up at a later date to verify that it was effective.

Corrective Action Request (CAR): A form initiated by any employee who has a problem that interferes with doing the work right the first time. Or, the CAR can be used to identify a work process that can be improved (to save time and money). The request initiates an investigation process to find and eliminate the root cause(s) of the problem.

Corrective Action Team (CAT): A specially created team with specific talents and experience that is formed temporarily to find a problem's root causes, develop corrective action solution(s), and ensure effective implementation.

Cost of Quality: The sum of the Price of Conformance (POC) and the Price of Nonconformance (PONC) (see separate entries).

Customer: Anyone who receives or uses the output of a process. There are both internal and external customers.

Deliverables: Documents identified in the scope of work of a contract to be prepared and submitted to the client.

Design: Refers to specifications, drawings, design criteria, or performance requirements for the components of a system from conceptual design through final design.

Diagnostic Arm: A group of employees who are assigned by management to solve a specific quality problem.

DIRTFT: Abbreviation for "Do it right the first time." Pronounced "Dirt Foot."

Drive Out Fear: Fear can be a major concern depending on business results, worry over organization change; the Quality Improvement Process must address issues of fear and encourage growth, risk-taking (one of W. E. Deming's 14 points).

Error Cause Removal (ECR): A formalized procedure that gives individuals a means of communicating to management about problems; a simple form is used and the ECR process is monitored closely to ensure quick response and resolution. (See Corrective Action Request and Bubble Up.)

Error-Free Costs: Expenses incurred to do the job or operate a process as it was designed to be done; material, equipment, and labor all exactly meet specifications.

Evaluate: To use a predetermined sign of completion in order to determine whether a corrective action has eliminated the root causes of a nonconformance.

Facilitator: An outside person brought in to increase the effectiveness of corrective action team meetings.

Finding: A lack of compliance with any element of a quality assurance program, including applicable codes, standards, or specifications.

Fishbone Diagram: See Cause-and-Effect Diagram.

Flow Chart: A graphic description of a work process that shows sequential work steps and their interrelationship, the output to the customer, and the input from suppliers.

Follow-Up: A required review conducted some time after a corrective action is put in place to ensure that it is effective and has not created new problems.

Force-Field Analysis: A technique used to identify factors that contribute to error-free performance and factors that contribute to nonconformances.

Four Absolutes of Quality: In Crosby-based quality systems, the general term for the key concepts of quality management:

1. The definition of quality is conformance to requirements.
2. The system for ensuring quality is prevention (causing nonconformances not to happen).
3. The performance standard is zero defects (the intent to meet requirements every time).
4. The measurement of quality is the price of nonconformance (what it costs to do things wrong).

Gantt Chart: A horizontal bar chart that illustrates various actions and their durations in a way that highlights overlapping actions.

Goal: A general statement describing a desired future condition. The statement focuses attention on the direction that the specific objectives must develop in order to support and attain that goal.

Histogram: A bar chart illustrating the frequency distribution of a measurement or value.

Hold Point: An activity that has been specified in a plan or procedure to be a point of inspection or surveillance. Work may not progress beyond that point until the inspection or surveillance has been completed.

Improvement: A change in a process that eliminates non-conformance, reduces variation, ensures that customer requirements are met more effectively, or reduces hassles, costs, or duration.

Input: The material, resources, and information needed to operate any process or perform any work task.

Inspection: Examination or measurement to verify whether an item or activity conforms to specified requirements.

Interdiscipline Review: Term used to describe design control activities between concerned project design disciplines, other responsible technical groups, and others, as required, so that the requirements of each discipline are consistent with those of the other disciplines.

Intradiscipline Check: Term used to describe control activities within each respective project discipline.

Lead Auditor: Individual who organizes and directs audits, reports audit findings, and evaluates corrective action.

Linking Pins: Individuals who are indirectly involved in a team decision who have been asked to attend or contribute to a team meeting to share their expertise. These people then have the responsibility to support team decisions and to communicate them back to their respective departments (see Facilitator).

Listen, Question, Restate: A technique for enhancing communication.

Mandatory Comment: Comments on a reviewed document that must be incorporated or resolved to the satisfaction of the reviewer before acceptance of the document is granted.

Measurement Chart: A graphic presentation of facts that highlights raw data, trends, or unusual activities or that presents information on status. It is used to focus attention on a nonconformance so that decisions can be made on the actions to be taken.

Meeting Minutes: A written record of the results of a formal discussion. Minutes are used to communicate the decisions and actions of a team and the assigned action items and their due dates.

Mistake-Proofing: Providing procedures that make it impossible for a nonconformance to be unknowingly generated or provided to a customer.

Multivoting: A means for quickly prioritizing a long list of problems or ideas. Each team member votes on one-half of the items on the list. Votes are tallied and the half with the fewest votes are eliminated. The process is repeated until the list has been reduced to a manageable size.

"Next Operation as Customer" (NOAC): The concept that anyone (inside or outside the organization) who must use the work product of someone else is that person's customer.

Nonconformance: Work that does not meet the previously agreed-to requirements of a customer.

Nonmandatory Comments: Comments on a reviewed document that are recommended but not mandatory.

Objective: A statement of a desired future condition. It details the measurable end results to be accomplished within specified time limits and budget. Objectives are more specific than goals.

Objective Evidence: Any documented statement of fact, other information, or record, either quantitative or qualitative, pertaining to the quality of an item or activity, based on observation, measurements, or tests that can be verified.

Observation: A minor deficiency detected and reported as the result of a quality assurance audit that, if not corrected, may become reportable as a finding or nonconformance.

Opportunity for Error: Any step in a work process that could produce a nonconformance, for example, a bad filing system. Looking for opportunities for error is one method of preventing problems and identifying root causes of a nonconformance.

Outlier Analysis: In a data set, an "outlier" is a point that falls outside the normal range. Outliers that represent substandard performance can be studied to reveal root causes of a problem. Outliers that represent superior performance can be studied to reveal innovative ways of improving a process.

Output: The results of a process. These products or services are provided to customers and are intended to meet their specified requirements.

Pareto Chart: A type of bar chart with its measurements arranged in order of descending frequency from left to right. A distinguishing feature of a Pareto chart is the presence of a cumulative percentage line that shows the additional percentage contributed by each measured value.

Pareto Principle: The "80/20" rule: 80% of the results (problems *or* successes) comes from 20% of the causes.

Partnering: A new concept in teamwork—the ultimate team. A special relationship created between a company and its client. After a project team has been selected from the company and client, the members of the whole team work as a single unit instead of the more typical "them" and "us."

Peer Reviews: Documented, fully traceable reviews performed by qualified specialists who are independent of the original work, but who have the expertise to perform the work.

Performance Standard: The basis for comparing performance against requirements; usually expressed as 100% conformance or zero defects. The performance standard must be determined for cost and schedule considerations as well as for output specifications.

Pie Chart: A graphic representation of percentages all summing to reflect the various components of a total product.

Pilot Program: Testing a potential solution on a small group to verify effectiveness prior to implementing the solution on the entire organization.

Policy: A formal guiding statement of goals to be accomplished.

Prevention: Actions that involve communicating, planning, proofing, and working in a way to eliminate opportunities for nonconformance.

Price of Conformance (POC): What it costs to get things done right the first time, to ensure that work processes conform to requirements.

Price of Nonconformance (PONC): What it costs to do things wrong; the cost of wasted time, effort, and money (See Churn).

Procedure: A document that specifies or describes how an activity is to be performed.

Process: A series of actions intended to produce a result (output) that meets its requirements.

Process Control: Operating a process, measuring against the requirements, comparing the results of the measurement according to a performance standard, and taking action (if needed) to correct or improve the process.

Process Model: In Crosby-based quality systems, a specific graphic display of all aspects of a work process, used to analyze and diagnose improvement needs and to clarify requirements.

Procurement Document: Purchase requisitions, purchase orders, drawings, contracts, specifications, or instructions used to define requirements for purchase.

Program Evaluation Review Technique (PERT) Chart: A chart used to communicate a flow of planned actions and corresponding dates so that everyone involved can know the order and dates when certain actions are to take place. For example, a project schedule.

Project Quality Committee (PQC): A committee that is set up for a particular project and that has a function similar to a department or division quality committee, except that the PQC addresses the project-specific quality activities.

Proof: The trial and evaluation of a process before full-scale operation to determine whether it can yield an output that conforms to the requirements every time.

Q/q: ("Big Q/little q") Big Q refers to "new" comprehensive approach to quality improvement through a formalized process of involvement, education, and participation; little q refers to "traditional," limited quality concepts applied primarily to inspection of completed products.

Quality: Conforming to defined and agreed-to requirements, fit for its intended use, predictable in uniformity and dependability. Any product, service, or process that conforms to this definition is a quality product, service, or process.

Quality Action Teams (QAT): Small ad hoc problem-solving groups, often cross-functional, which are formed to deal with problems beyond an individual's job scope (see Corrective Action Teams).

Quality Assurance (QA): All those planned and systematic actions necessary to provide adequate confidence that a system and its subsystems or components will perform satisfactorily in service.

Quality Assurance Record: A completed document or item that furnishes evidence of the quality and completeness of data (including raw data).

Quality Control (QC): Checking a product to determine if it conforms to requirements.

Quality Improvement Process (QIP) Elements: The series of actions that aids each employee in producing higher quality work. The elements are:

- Organization.
- Education.
- Awareness.
- Recognition.
- Definition of requirements.
- Measurement.
- Corrective action.

Quick Fix: In problem solving, taking immediate, short-term steps to keep a job or process running while the root cause of the problem is analyzed and eliminated.

Requirement: Expectations for a product, service, or work process, which should be mutually agreed upon by suppliers and customers.

Resolution Date: The date when a corrective action to eliminate a nonconformance should be operational.

Ripple Effect: When adding up the price of nonconformance (PONC) for a given problem, the hidden (ripple) effects, which are created by the problem, must also be identified. In many cases, this hidden "ripple" cost is the major factor, outweighing the more obvious tip of the iceberg.

Root Cause: The source from which a nonconformance originates.

Run Chart: A measurement chart used to record the data

gathered (usually on the vertical axis) over a period of time (on the horizontal axis).

Scope: A selected beginning and end point of a process for the purpose of analysis (from an initial activity to a final activity).

Statistical Process Control (SPC): A system using statistical methodology to determine whether a process is predictable and is capable of meeting its requirements.

Steering Arm: The role of senior management in guiding the solution of a quality problem.

Stop Work Order: Documented directive from a designated authority to terminate specified activities associated with an item or activity on which a significant condition adverse to quality has been reported. The order remains in full effect until withdrawn by documented directive from the same authority who originated the order, after corrective action has been taken and approved.

Supplier: Anyone who provides the input to a process. Suppliers can be external or internal to an organization.

Surveillance: The act of monitoring or observing to verify whether an item or activity conforms to specified requirements.

Synergy: Blending of different human skills, talents, and experiences to produce a total effect greater than the sum of the individual skills, talents, and experiences.

System: A series of steps, tasks, or procedures developed to accomplish an objective.

Ten/Four (10/4) Vote: A means of quickly prioritizing a list of problems or ideas. Each team member is given ten votes to cast. Up to four votes of the ten can be given for only one problem on the list. The remaining six votes are allocated as the voter wishes. After all of the items on the list have been presented for voting, the chairman of the team then totals the votes to reflect the team's assignment of priorities.

Technical Specialists: General term to include engineers, architects, planners, scientists, and technicians performing specialized work on a project.

"That's Close Enough": Phrase used to describe conventional performance standards by which results are compared to something *other than* the requirement(s). In Total Quality Project Management, close enough is not good enough!

Threads of Similarity: A method for identifying similar conditions responsible for producing either conforming or nonconforming output in an effort to identify the root cause(s) of nonconformance.

Total Quality Project Management: The integration of effective methods for Quality Control, Quality Assurance, and Quality Improvement.

Traceability: The ability to trace the history, application, or location of an item and like items or activities by means of recorded identification.

Verification: The act of reviewing, inspecting, testing, checking, auditing, or otherwise determining and documenting whether items, processes, services, or documents conform to specified requirements.

Waiver: Documented authorization to depart from specified requirements.

Witness Point: An activity that has been specified in a plan or procedure to be a point of inspection or surveillance. Work may not progress beyond that point unless a waiver to the inspection or surveillance is first obtained, or the inspection or surveillance has been performed.

Work Process Model: An analytic tool used to identify all the customer's requirements for the output of a work process and all the input processes and their requirements necessary to produce the output right the first time.

Zero Defects: The concept of working to a performance standard of 100% correctness, each time, every time. One of Crosby's Four Absolutes, zero defects describes the intent to meet requirements the first time, every time.

B CHECKLISTS FOR DESIGN REVIEWS

The vast majority of design errors and omissions are not new; they are repetitions of similar mistakes made on many previous projects. If we are to learn from past mistakes, there must be a systematic way of identifying and avoiding them.

This appendix presents a comprehensive set of design checklists based on commonly observed design errors and omissions. The checklists are organized by discipline so that each reviewer can use them as a convenient reference while checking a portion of the design. Designs that pass these checklists will probably be easy to build, operate, and maintain.

CALCULATION REVIEW CHECKLIST

Questions	Yes	No	N/A
1. Has the originator listed his or her name, department, the date, and the job number? Has the checkcopy been indicated as being for checking?	_____	_____	_____
2. Has the originator referred to the drawing number, specification, or tag number to which the calculations pertain?	_____	_____	_____
3. Have you studied the design criteria, the general arrangement drawings, the designer's drawings and sketches to gain familiarity with the problem and to determine any parameters that pertain to the calculations, such as design stresses, safety factors, flow rates, or space restrictions on member size?	_____	_____	_____
4. Have applicable codes been followed?	_____	_____	_____
5. Study the calculations and the design to which they pertain. Have all required calculations been included?	_____	_____	_____
6. Where possible, has the originator used standard calculation methods, such as formulas, tables, or computer programs? If there is no such standard method, has the originator used an acceptable engineering approach?	_____	_____	_____
7. Follow through the steps of the calculations. Have you verified any information that comes from another source?	_____	_____	_____
8. For each step, are all assumptions valid?	_____	_____	_____
9. For each step, are all arithmetic calculations correct?	_____	_____	_____
10. Is the presentation neat and clear?	_____	_____	_____
11. Has coordination with utilities been completed and have agreements been documented in writing?	_____	_____	_____
12. Have you verified that computations support equipment selection?	_____	_____	_____

ARCHITECTURAL DRAWING REVIEW CHECKLIST

Questions	Yes	No	N/A
1. North arrow orientation is shown on all plans.	_____	_____	_____
2. Using overlays, verify that property line on architectural site plan matches civil site plans.	_____	_____	_____
3. Buildings are located behind required setbacks.	_____	_____	_____
4. Using overlays, verify that columns, walls, and dimensions on plans match structural.	_____	_____	_____
5. Building elevations match floor plans; in particular, roof lines, windows, doors, louvers, and expansion joints.	_____	_____	_____
6. Architectural wall sections match structural.	_____	_____	_____
7. Sizes of openings for windows and doors match structural.	_____	_____	_____
8. Expansion joints are continuous through building.	_____	_____	_____
9. Using overlays, verify that reflected plan matches electrical and mechanical plans.	_____	_____	_____
10. Room schedule information matches plan and elevation information such as room names, room numbers, finishes, and ceiling heights.	_____	_____	_____
11. Door schedule information matches plan and elevation information such as size and type.	_____	_____	_____
12. Locations of fire rated walls match locations of dampers on mechanical plans.	_____	_____	_____
13. Cabinets will fit in available space.	_____	_____	_____
14. Door swings are correct.	_____	_____	_____
15. Flashing material, gauge, and construction match specifications.	_____	_____	_____
16. Sealants are coordinated with specifications.	_____	_____	_____
17. All previous check prints have been properly signed.	_____	_____	_____
18. All required calculations have been checked and approved.	_____	_____	_____
19. Building heights comply with zoning regulations.	_____	_____	_____
20. Sufficient exists have been provided.	_____	_____	_____

CIVIL DRAWING REVIEW CHECKLIST

Questions	Yes	No	N/A
1. Have all structures and facilities been located?	————	————	————
2. Have property lines and ROW lines been located?	————	————	————
3. North arrow orientation is shown.	————	————	————
4. Using overlays of site plans of all disciplines, verify that there are no interferences.	————	————	————
5. Using overlays of site plans of all disciplines, verify that appurtenances do not interfere with roadways and parking.	————	————	————
6. Using overlays of site plans of all disciplines, verify that limits of construction presented are valid.	————	————	————
7. Using overlays of site plans of all disciplines, verify that hydrants, valves, manholes, power poles, and lighting poles do not conflict with other items.	————	————	————
8. Profile sheets show other underground utilities and avoid conflict.	————	————	————
9. Horizontal distances between appurtenances match scaled and stated dimensions on plans and profiles.	————	————	————
10. All existing and proposed grades are shown.	————	————	————
11. All previous check prints have been properly signed.	————	————	————
12. All required calculations have been checked and approved.	————	————	————
13. Is flood plain shown correctly?	————	————	————
14. Are specified materials available locally?	————	————	————
15. Guard rails are provided where needed.	————	————	————

STRUCTURAL DRAWING REVIEW CHECKLIST

Questions	Yes	No	N/A
1. North arrow orientation is shown.			
2. Using overlays, verify that column grid lines match architectural plans.			
3. Using overlays, verify that column locations match architectural plans.			
4. Using overlays, verify that dimensions match architectural drawings.			
5. Using overlays, verify that concrete structural slab matches architectural drawings.			
6. Using overlays, verify that depressed or raised concrete slabs match architectural plans.			
7. Using overlays, verify that slab elevations match architectural plans.			
8. Using overlays, verify that openings in floor, roof, and walls match other disciplines.			
9. Using overlays, verify that clearance is adequate for platforms, piping equipment, and doors.			
10. Member sizes and spacing match calculation sketches.			
11. Concrete footings and columns are sized and identified on a schedule or plan.			
12. Concrete beams are sized and identified on a schedule or plan.			
13. Using overlays, verify that column lines and columns foundations match all floors and roofs above.			
14. All columns and beams are listed in schedules.			
15. Lengths of beams in schedules match plans and sections.			
16. Heights of columns in schedules match plans and sections.			
17. Sections are properly labeled and oriented.			
18. Expansion and construction joints match other discipline drawings.			

STRUCTURAL DRAWING REVIEW CHECKLIST—CONTINUED

Questions	Yes	No	N/A
19. Are materials weldable and weld symbols correct?			
20. Is bracing provided for structural steel?			
21. Are adequate connection details provided?			
22. Any special foundations required for rotating equipment are adequately specified.			
23. Are all drawing notes consistent with specifications?			
24. Have all previous check prints been properly signed?			
25. Have all required calculations been checked and approved?			

BUILDING SYSTEMS MECHANICAL DRAWING REVIEW CHECKLIST

Questions	Yes	No	N/A
1. North arrow orientation is shown on all plans.	_____	_____	_____
2. Using overlays, verify that plumbing plans match architectural plans.	_____	_____	_____
3. Using overlays, verify that HVAC plans match architectural plans.	_____	_____	_____
4. All new utility piping and drains connect to either existing or new utilities on site plan.	_____	_____	_____
5. Plumbing fixtures match plumbing schedules and architectural locations.	_____	_____	_____
6. Using overlays, verify that roof drain locations and roof slopes match architectural roof plan.	_____	_____	_____
7. Pipes and drains do not interfere with foundations.	_____	_____	_____
8. Wall chases are provided on architectural drawings to conceal vertical piping.	_____	_____	_____
9. Fixtures are connected to sanitary drains.	_____	_____	_____
10. Using overlays, verify that sprinkler heads are in appropriate rooms and that they do not interfere with architectural or structural features.	_____	_____	_____
11. Ceiling height is adequate at worst-case duct intersection with largest beams.	_____	_____	_____
12. Structural supports for HVAC equipment are indicated on structural drawings.	_____	_____	_____
13. Dampers are provided at smoke and fire walls.	_____	_____	_____
14. Building complies with fire code.	_____	_____	_____
15. Using overlays, verify that openings for roof penetrations are indicated on structural roof plan.	_____	_____	_____
16. Using overlays, verify that air conditioning units, heaters, and exhaust fans match architectural roof plan location.	_____	_____	_____
17. HVAC equipment will fit space allocated; adequate space is provided for maintenance such as removing filters or tubes.	_____	_____	_____

BUILDING SYSTEMS MECHANICAL DRAWING REVIEW CHECKLIST—CONTINUED

Questions	Yes	No	N/A
18. Building complies with noise control requirements.	_____	_____	_____
19. Using overlays, verify that thermostat locations have been coordinated with architectural drawings.	_____	_____	_____
20. Building complies with energy conservation requirements.	_____	_____	_____
21. Using overlays, verify that electrical power is provided to all equipment.	_____	_____	_____
22. Adequate floor drains are provided for equipment.	_____	_____	_____
23. There are adequate provisions for draining pipelines.	_____	_____	_____
24. All specified products are compatible.	_____	_____	_____
25. Shut-off valves and/or bypasses are provided for all equipment.	_____	_____	_____
26. All previous check prints have been properly signed.	_____	_____	_____
27. All required calculations have been checked and approved.	_____	_____	_____
28. Safety showers are provided where needed.	_____	_____	_____
29. Hazardous areas are adequately ventilated.	_____	_____	_____
30. Backflow preventers and/or air gaps are provided where needed.	_____	_____	_____
31. Are necessary pressure relief valves/blow-offs provided?	_____	_____	_____

PROCESS MECHANICAL DRAWING REVIEW CHECKLIST

Questions	Yes	No	N/A
1. North arrow orientation is shown on all plans.			
2. Using overlays, verify that equipment and piping do not conflict with structural members.			
3. Using overlays, verify that electrical power is provided to all equipment.			
4. Using overlays, verify that piping locations are coordinated with conduit and cable trays.			
5. Verify wall pipe or sleeve size and location on structural drawing.			
6. Structural supports and pads required for mechanical equipment are indicated on structural drawings.			
7. Structural supports required for piping and valves are indicated on structural drawings or specified adequately.			
8. Adequate space is provided between structures and pipes for installation and assembly.			
9. Adequate space is allocated for equipment maintenance and repairs.			
10. Adequate structural members are provided for hoist removal of major equipment.			
11. Adequate doors or block-outs are shown on architectural drawings for installation/removal of major equipment.			
12. Adequate floor drains are provided for equipment.			
13. Adequate provisions are included for draining pipelines.			
14. There are adequate pressure gauges.			
15. Shut-off valves are provided for all equipment.			
16. Bypass valves are provided for equipment, if required.			
17. Equipment names and numbers match those on instrumentation drawings and in equipment specifications.			

PROCESS MECHANICAL DRAWING REVIEW CHECKLIST—CONTINUED

Questions	Yes	No	N/A
18. Adequate thrust restraints are provided.			
19. Drawings locate equipment with respect to columns and elevation.			
20. Adequate width and headroom have been provided on equipment walkways and passages.			
21. All previous check prints have been properly signed.			
22. All required calculations have been checked and approved.			
23. Are necessary sample valves provided?			
24. Are necessary guards provided on rotating equipment?			
25. Are necessary pressure relief valves/blow-offs provided?			
26. Are mixers properly supported?			
27. Are mixers long enough to mix tanks at minimum level?			

INSTRUMENTATION DRAWING REVIEW CHECKLIST

Questions	Yes	No	N/A
1. All symbols and line designations are shown in legend and used in all P&ID drawings.			
2. All equipment names and major flow patterns match those on process flow diagrams.			
3. Power or air is provided to actuate all instruments.			
4. Using overlays, verify that all control wiring and instrument air are coordinated with structural plans.			
5. Structural supports are provided for instruments and panels.			
6. Sufficient space is provided for access to instruments and panels.			
7. Equipment names and numbers match those on process mechanical and HVAC drawings.			
8. Line size and designation match process mechanical and HVAC drawings.			
9. Is pipe insulation designation provided, if required?			
10. Has heat tracing been provided?			
11. All drawing reference continuation arrow numbers are verified.			
12. All instruments listed in specification are shown on P&ID drawings.			
13. Pipe sizes designated on P&ID drawings match process mechanical drawings.			
14. All previous check prints have been properly signed.			
15. All required calculations have been checked and approved.			
16. Isolation valves are provided for gauges and instruments.			

ELECTRICAL DRAWING REVIEW CHECKLIST

Questions	Yes	No	N/A
1. North arrow orientation is shown on all plans.	_____	_____	_____
2. Using overlays, verify that floor plan columns and walls match other disciplines.	_____	_____	_____
3. Using overlays, verify that floor plan equipment matches process mechanical drawings.	_____	_____	_____
4. Using overlays, verify that light fixtures match architectural reflected ceiling plan.	_____	_____	_____
5. Using overlays, verify that light fixtures do not conflict with structural, process mechanical, or HVAC systems.	_____	_____	_____
6. Using overlays, verify that locations of conduits, cable trays, floor trenches, and openings are coordinated with structural plans.	_____	_____	_____
7. Using overlays, verify that panelboard locations are consistent with other disciplines.	_____	_____	_____
8. Using overlays, verify that exterior electrical equipment does not conflict with features on civil/sitework drawings.	_____	_____	_____
9. Structural supports are provided for electrical equipment.	_____	_____	_____
10. Electrical panels are not recessed in fire rated walls.	_____	_____	_____
11. Sufficient space is provided for access to electrical panels.	_____	_____	_____
12. Verify that electrical connections are provided for all process equipment, HVAC equipment, and instrumentation devices.	_____	_____	_____
13. Verify that horsepower ratings on single line diagrams match specified equipment.	_____	_____	_____
14. Equipment names and numbers match those on process mechanical and HVAC drawings.	_____	_____	_____
15. Instrument names match those on instrumentation drawings.	_____	_____	_____
16. Electrical schematics are provided for all equipment.	_____	_____	_____

ELECTRICAL DRAWING REVIEW CHECKLIST—CONTINUED

Questions	Yes	No	N/A
17. Design conforms to power company requirements.	————	————	————
18. All previous check prints have been properly signed.	————	————	————
19. All required calculations have been checked and approved.	————	————	————
20. Electrical equipment is protected from flooding.	————	————	————

SPECIFICATION REVIEW CHECKLIST

Questions	Yes	No	N/A
1. Bid item measurement and payment explicitly states what is intended and how measured.			
2. Architectural schedules match specifications.			
3. Check equipment items and verify that they are coordinated with drawings.			
4. Verify that items specified "as indicated" or "where indicated" in the specification are in fact indicated on drawings.			
5. Verify that no asbestos-containing material is specified.			
6. Have equipment manufacturers reviewed specifications to verify that they will provide equipment?			
7. Are most recent codes and standards listed in specifications?			
8. Do operating descriptions in mechanical, electrical, and instrumentation sections agree?			
9. Do electrical enclosures and voltages match specifications for equipment?			
10. Are materials specified locally available?			
11. Are specified products compatible?			
12. Have equipment test procedures been specified?			
13. Have shop drawing submittal requirements been indicated?			
14. Have appropriate codes and standards been listed on specified items?			
15. Have installation requirements been described?			
16. If performance specifications are provided, have adequate ranges of each important parameter been provided to supplier?			
17. If performance specifications are provided, have details been minimized to maximum possible extent?			

SPECIFICATION REVIEW CHECKLIST — CONTINUED

Questions	Yes	No	N/A
18. Have all specifications been reviewed and approved?	————	————	————
19. Have required calculations been checked and approved?	————	————	————
20. Have requirements for as-built drawings been specified?	————	————	————

OPERABILITY AND MAINTAINABILITY CHECKLIST

Questions	Yes	No	N/A
1. Are necessary drain valves provided for pumps, tanks, etc.?			
2. Are necessary cleanout valves provided?			
3. Are all necessary valves included to provide adequate operating flexibility?			
4. Are all valves accessible?			
5. Are check valves provided where necessary?			
6. Are bypasses provided to allow equipment and instrumentation to be removed for maintenance without disturbing critical processes?			
7. Are pressure gauges provided on all pumps?			
8. Are pumps sized to provide entire range of required flow?			
9. Are means provided to lift pumps from pits or vessels?			
10. Are controls in convenient locations for operators?			
11. Are additional instruments or controls required?			
12. Are necessary stairways, ladders, and access platforms provided?			
13. Are necessary manways provided?			
14. Are overflow lines provided?			
15. Are required containment dikes and walls provided?			
16. Are sight glasses provided and protected?			
17. Are calibration containers provided for chemical feed systems?			
18. Are sufficient access ramps, ladders, steps, or walkways provided?			
19. In cold climates, are provisions made to minimize dangers of slipping on walkways?			
20. Are sufficient water outlets provided in all locations?			
21. Are roadways or pathways provided to allow equipment to be removed or added?			

C

CLAIMS DISCOVERY CHECKLIST*

Contractor claims cause cost overruns for owners and ulcers for design professionals. It often seems that the owner and designer are taking turns in a spear catching contest in which the contractor has an endless supply of spears.

This appendix presents a checklist of common causes of contractor claims. It should be used during the constructability review of each design before it is issued for bids. Where "red flags" are noted, additional design efforts should be considered to reduce the potential for claims.

*Reproduced with permission of Engineering-Science, Inc., Pasadena, Calif.

CLAIMS DISCOVERY CHECKLIST

Constructability Review Item	Red Flag?

I. Site Conditions

A. Grades, Elevations, and Contours _____
  - Has the entire site been photographed before any work has begun?
  - Having the existing grades been spot-checked for accuracy? If so, have any discrepancies been discovered? If so, has a detailed check been arranged?
  - Have the locations of existing telephone, water, sewer, fuel tanks and lines, and gas lines been verified?
  - Have manholes been opened to spot-check actual pipe invert elevations?

B. Utilities _____
  - Have the characteristics of all existing utilities been verified with each respective company?
  - Has each utility company representative reviewed the design?
  - Have the locations of telephone poles, street signs, pole guys, and any other constructions been checked to avoid interference with site improvements?
  - Have the actual horizontal distances among telephone poles, light poles, manholes, drainage structures, etc., been checked for accuracy?
  - Have any discrepancies discovered been documented in the most accurate and unquestionable manner available?

C. Easements/Rights of Way _____
  - Are there designated easements? If so, will they adversely affect construction?
  - Do local traffic patterns restrict access?
  - Are there parking areas, traffic patterns, businesses, etc., at the contract limit line that will restrict construction operations in any way?

D. Inland Wetland Approvals _____
  - Does any portion of the site encroach on inland wetlands? If so, are all appropriate approvals in place?

E. Subsurface Data _____
  - Are boring depths inconsistent?
  - Are boring locations erratic or unusual?
  - Are boring locations relevant to construction?
  - Are borings provided outside the area?
  - Are gaps left within the building area?
  - What time of year were the borings taken?

CLAIMS DISCOVERY CHECKLIST—CONTINUED

Constructability Review Item	Red Flag?

F. Changed Existing Conditions _____
- Have the designers involved met at the site to inspect the site for changes that have occurred since design?
- Have any changes between conditions existing now and those existing at the time of design become apparent?

G. Adjacent Properties _____
- Have all properties adjacent to the site perimeter been reviewed in detail?
- Are there seasonal watercourses? Heavy traffic patterns? Other independent construction activities?

II. Contract Documents

A. Contract Time _____
- Does the first schedule draft drastically exceed the allowed contract time?
- Do subsequent schedule drafts incorporate unusual or excessive compressions and accelerations?
- Do any long lead time purchases dramatically exceed the originally anticipated deliveries. If so, were they for specified items?
- Has the contract award date been extended?
- Has the site start date been extended for an owner-caused reason? If so, will extra work result?
- Can clear cause-effect relationships be demonstrated to justify more contract time?

B. "Fat" Specifications _____
- Does a review of the documents reveal an unusually fat "front end"?
- Is there extensive duplication in the general provisions?
- Are there long and/or labored descriptions and instructions?
- Are there "catch-all" phrases and boilerplate not specifically applying to project conditions?

C. Specification Section on "Scopes" _____
- Are the rules of precedence described adequately?
- Does the design coordination process appear to have been done correctly?
- Are specific cross-references included?
- Does the scope section appear to be complete?

D. Named Subcontractors _____
- Are there owner-selected subcontracts on the projects?

CLAIMS DISCOVERY CHECKLIST—CONTINUED

Constructability Review Item	Red Flag?

- Does any disclaimer exist that limits the owner's liability for subcontractor selection?
- Are the subcontract agreements themselves owner-defined?
- Is any specific procedure in place to resolve disputes between two owner-defined subcontracts?
- Will the owner make decisions (or will there be constant attempts to drop the responsibility on the general contractor)?

E. Price/Bid Allowances _____

- Are there allowances anywhere in the contract? If so, will all allowance items be awarded in time to prevent schedule interruption?

F. Proprietary Restrictions (Public Sector Projects) _____

- Does the specification being considered name fewer than three acceptable suppliers? Does it include the words "or equal"?
- Does the contractor intend to use an "equal" product?
- If so, will the owner want a credit change order?
- Will the owner reject an "equal" submission?

G. Division of Work Among Trades _____

- Are all affected plans noted to be the responsibility of the affected subcontractor(s)?
- Should any contractor aware of the work have reasonably construed it to be included by another trade?
- Did anyone request clarification from the owner before the bid? If so, is the request and/or response documented?
- Is each duplication clear and complete in itself?

III. Technical Plans and Specifications

A. Performance and Procedures Specifications _____

- Are there any instances in which both performance and procedure specifications occur for the same item? If so, are they mutually exclusive?
- Is one or the other more expensive?
- Is one preferred over the other?
- Has one been included in the Schedule of Values?
- Is it cost-prohibitive to accomplish both?
- Is time or material availability a factor?
- Is one more complete or otherwise more appropriate?

B. Clarity of Drawings and Specifications _____

- Are notes without specific references common (such as "As Indi-

CLAIMS DISCOVERY CHECKLIST—CONTINUED

Constructability Review Item	Red Flag?

cated," "See Specs," "See Plans," etc.)? If so, has time been taken to research each one to confirm that the referenced details do in fact exist? If so, have incomplete, conflicting, or missing references been discovered? If so, has each instance been cataloged for individual consideration?

- Are existing facilities clearly distinguished from new work?
- Are demolition requirements clearly shown and described?

C. Design Discipline Interfaces and Duplications   _____

- Does a spot-check reveal any problems at the points where design disciplines cross each other?
- Have any duplications been observed during a spot-check? If so, is each description complete?

D. Design Change Telltales   _____

- Are there a large number of apparent last-minute design changes?
- Are there different styles of type or handwriting in the specifications?
- Are there incomplete erasures?
- Are there out-of-sequence reference marks or inserted pages in the specifications?
- Is there different handwriting on the plans?
- Is the use of language different for the same or similar remarks?
- Do random spot-checks of dimension strings reveal any discrepancies?

IV. Construction Requirements

A. Plan Approvals (Building Permit)   _____

- Has the building permit been applied for at the earliest possible time? Were there any problems? Were any notes or corrections made on the plans?
- Has the permit been delayed in any way?
- Is a permit required (and a Certificate of Occupancy necessary) for temporary field offices?

B. Temporary Utilities   _____

- Are telephone, power, and water available during construction? Are they adequate?
- Are there adequate provisions for construction trailers?
- Are there adequate provisions for equipment lay-down areas?

C. Borrow and Spoils Disposal   _____

- Are spoils disposal areas reasonably available?
- Are borrow areas required? If so, are they reasonably available?

D
GUIDELINES FOR SHOP DRAWING REVIEW*

Too often, designers are given a set of shop drawings and told to, "review these and mark anything that's wrong." Such vague instructions can result in nonconformances slipping through the review process and creating major problems when they are finally discovered in the field. Reviewers of shop drawings should be provided with checklists (such as presented here) in order to assure a thorough, efficient review.

I. Structural

    A. Reinforced Concrete

        1. Concrete mix design—strengths, proportions, aggregates, cement, admixtures, etc.

        2. Aggregates—gradation, source, inactivity, abrasion, etc.

        3. Waterstop catalog cuts—size, shape, material

        4. Curing compound literature—general review

        5. Floor hardener—general review

        6. Grout mix—strength, proportions, contents, etc.

        7. Rebar drawings

          • Bar size, number, spacing, and location

          • Splice locations and type

          • Construction joint locations

          • Pour sequences

        8. Type of joint—keyway and waterstop details

B. Foundation Piles
    1. Type and size
    2. Splice details
    3. Hammer test results

C. Sheeting
    1. Type
    2. Section
    3. Anchorage
    4. Bracing
    5. Utilities
    6. Location

D. Structural Steel
    1. Mill test reports
    2. Erection drawings—sizes and strengths of members and types of fasteners
    3. Compare piece marks—erection vs. detail drawings
    4. Special nonstandard connection and bearing details
    5. Shop coat painting details
    6. Critical portions of design as deemed necessary

E. Miscellaneous Metals, Deck, Etc.
    1. Size and strength of members
    2. Stair details—treads, risers, handrails, kickplates, etc.
    3. Grating—material, sizes, finish, banding, coverage
    4. Lintel schedule
    5. Specify details as deemed necessary

F. Earthwork
    1. Laboratory report review for conformance to compaction requirements

II. Architectural

A. Landscaping
    1. Size, location, and species of plants
    2. Type of sod or grass seed
    3. Type of fertilizer and/or lime

B. Specially Finished Concrete
    1. Finish and texture of sandblasted surfaces
    2. Procedures for forming, placing, and finishing concrete

C. Masonry

1. Quality and type of units—color selection
2. Mortar and grout mixes—strength, type, proportion, admixtures, etc.
3. Approve sample panel if required
4. Embedded items—review submittal in general

D. Wood and Plastics

1. Review reports (certificates) for fire protection and preservative
2. Review details and features of construction for casework
3. Approve hardwood samples and finishes for casework

E. Thermal and Moisture Protection

1. Waterproofing—material, quantities, thickness, coverage, etc.
2. Built-up roofing—approve samples, materials, coverage, procedures, etc.
3. Metal siding—review shop drawings for layout, details, closures, gauges, caulking, and color selection
4. Sheet metal—check materials and sizes
5. Skylights—check shop drawings for materials and details of construction
6. Building insulation—materials, sizes, and R-values
7. Caulking—materials, application, coverage

F. Doors and Windows

1. Hollow metal doors and frames—materials, gauges, types, sizes, finishes, details of construction, door schedules, swing direction, louver requirements
2. Wood doors—details of construction, materials, sizes, types, trim, louvers, etc.
3. Overhead service doors—materials, gauges, type, sizes, hardware, finish, type and details of operator, method of attachment, electrical requirements, (if any)
4. Finish hardware—materials, samples, catalog cuts, finishes, hardware
5. Glass and glazing—approve glass samples and usage (safety)
6. Windows—materials, gauges, details of construction, approve sample of finish

G. Metal Furring, Lathing, and Plastering

1. Catalog cuts of materials
2. Method and procedures as required

H. Tile, Vinyl Wall Covering, and Acoustical Treatment
   1. Samples
   2. Select colors

I. Resilient Flooring and Carpeting
   1. Approve samples
   2. Select colors

J. Painting and Coatings
   1. Coating materials schedule
   2. Color samples
   3. Coating schedule
   4. Certification of applicator

K. Architectural Specialty Items
   1. Catalog cuts
   2. Ventilation requirements

L. Laboratory Equipment and Furniture
   1. Catalog cuts

M. Elevators
   1. Materials
   2. Opening dimensions
   3. Finishes
   4. Loads
   5. Electrical requirements

III. Mechanical

A. Equipment
   1. Materials of construction
   2. Performance: output, capacity, size, speed, etc.
   3. Compliance with specifications
   4. General review of dimensions and interfaces with other portions of the work
   5. Shop painting requirements
   6. Electrical requirements
   7. Control and operations

B. Piping
   1. Materials for each service
   2. Method of installation, supports, joints, testing, etc.
   3. Coatings

C. Layout

1. Review floor and wall opening drawings for completeness but not exact location or dimensions
2. Review anchor bolt and pad layout for completeness and contractibility but not exact dimensions

D. HVAC

1. Duct sizes
2. Damper locations
3. Low headroom clearances

IV. Electrical and Instrumentation

A. Equipment and Products

1. Materials of construction
2. Performance—capacity, sizes, ratings, etc.
3. Compliance with specifications

B. Wiring Diagrams, Functional Schematics, and Descriptions

1. Limits of responsibility
2. Completeness of circuits
3. Compliance with single-line drawings
4. Correct interface between areas of system responsibility and general project electrical work
5. Logic, function, and operation
6. Compliance with specifications
7. Correct interface between areas of system responsibility and general project electrical work

E QUALITY BIBLIOGRAPHY

Albrecht, Karl, *Service America,* ISBN 0-87094-659-5, Dow Jones - Irwin.

Bhote, Keki R, *Next Operation as Customer (NOAC): How to Improve Quality, Cost and Cycle Time in Service Operations,* ISBN 0-8144-2346-9, American Management Association, Membership Publications Division.

Block, Peter, *The Empowered Manager*, ISBN 1-55542-01Q-2, Jossey-Bass Inc.

Burstein, David and Frank Stasiowski, *Project Management for the Design Professional*, Whitney Library of Design, New York, 1991.

Crosby, Philip B., *Quality Without Tears*, ISBN 0-07-014530-Y, McGraw-Hill.

Deming, W. Edward, *Out of the Crisis*, ISBN 0-911379-01-0, MIT Caes.

Drucker, Peter F., *Managing in Turbulent Times*, ISBN 006-011094-5, Harper & Row.

Guaspari, John, *I Know It When I See It*, ISBN 0-8144-4787-8, AMACOM/AMA.

Huber, George P, *Managerial Decision Making*, ISBN 0-673-1S141-7.

Imai, Masaaki, *Kaizen (Ky'Zen)*, ISBN 0-394-55186-4, Random House.

Juran, Joseph R., *Leadership for Quality,* ISBN 0-02-916682-9, Free Press.

Juran, Joseph R., *Planning for Quality*, ISBN 0-02-916681-0, Free Press.

Nemoto, Masao, *Total Quality Control for Management.* ISBN 0-13-925637-7, Prentice Hall.

Peters, Tom, *Thriving on Chaos,* ISBN 0-394-56784-6, Alfred A. Knopf.

Rowntree, Derek, *Statistics Without Tears*, ISBN 0-02-404090-8, Macmillan.

Schenkerback, William W., *The Deming Route To Quality and Productivity*, ISBN 0-941893-00-6, Mercury Press.

"The Quality Imperative," *Business Week*, January 15, 1992.

INDEX